W9-BRZ-600

Baking
from the
Heart

A Share Our Strength Book
to Fight Hunger

Broadway Books, New York

Baking
from the
Heart

Our Nation's Best Bakers Share Cherished Recipes
for The Great American Bake Sale®

Michael J. Rosen

First edition published 2004

Book design by RLF Design
Photography by Sang An

Library of Congress Cataloging-in-Publication Data
   Rosen, Michael J., 1954–
      Baking from the heart : our nation's best bakers share cherished recipes
     for The Great American Bake Sale® / Michael J. Rosen.
         p.   cm.
      "A share our strength book to fight hunger."
      1. Baking.   I. Title.

   TX765.R678 2004
   641.8'15—dc22   2003065516

ISBN 0-7679-1639-5

10 9 8 7 6 5 4 3 2 1

Contents

------------------------- ◇ ◆ ◇ -------------------------

Acknowledgments

As with any major collaborative undertaking, there are many individuals whose generosity, commitment, and passion warrant more than inclusion on a brief listing of names. I must trust that my devoted colleagues at Share Our Strength and my creative allies at Broadway Books know that my appreciation of their support and confidence far exceeds anything than might be written here. Likewise, I hope that the privilege of working with fifty-four of the country's most accomplished culinary talents is at least partially honored by the beauty and success of this finished book.

That said, Sharon Reiss's expertise and talents deserve special mention. Her contributions to this book go well beyond testing recipes and tempting neighbors and siblings with each success. Her ideas and companionship finessed the mechanics and ingenuity of cooking into the joyful art of friendship and its lucky communion.

On an even more personal note, the recipes in the introduction pay some small tribute of love to my mother and to my aunt Sylvia. To Mark, and to the friends who so often gather around the table at Hopewell Springs, there is only the guarantee of future occasions to excuse that I have not detailed here my love and gratitude to each of you.

Finally, the publication of *Baking from the Heart* coincides with the twentieth anniversary of Share Our Strength's founding and two decades of fighting this winnable battle against hunger. To the thousands of volunteers, community leaders, sponsors, staff members, bake sale coordinators, and contributors, this book is yet another toast to your unflagging spirit. It's a toast spread with Dorie Greenspan's Lemon Marmalade or Jacques Torres's Blueberry Jam. It's a toast sweetened with all the successes we've preserved in our hearts and with all the successes we're pledged to create in the coming seasons.

The Most Important Baking Secret

An Introduction with Recipes

More than any other kind of cooking, baking is about heirlooms: recipes handed down either on actual recipe cards or from the memories of someone who cooked alongside someone else who measured by handfuls or added water to a dough until "it just feels right."

How often sweets are bound up in our emotional life: They're how we reward ourselves or our children, how we celebrate and symbolize holidays and anniversaries, how we honor guests and welcome travelers, how we unwind after a day's tumult or settle into an evening at home.

So often our baking is about capturing familiar tastes, textures, and aromas, partly because great baking requires skill and science rather than experimentation. But as you read the stories that accompany these recipes, you'll hear the greater reason, the refrain of longing, of savoring, of cherishing childhood favorites and traditional treats that informed the character of these bakers' families and homes. It's almost as though

baking hints at our identities, permitting us to feel a little proud—a little proprietary, even—about the way something as dear as daily bread, as profound as homemade peach pie, as heavenly as grandmother's box of holiday sweets, ought to taste. Perhaps this sense of integrity or provenance comes from the way those "primal" baked goods are imprinted upon our sense of taste.

You've had the experience: You're at a concert and the orchestra is performing a piece you love, a work you've known since college. You have a recording of it, which you've played countless times. But from the first note, you can tell: This performance is off! The music is faster/slower than your memory of it. Why, the horns are too brash/too muffled! The vocalist is rushing/slurring/emphasizing different notes. The whole work sounds "off" in some way, even though you know the orchestra members must be following the composer's score. You dismiss the performance as unskilled, inattentive, rash. But then you also wonder:

Could this performance's unfamiliarity obscure the fact that this version might, in fact, be more passionate, sensitive, powerful, even better than the version you've grown accustomed to enjoying? You give up. It's all a little disorienting.

A similar thing happens with baked goods, although not every cook's recipe for a given dish is the same "score." "Peach pie," for instance, can signify many things: a lattice top, a crumble top, an almond or vanilla flavoring, a chunky or a mushy or a buttery filling . . . *Your* ideal peach pie, the one you've come to love, is modeled on this ideal pie you keep in your memory's pie safe.

"The soda bread's missing caraway seeds" is a realization based on the loaves your aunt brought from Pittsburgh whenever she visited. "The pecan rolls should have *whole* pecans, not bits!" is a declaration you can't help but make, having learned to bake them with Miss Booth's recipe in junior high home ec.

The sweets that we have each come to cherish may have generic names, but each one's specific textures and tastes prompt something almost reverential among its appreciators.

My dear friend and cooking partner, Sharon Reiss, who tested all the recipes

Smooshed Apple Pie

Makes one 10 x 15-inch pan, serving 15 to 20

For the pastry

4 cups all-purpose flour
1 teaspoon salt
1½ cups vegetable shortening, cold, cut
    into ½-inch pieces
1 large egg
2 teaspoons cider vinegar

For the apples

8 cups ⅓-inch-thick slices peeled
    McIntosh or other apple that breaks
    down to a sauce when cooked (6
    large apples)
¾ cup sugar

2 tablespoons all-purpose flour, plus
    extra for rolling the dough
1 teaspoon ground cinnamon
¼ teaspoon freshly grated nutmeg

¼ cup sugar, for topping, optional

For the optional glaze

2 tablespoons unsalted butter, softened
2 tablespoons pure maple syrup
1 cup confectioners' sugar

1. Combine the flour and salt in a large bowl. Add the shortening and cut it into the flour using two knives or a pastry blender. The mixture should resemble coarse meal.

2. In a small bowl, stir together the egg, vinegar, and ½ cup cold water and pour into the flour mixture, stirring just until the dough comes together and forms a ball. Divide the dough in half and seal each piece in plastic wrap. (Alternatively, you may make the dough in a food processor: Pulse the flour and salt together briefly. Add the shortening and pulse until the mixture resembles coarse meal. Add the wet ingredients all at once and pulse four to five times. Dump the mixture out onto a lightly floured work surface and knead the dough several times until it comes together.)

Refrigerate the dough for at least 20 minutes; it can also be prepared 1 day in advance or frozen for up to 1 month.

3. Preheat the oven to 400°F. Lightly mist a 10 x 15-inch baking pan with non-stick cooking spray.

4. In a large bowl, combine the apples, sugar, 2 tablespoons flour, cinnamon, and nutmeg. Toss to coat.

5. On a lightly floured work surface, roll out a piece of dough to an 11 x 16-inch rectangle. (If the refrigerated dough is too firm, allow it to sit at room temperature for 5 to 10 minutes.) Carefully run a long knife around the dough's edges to ensure that it has not stuck to the work surface. Lightly flour the rolling pin, roll the pastry back onto the rolling pin, then unroll it inside the pan. The dough does not need to extend up the sides of the baking pan. (This is a forgiving dough: Patch any tears or thin places with extra dough from an outside edge.)

6. Spread the apple slices evenly across the dough-lined pan, leaving a small border of dough around the edges.

7. Roll out the remaining piece of dough as directed above and cover the apples with a top crust. Trim any excess dough, then crimp the two crusts together with your fingers. Cut 6 slits across the top so the steam can escape. Sprinkle the top with ¼ cup of sugar unless you are making the optional glaze.

8. Bake for 35 to 40 minutes, until the pastry turns a light golden brown and the juices are bubbling inside. (They need not reduce to a thick syrup as in a pie.) Transfer the pan to a wire rack and cool to room temperature.

9. To make the glaze, if using, combine the butter, maple syrup, and confectioners' sugar in a small bowl. Mix until smooth, then cover the surface with plastic wrap until ready to use.

10. Drizzle the glaze over the top of the pastry and allow it to set for 1 hour before cutting into individual squares.

❖ Bake Sale Tips

Wrap the squares individually in wax paper or tuck each in a vellum envelope and seal with a sticker.

To make two "pies," complete the recipe two separate times.

Pecan Prune Cake

Makes one 10-inch cake, serving 12 to 16;
an easy recipe to double

For the cake

1 cup pitted prunes

1 cup vegetable oil

2 cups sugar

3 large eggs

1 teaspoon pure vanilla extract

1 teaspoon baking soda

1 cup buttermilk

2 cups all-purpose flour

½ teaspoon ground cloves

½ teaspoon ground nutmeg

½ teaspoon ground allspice

½ teaspoon ground cinnamon

½ teaspoon salt

2 cups chopped pecans

For the optional glaze

½ cup sugar

½ cup buttermilk

¼ teaspoon baking soda

3 tablespoons unsalted butter

1. In a medium saucepan, combine the prunes with 1 cup water and bring to a boil. Remove from the heat, cover, and allow the prunes to steep for 15 minutes. Drain any remaining liquid and coarsely chop the prunes. (You may substitute an equivalent amount of store-bought stewed prunes; drain well.)

2. Preheat the oven to 350°F. Lightly mist a 10-inch tube cake pan with a removable bottom with nonstick cooking spray.

3. In a large bowl, whisk together the oil and sugar until smooth. Add the eggs and vanilla, and mix until thoroughly incorporated.

4. In a separate bowl, whisk together the baking soda and buttermilk.

5. In another large bowl, combine the flour, spices, and salt. Alternately add one-third of the flour mixture and half the buttermilk mixture, stirring just until incorporated after each addition; begin and end with the flour mixture. Fold in the prunes and the pecans. Spoon the batter into the prepared pan and bake for 55 to 60 minutes, or until a toothpick inserted into the center of the cake comes out clean. Transfer the cake to a wire rack and glaze, if desired.

6. While the cake is baking, make the glaze, if using, by combining all the ingredients in a medium saucepan. Cook over medium-low heat, stirring until all the sugar melts. Do not bring to a boil.

7. Prick the baked cake's surface with a fork, and pour half the glaze over the top; reserve the rest, warmed slightly, for serving. Allow the cake to cool in the pan for 30 minutes. Remove the sides of the pan and turn the cake upside down. Remove the center of the tube pan. Turn the cake right side up and cool completely. Transfer to a cake plate and wrap in plastic if not serving immediately.

in this book, considers her family recipe box even more of a direct link to the past than a family photograph album. "Both contain information, mark experiences, and recall family history. But so often, when I'm looking at a snapshot with one of my siblings, we have different versions of what's been documented there because of our selective personal-history buttons. The photo may have captured the moment, but the *feeling* of the experience isn't recreated there. But cook up one of my mother's desserts, and we all *feel* that same sense of familiarity, fondness, warmth.

"All five of us kids have copies of our favorite recipes from Mom's recipe box, but we're always misplacing them," Sharon says. "So that's an extra reason to call one another: while my sister or brother is rummaging for a copy of the recipe, we catch up on whatever's been happening in our lives. Our mother's recipes are a medium through which her children continually communicate."

For Sharon, as for many others, there must be dozens of prized desserts in that family recipe box. For this collection, Sharon chose her mom's sliced apples baked between two crusts in a cake pan. "We were always piling into the sedan for one family activity or another: all of us bundled up in layers of clothing, going to see the spectacular holiday windows in Chicago, all of us driving on an early spring morning to a lilac park, all of us venturing to an orchard to bring home loads of apples—and I mean *loads,* since there were seven of us picking. Then my mother set to baking pies, making applesauce, and preparing the giant, deli-

cious Pop-Tart we call 'apple slices,' which most resembles a smooshed apple pie. Although my mother prepared this snack throughout the year, it seemed to taste best with apples that we'd picked and carried home in those paper bags with the handles and the grower's name printed on the side."

In my own family's recipe box, there are somewhat fewer treats. To be specific, there are two.

My parents had been married a month when they moved from Columbus, Ohio, to Henderson, Kentucky, as part of my father's tour of duty for the army. As an officer—Dad taught artillery—he had to live off the base, so my parents found a log cabin home to rent for $61.50 per month. Their new landlords, Shirley and Saul Bernstein, became dear friends and were the only other Jews they'd meet in the area. They were also my mother's cooking guides for the next eighteen months: Southern cooking, Jewish cooking, and just plain old cooking, none of which my mother knew anything about.

Officers' wives weren't supposed to work; a $375 paycheck was to last the month. But my folks were also making payments on a 1952 Plymouth and a hide-away bed that doubled as their couch. For social occasions, the wives pooled whatever they had in their refrigerators.

Early on, the Bernsteins invited my parents for a Friday night Sabbath-eve dinner, and Shirley completed the meal with a pecan prune cake. My father flipped over it. My mother asked for the recipe, and Shirley

Aunt Sylvia's Rugelach

Makes 100 pieces

For the dough

16 tablespoons (2 sticks) margarine, cold, cut into 1-inch pieces

16 tablespoons (2 sticks) unsalted butter, cold, cut into 1-inch pieces

Two 8-ounce packages regular cream cheese

4 large egg yolks

5 cups all-purpose flour, plus extra for rolling out the dough

4 teaspoons baking powder

For the filling

1½ cups sugar

2 tablespoons cinnamon

1 cup apricot or raspberry preserves

2 cups finely chopped pecans or walnuts

Toasted sweetened coconut flakes, optional

For the topping

2 large egg whites

1 tablespoon cinnamon

1 cup sugar

1 cup chopped pecans or walnuts

1. In the bowl of an electric mixer fitted with the paddle attachment, combine the margarine, butter, and cream cheese and mix on medium speed until blended. Add the egg yolks and mix until incorporated. Scrape the inside of the bowl. Reduce the speed to low, add the flour and baking powder, and mix until dough forms a ball. Remove the mass of dough from the bowl. Knead briefly, if necessary, to bring it all together into a ball.

2. Divide the dough into 8 even pieces. Press each piece into a flat disk

wrote it out on a small card, which sits on my desk as I write this.

With this yet untried recipe card in her hand, my mother went to the commissary to buy her first tube pan: the same kind that Shirley owned, with the handle that slides around the bottom to release the cake. She bought the same measuring spoons that Shirley had used to ensure that she would measure correctly. She shopped for each ingredient, since she had nothing in her pantry. That afternoon, my mother worked her way through the recipe. "It took me a very long time to make the cake," she told me, "because I was so afraid. I had never baked a thing in my life."

When my father arrived home, he spied the glistening cake and the pool of glaze, and immediately grabbed the phone to invite a few couples from the base to come for coffee. He was so proud of my mother that "from that time on," my mother tells me, "I and seal it individually in plastic wrap. Refrigerate the dough for 4 hours or overnight. (The dough may be frozen for up to 1 month.)

3. Preheat the oven to 350°F. Line two to four baking sheets with aluminum foil or silicone mats.

4. To make the filling, combine the sugar and cinnamon in a small bowl and mix well.

5. Place one piece of dough on a lightly floured work surface and roll it into a 10- to 12-inch circle. Gently spread 2 tablespoons of the desired jam over the entire surface of the dough and sprinkle with 2 tablespoons of the cinnamon-sugar mixture. Top with 2 tablespoons of the chopped nuts and the coconut flakes, if using. Slice the circle, as you would a pizza, into 12 wedges. Roll each wedge from the outside edge to its point. Transfer each cookie to the prepared sheets,

placing them 1 inch apart, pointed flap down so that the cookie seals. Repeat the process with the remaining pieces of dough.

6. In a small bowl, combine the egg whites with 1 tablespoon water; whisk until frothy. In another bowl, combine the cinnamon, sugar, and nuts. With a pastry brush, generously paint each cookie with the egg wash, then sprinkle on a dense coating of the cinnamon-nut mixture.

7. Place the baking sheets on the top rack of the oven and bake for 30 to 35 minutes or until the pastry is browned and the preserves have caramelized at the edges of the pastry. Rotate the pans, front to back, halfway through the baking process.

8. Transfer the pastries to a wire rack to cool. Store in an airtight container for up to 1 week.

made pecan prune cake again and again and it was probably the only thing I baked until you kids were born."

After we were born, the pecan prune cake resurfaced, now and then, to signal a holiday or company for dinner. Otherwise, baking was what the bakery did. It's what David Hameroff's mother did, keeping her double-fork-crossed peanut butter cookies in a tin in the narrow cupboard beside the fridge. It's what the babysitter did—letting

us stir Rice Krispies into Marshmallow Fluff—so we could watch television way past our bedtimes. No other homemade dessert—with the exception of some far-fetched Jell-O-mold concoctions—ever really expanded her repertoire.

This, then, is the lone dessert that spans fifty-plus years in my small family, the one dessert that hints at who my parents were when they were younger than I knew them, the one dessert that brings back the image of my father's face beaming over his wife's, or one of his children's, accomplishment. A slice of this fragrant, moist, pecan-rich cake bears a deliciousness that ingredients alone cannot account for: It is memory, like salt, that brings the taste forward . . . forward into the future, "forward, you understand, and in the dark," as Robert Frost once wrote of a poem's captivating power.

Only one other sweet has eclipsed that cake. When my uncle remarried, Aunt Sylvia joined our Ohio family with an exuberant Manhattan spirit, a contagious sense of humor, and boundless affection. Despite her vivaciousness and youthful spirit, she is now the elder of our family—not because she presides at the religious holidays, not because she can speak the language of the old country, not because she can recall my grandparents as if they were her next-door neighbors—but because she's the muse of our family's culture: the raconteur, the re-memberer, *and* the bringer of *rugelach*.

Maybe every family boasts about that one relative who cooks the classic version of a certain food. The moment Aunt Sylvia's rugelach arrives on the sideboard, everyone in our family heralds these pastries as if we'd been wandering in the desert and they were the gift of manna.

No matter how many batches Aunt Sylvia rolls out, there are never enough rugelach. We devour them. We hoard them. We hide them, shamelessly, from one another. We feel guilty about inviting her over, since we know that will mean she will spend hours standing at the kitchen counter,

her back aching, as she rolls out more and more rugelach to bring along.

The last of the many times I asked Aunt Sylvia to teach me to make *her* rugelach, we were in my sister's kitchen; it was the final day of sitting shiva after my father's funeral. We had all spent a grief-driven week receiving friends, trading small, endearing anecdotes, and sharing in the waves of generously prepared meals and baked goods that arrived throughout the day, each with someone's name taped under the plate as though the act of returning this mound of dishes would reconnect us to the community of people whom we would love even harder.

My aunt had two answers for my request: "My mother was very strict when I was growing up," she began. "When I told my mother, finally, that I wanted to get married, she said to me, 'Well, then, Sylvia, I guess I better tell you the facts of life.' And so, *I* said"—and here my aunt switched to Yiddish, so it wouldn't sound quite so vulgar—"*Ma! I know* how to make *babies; how do you make rugelach?*"

Later, after another wave of visitors left, she told me: "You really want the secret of my rugelach? *Just keep me as your aunt.* People always ask me for my recipe, and I write it out for them, of course. I tell them how to roll the dough just right. But for whatever reason, they don't listen right or they get home and the phone starts ringing—they get confused, and the results aren't the same. So at the bottom of the recipe, I just write, like it's the last step in the baking, '*OR . . .*

you can just keep being my friend.' That's the secret to my rugelach; I'll always bring you some."

I know, I have just spent the last few pages touting the sacredness of one's own family's baked goods. That is the pleasure of recognition. But there is also the pleasure of surprise: the ever enticing opportunity to take a recipe or a flavor and welcome it to your table like your daughter's new best friend from college or a childhood friend you haven't seen in decades. Here are more than a hundred undemanding, authentic, beguiling, and entirely beloved baked goods well worth trying.

I know I can speak for everyone in this book when I say that we hope you'll not only discover a few new treats for your next bake sale, block party, birthday party, or lunch box, and pick up some practical baking tips and sound techniques from this pantheon of veteran bakers, but that you'll also pass along the one secret my aunt Sylvia and any other baker in this book would have you know: Keep near the ones you love, and—why not?—bring them something you've baked, something your love has sweetened, something their memories, in time, will salt.

—**Michael J. Rosen**
Hopewell Springs
Glenford, Ohio

The Great American Bake Sale®

All across America, kindergarteners and garden clubs, businesses and babysitters, farmer's markets and marching bands, sisterhoods and neighborhoods—people everywhere hold bake sales. Whether a sale takes the shape of a cake walk, pie auction, best-ever-brownies bake-off, block party, Kool-Aid stand, ice cream social, annual Irish soda bread sale before the Saint Patrick's Day parade, or a cake-decorating contest, the idea of baking some family specialty and offering it for sale must be the most popular, democratic, and downright delicious way that people of all ages raise funds and awareness for their communities and causes.

In 2003, Share Our Strength, one of this country's most inspired and effective anti-hunger agencies, along with *PARADE* magazine, the largest-circulation magazine in the United States, launched a nationwide grassroots effort to inspire thousands of bake

sales in the spring of each year. The clear and unified goal of these volunteer efforts: ending childhood hunger in America— something that needs no breakthrough cure, no controversial political win, no unattainable sum of money. Ending hunger simply requires that we "choose our battle": refuse to allow nearly 18 million American children to go hungry each day. And 18 million adults. That's 12 percent of the people we consider our neighbors, our fellow citizens, our future.

Share Our Strength grants the proceeds from all these bake sales to the most effective anti-hunger efforts throughout the nation. (See page 295 for more information on Share Our Strength's programs.) The sixty celebrity bakers, pastry chefs, chocolatiers, and cookbook authors gathered here have contributed their stories and recipes as part of this pledge to end hunger. Their cinnamon rolls, cheesecakes, pound cakes, scones, chocolate cookies, and peppermint patties are meant for your next bake sale or family gathering. Rather than offer exotic or complicated dishes, these renowned chefs have chosen recipes that express the essential character of family get-togethers, neighborhood block parties, and cherished holidays.

You, too, have a part to play in The Great American Bake Sale™ and in ending hunger in your community. You already have the compassion in your heart. You already know those perennial treats in your family's treasury of recipes. And here are more than 100 classic, original, delicious, and inspired treats vying to become one of your own family's most requested recipes.

To learn more about attending, hosting, or contributing to a future bake sale, please visit *www.greatamericanbakesale.org*, or Share Our Strength's own Web site, *www.strength.org*, or telephone: (800) 969–4767.

Before You Get Started

Unless otherwise directed in specific recipes, these ingredients are used for the recipes in this book.

Ingredients

All-purpose flour: This is the principal flour used throughout this book, although several recipes specify other types. All-purpose flour is not the same thing as self-rising flour or bread machine flour. To measure the flour, spoon it into a measuring cup, then remove the excess by passing a knife or other flat edge across the cup's rim.

Brown sugar: The recipes specify how to measure brown sugar, since its coarseness and moisture can make a light or heavy cup of sugar, depending on how tightly you pack the sugar in the measuring cup. With both dark and light sugar, follow directions as to whether the sugar should be lightly packed into the measuring cup, packed, or simply scooped and leveled with a knife, like flour.

Butter: Use good-quality, fresh, unsalted (also known as "sweet") butter. The package should be labeled U.S. Grade AA. Margarine cannot be substituted for butter; the taste and texture of the dessert will be altered. (Some recipes may call for a combination of both.) Unless the recipe specifies "softened butter," which is butter at room temperature, butter should come directly from the refrigerator. Butter can be stored in the freezer for several months.

Cake flour: Made from a softer wheat than all-purpose flour, cake flour gives a lighter texture. For a substitution, measure 1 cup bleached all-purpose flour according to the spoon-and-level method described in "all-purpose flour," and then remove 2 tablespoons. Use this scant cup of flour to replace 1 cup cake flour.

Chocolate: Use premium-quality chocolate, whether domestic or European, for the most intense chocolate flavor and the best results in baking.

Cocoa: Use Dutch-process cocoa powder, either domestic or European.

Confectioners' sugar: Also known as powdered sugar or 10x (ten times as fine as granulated sugar), it is often measured by weight when more accuracy is required.

Cream: This indicates heavy cream ("whipping" cream), which contains at least 36 percent butterfat. The higher fat content allows air to be incorporated into the cream when whipped.

Cream cheese: Use regular cream cheese, which has a high fat content. Low-fat or nonfat versions will result in a different texture and taste.

Eggs: Use AA large eggs.

Leavening agents (baking soda, baking powder, and yeast): Always check the expiration dates for these agents; if they are expired, their effectiveness is likely to be weakened, causing flatter, denser baked goods. They are not interchangeable in any recipe.

Milk: Use whole milk. Although many home bakers freely substitute lower-fat milk, soy milk, buttermilk, or yogurt, such changes may have an undesirable effect on a recipe's success and cannot be recommended.

Nuts: Nuts should be stored in airtight containers in the freezer and brought to room temperature before using. Taste a sample nut before incorporating the full amount into a dough or batter; nut oils can take on undesirable flavors.

Pastry flour: Pastry flour is carried in specialty markets and larger food emporiums. It can also be ordered from King Arthur Baking Company. For a substitution, use a ratio of 3 parts all-purpose flour to 1 part cake flour (for example, ¾ cup all-purpose flour and ¼ cup cake flour can replace 1 cup pastry flour).

King Arthur Flour Company
P. O. Box 876
Norwich, Vermont 05055–0876
(800) 827–6836
www.kingarthurflour.com

Salt: Use fine salt, which dissolves more quickly. Kosher salt or other large-grain salts will measure differently and may not distribute evenly.

Sugar: Use granulated sugar unless directed otherwise, preferably from sugar cane rather than beets. Cane sugar caramelizes more readily and is widely available at a similar price.

Vanilla beans: Although whole beans are expensive, they create the necessary vanilla character the contributing chefs desire in these recipes. Choose moist, aromatic beans, which will provide the best flavor. Premium beans from various countries can be ordered from many gourmet purveyors such as King Arthur's Baking Catalog or Penzeys.

Penzeys Spices
P. O. Box 933
Muskego, Wisconsin 53150
(292) 679–7207
www.penzeys.com

Equipment

Baking pans and pots: Baking and cooking times vary depending upon the quality, thickness, and material of your cookware. Heavy-gauge equipment, which holds a consistent heat and distributes it evenly, is specified in most of these recipes. If you use glass baking dishes, reduce the baking temperature by 25°F and anticipate a shorter baking time.

Baking parchment paper or silicone mats: Baking parchment can be purchased in rolls or sheets and cut to fit almost any size pan. The paper will reduce sticking as well as offer a means of lifting baked goods from the pan. Silicone mats, which can be reused a thousand times, serve the same purpose. Simply wipe them down with a damp cloth and dry them between uses. Although many recipes suggest aluminum foil or one or both of these nonstick alternatives, they cannot always be used interchangeably; simply choose the option presented by the contributing chef in each recipe.

Baking sheets: Also known as jelly roll pans, these are the flat metal pans with rims or upturned edges. A cookie sheet has only two upturned edges.

Candy thermometer: Small changes in sugar temperature can change the structure of melted sugar. Most candy thermometers can be clipped to the inside of a pot with the tip immersed in the sugar. Clean after each use by soaking the thermometer in tepid water to dissolve the sugar. Store in a safe place to protect the glass tube.

Electric mixer: For the most consistent results, use a heavy-duty standing electric mixer with a paddle, whisk, and dough-hook attachments. A mixer with too little

Bake Sale Tips

Many recipes throughout the book are followed by a short paragraph with suggestions on how to wrap, transport, or present the dessert at a bake sale. Some are simply styling suggestions, while others offer precautions: All the recipes presented here can be brought to a bake sale, but a few have "home" versions, in which a dollop of whipped cream, sorbet, or sauce might enhance the dessert plate. A few *require* refrigeration. If transporting baked goods will require an extended journey in a car or prolonged exposure to warm weather or high humidity, either choose one of the desserts that won't be affected by these conditions, or take pains to package and pad the item in a cooler filled with ice packs.

Although cakes and pies are intended to be sliced into individual portions, the baking tips suggest leaving whole any desserts that might be rather sticky, crumbly, or moist.

power can cause a range of problems: The beaters can overwork the dough, heat rather than cream the butter, or fail to beat enough air into a batter or egg whites.

Food processors: Use the steel blade for all the recipes in this book. A food processor cannot be used interchangeably with an electric mixer.

Nonreactive bowl: Many recipes specify nonreactive bowls such as glass or stainless steel because they do not stain, retain flavors, or chemically react with ingredients.

Nonreactive pots and pans: In general, use stainless steel, enamel-coated cast iron (such as Le Creuset), or anodized aluminum equipment. Heat and acids, such as lemon juice, can react with aluminum pans to create off-flavors and colors.

Ovens: Preheat the oven for 20 minutes prior to baking; a proper, consistent temperature is critical in many baking recipes. In addition to programming or setting the oven's temperature, use an interior thermometer to confirm baking temperature. Unless directed otherwise, place your baking sheet or cake pan on the middle rack of the oven for baking. To ensure even baking, many recipes specify rotating the pan from front to back midway through the baking process; when two racks and two baking pans are being used, rotation also means switching positions from one rack to the other.

Rolling pins: Whether wood or marble, rolling pins should by wiped clean with a damp cloth rather than immersed in water.

Techniques

Doubling recipes: Although a bake sale might signal the perfect chance to double a recipe, doubling or tripling a recipe may change the results. Your food processor's or mixer's capacity, likewise, determines whether the increased volume of ingredients will be handled effectively without taxing the machinery or warming the mixture. Whipping egg whites or heavy cream often requires a large-capacity bowl. Specific times are often given for steps throughout these recipes; these times may differ if the size of the pan or the quantity of its contents is increased. It can be difficult to divide cake batters evenly among several baking pans. Therefore, in the baking tips paragraph, we note the recipes that are more dependably doubled if you make them two separate times. If it is especially easy to double a recipe, this is noted in the yield.

Measuring dry ingredients: Use dry measuring cups and spoon the dry ingredient into the cup. Mound more than will fit into the cup, then scrape off any excess by passing a knife or straight edge across the lip of the cup.

Melting chocolate: Several recipes require melting chocolate. Often it can be melted by the addition of a hot liquid. But when melting on its own, a double boiler can be used. Take extra care not to splash any water into the chocolate, which can make it seize up and harden. A microwave oven can also be used. Depending on the wattage of the particular machine, chocolate can melt very quickly. In general, break up the chocolate in a microwave-safe bowl, and use half power for a short burst of time (30 seconds). Check the chocolate, stir the chips, and microwave for another 30 seconds. Continue as needed, stopping when the chocolate is half melted; stirring will finish the process.

Starting: Read the entire recipe before starting. Check to see that you have all the ingredients, equipment, and necessary time required to complete the dish.

Gather all ingredients 30 minutes before you begin baking or mixing to bring them within reach and to a similar temperature, which will create a smoother batter. Placing eggs in a bowl of warm water will bring them to room temperature in about 5 minutes.

Cookies
and Bars

Michel Richard's Hazelnut Grahams

Miguel Ravago's Polvorones con Canela (Mexican Wedding Cookies)

Elizabeth Falkner's Browned Butter–Walnut Tea Cakes

Judy Rosenberg's Almond Raspberry Bars

Greg Patent's Apricot-Cherry Coconut Bars and
his mom's Walnut Fudge Brownies

Joanne Chang's Homemade Oreos®

Dorie Greenspan's Choco–Peanut Butter Oatmeal Chipsters

François Payard's Flourless, Butterless Chocolate Cookies

Susan and Cassandra Purdy's Apricot Crumb Bars

Judy Zeidler's Korjas (Crisp Poppy Seed Thins) and
Poppy Seed Hamantaschen

Lora Brody's grandmother's Mohn Kickle (Poppy Seed Cookies)

Jacques Torres's Blueberry Dame Blanche

Nicole Kaplan's Most Favorite Cheesecake Brownies
and Best-Ever Hot Fudge Sundaes

Lindsey Shere and Kathleen Stewart's Gingersnap Ice Cream
Sandwiches with Wild Plum Ice Cream

Fran Bigelow's Chocolate Wafer Cookies (page 195)

Nick Malgieri's Biscotti di Pasta Frolla (page 121)

Michael J. Rosen's Aunt Sylvia's Rugelach (page 6)

Crescent Dragonwagon's Grandma Hat's Butter Cookies (page 284)

Hazelnut Grahams

◇◆◇

I was born in Brittany and raised in Ardens. We had an apricot tree across the street from our home. When the fruit covered the tree, my friend and I would tuck our T-shirts inside our pants and load them up with apricots, dropping the fruit inside the collar until the fruit gave us each a big belly brimming over our pants. The *garde de campagne,* the country policeman, found us one time: "What do you have in your belly there?" he asked us. He tugged at our T-shirts, pulling them from our pants and spilling all the apricots out onto the ground. He gave us each a ticket; I think my mother had to pay something like a quarter as a fine. But I feasted on a ton of apricots for that quarter.

The other crop that was free for the taking was the fresh hazelnuts that bordered a forest on the way to school. We had no money to buy candy, but here was the candy offered by God. You have to pluck off the green case with your fingers, and then pop the hard shell into your mouth and crack it open with your teeth—at least, if you're a kid walking to school. The nut meat inside is soft, like a fresh pea; they have a wonderful milky texture. The typical hazelnut aroma comes from roasting them, but we had no time to take them home to the oven; my stomach had to be my oven!

This hazelnut graham cracker, something I invented many years later, brings back the memory of those hazelnut trees, as well as the very best of the hazelnut's flavor. The nut's buttery texture is enhanced with a little more butter and the graham cracker's own nuttiness. And they're simple enough for your own kids to make and take to school.

Michel Richard's Basque Custard Cookie Cake appears on page 117.

Hazelnut Grahams

Makes 3 dozen cookies

½ cup hazelnuts

2 cups graham cracker crumbs

16 tablespoons (2 sticks) unsalted butter

½ cup dark brown sugar (packed)

1 large egg, at room temperature

1. Preheat the oven to 350°F and place the hazelnuts on a baking sheet. Toast the nuts for 7 minutes, or until they just begin to brown; lightly shake the pan midway through the toasting to turn the nuts. Remove the nuts from the oven. If your hazelnuts were not "husked" and still possess a papery outer skin, place them in a tea towel, and rub briskly to dislodge this darker outer covering from the nuts.

2. Combine the hazelnuts and crumbs in a food processor and grind to a fine powder.

3. In the bowl of an electric mixer fitted with the paddle attachment, combine the butter and brown sugar on low speed and mix until just blended. Add the egg and mix until just incorporated. On low speed, add the crumb mixture and blend until just incorporated.

4. Cover the bowl with plastic wrap and refrigerate the dough for 15 to 30 minutes or until it is firm enough to shape.

5. Divide the dough into 2 equal portions. Place each portion on a 12-inch piece of plastic wrap and form two logs with a diameter of 1½ inches. Seal the plastic around the logs and refrigerate for 4 hours or until firm. You can also freeze the dough for 2 months; defrost in the refrigerator before continuing with the recipe.

6. When ready to bake, preheat the oven to 350°F. Line two baking sheets with parchment paper or silicone mats.

7. Slice the dough into ¼-inch coins and arrange them on the prepared sheets, leaving a bit less than an inch between each cookie. Bake the cookies on the middle rack of the oven for 8 to 10 minutes or until the edges of the cookies are browned; rotate the pans halfway through the baking. Allow the cookies to cool slightly on the baking sheet before transferring them to a wire rack to cool completely. Store in an airtight container.

Michel Richard is an internationally acclaimed chef and restaurateur. He has been the recipient of the most prestigious culinary honors and appears frequently on nationally televised cooking shows. Born in France, Michel came to the United States in 1974 to open Gaston Lenôtre's New York City pastry shop. Michel then moved to Santa Fe before opening his own pastry shop in Los Angeles. He opened his famed restaurant Citrus in 1987. In September 1997, Michel moved to Washington, D.C., to create Citronelle. He is co-author with Judy Zeidler of Michel Richard's Home Cooking with a French Accent.

Miguel Ravago's

Polvorones con Canela

(Mexican Wedding Cookies)

This recipe is my mother's, but its origin is certainly Arabic, taken to Mexico by the Spaniards at some point in their long mutual history. *Polvorones* comes from the Spanish word for "dust," *polvo,* because the cookies are dusted with powdered sugar. And the cookies have to be small enough to just pop in your mouth whole, because if you bite into one, the dust of the powdered sugar will make you cough.

My mother baked these cookies every week, and we'd have them after church on Sunday: We'd walk in the door and the cookies would be sitting on a plate, cooled to room temperature, and all we'd need to do was stir up a batch of Mexican chocolate drink to accompany them.

But polvorones are also part of most every Mexican wedding, mounded into in a pyramid at the reception. They make a beautiful white centerpiece: all the little balls carefully stacked into a tower as high as someone can reach. With all the dressed-up people hugging and rushing over to see relatives, the table is always jostled and the tower of cookies inevitably falls over, the balls rolling across the tablecloth. It doesn't matter. Each guest has a few polvorones with a glass of liqueur—my grandfather insisted that anise was perfect—or a glass of Mexican chocolate, and the celebration continues for hours.

These cookies are also just right for bake sales or with a gulp of milk drunk right from a little school-size carton.

Miguel Ravago's Capirotada (Mexican Bread Pudding) and his
unusual Almond Flan begin on page 143.

Polvorones con Canela

(Mexican Wedding Cookies)

Makes 4 dozen cookies

---

16 tablespoons (2 sticks) unsalted butter,
   softened

1½ cups sifted confectioners' sugar

1 tablespoon pure vanilla extract

2 cups all-purpose flour

¼ teaspoon salt

⅔ cup ground or finely chopped
   pecans

1 teaspoon ground cinnamon

1. In the bowl of an electric mixer fitted with the paddle attachment, beat the butter on medium speed for 1 minute or until creamy. Add ½ cup of the confectioners' sugar and the vanilla; mix for 1 to 2 minutes or until creamy.

2. In a large bowl, combine the flour and salt. With the mixer on the lowest speed, add the flour mixture to the butter, 1 tablespoon at a time. Add the nuts with the final addition of the flour and mix just to combine. Cover the bowl with plastic wrap and chill for 2 hours, or until the dough is firm.

3. Preheat the oven to 345°F.

4. Form the dough into ¾-inch balls by rolling small pieces between your palms. Place the balls 1 inch apart on an ungreased baking sheet. Place the sheet on the middle rack of the oven and bake for 15 minutes until the edges of the cookies turn a golden color. Rotate the pan front to back halfway through the baking process.

5. Put the remaining 1 cup confectioners' sugar and the cinnamon in a large bowl. Remove the cookies from the oven and, while they are still warm, put the cookies into the sugar mixture and cover completely. Allow each powdered cookie to cool on a wire rack set on a pan to catch the sugar. When the cookies are completely cooled, dust them again with the sugar mixture. Store the cookies in an airtight container at room temperature.

Miguel Ravago's dedication to the cuisines of Mexico in their authentic preparations have made him an authority on the regional dishes of Mexico. He began his culinary knowledge working with his grandmother, a native of Sonora, Mexico, and continued to refine his understanding of Mexico's culinary heritage during his twenty-eight years in the restaurants he co-founded with Thomas Gilliland—San Angel Inn in Houston and Fonda San Miguel in Austin—and other Mexican food authorities in consultation with Diana Kennedy and Patricia Quintana. With Marilyn Tausend, Miguel co-authored Cocina de la Familia, *which won an IACP/Julia Child Cookbook Award.*

Browned Butter–Walnut Tea Cakes

 love to eat and bake with all kinds of nuts. Hazelnuts, pistachios, pecans, peanuts, macadamias, almonds, walnuts—they all have a place in our baking and the savory food at Citizen Cake.

A couple of years ago, I was invited by the California Walnut Board to teach some California-style pastry classes throughout Japan. The Japanese love and consume loads of walnuts (they've long been aware of their nutritional properties), but their taste in sweets is very different from the typical American's. Japanese confections are usually consumed with tea, and they are less sweet and more subtle in flavor than Western desserts. Traditional Japanese confections are rice crackers or baked goods with various bean pastes or sweet potato rather than frostings or buttercream. Even fruit fillings are more delicate. Also, most of their baked goods are finely textured or flaky, with a buttery richness; a crusty baguette was never as popular as a smooth Wonder Bread–like bun. (And the Japanese can't fathom America's jumbo bags of cookies or grand samplers of candy; their treats are packaged individually or in small clusters, with miniature boxes or wrappers that add that extra element of expectation.)

But around the middle of the last century, the Japanese fascination with Western-style baking and pastry-making became a passion, and talented chefs began to showcase classic European baked goods. The country also began to plant decorative walnut trees. (California is their preferred source of consistently superior walnuts.) And I heard a story there about how the Japanese crows, too, came to love walnuts. I know this sounds like folklore, but I was told many stories about these wise birds around several dinner tables. The crows have figured out how to get the meat from the walnut's very hard shell: They drop the whole nuts into busy intersections where cars are waiting at red lights. The car tires crack the shells when the traffic rushes ahead at the green light, and then, when the light changes to red again, the crows hop into the road with the pedestrians and pluck up the shattered nut bits.

Among the two dozen recipes I created for this new niche were Rocky Road Brownies with homemade marshmallows, milk chocolate chunks, and walnuts; a Walnut-Cheddar-Olive Shortbread; and a Citrus and Walnut "Salad" with a chocolate crottin and espresso-walnut vinaigrette.

But I especially love the idea of these tea cakes, which afford just a single bite of cake. Like a truffle, each one possesses a single burst of flavor, but with less intensity. I think of them as modern, California-style petits fours that don't need the fondant and jam, and they were a big hit in Japan. The subtle taste of brown butter, which is more typical in a savory or sautéing application, really enhances the richness of walnuts. They're an ideal treat for Japanese or Western teatime.

Elizabeth Falkner's Rhubarb-Strawberry-Rose Pie and her biography begin on page 98.

Browned Butter–Walnut Tea Cakes

Makes 3½ dozen tea cakes (see Bake Sale Tip)

----

32 tablespoons (4 sticks) unsalted butter, browned and cooled to room temperature (see page 253 on browning butter)

1¾ cups sugar
6 large eggs
2 cups ground walnuts
2¼ cups pastry flour
½ teaspoon kosher salt

1. Preheat the oven to 325°F. The recipe will make 3½ dozen tea cakes, so lightly butter as many 12-cup small muffin tins or madeleine pans as you have and make the

tea cakes in batches. You may also use one 12½ x 17-inch rimmed baking sheet, lined with parchment, and cut the cooled tea cakes from that one large sheet.

2. In the bowl of an electric mixer fitted with the paddle attachment, cream the browned butter and sugar on medium speed for 1 minute. Reduce the speed to low and add the eggs all at once. Mix for 1 to 2 minutes. Scrape down the inside surface of the bowl.

3. In a medium bowl, combine the walnuts, flour, and salt and add to the egg batter; mix on low speed just to combine.

4. Transfer the batter to a large pastry bag fitted with a wide plain pastry tip and pipe into the molds, or spread the batter evenly across the entire baking sheet.

5. Bake for 10 to 15 minutes or until the tea cakes are firm to the touch and have pulled away from the sides of the pan. Allow the cakes to cool slightly and then invert the tins. (If using a baking sheet, you may need to extend the cooking time another 5 to 7 minutes. Cut the cake into small squares after the sheet has cooled.) Transfer the tea cakes to wire racks and cool completely. Store in an airtight container at room temperature for up to 3 days.

❖ Bake Sale Tip

Making many small tea cakes would be ideal. But this batter will also fill one rimmed baking sheet, so you can bake the tea cakes in one "batch" and cut them into small squares.

Judy Rosenberg's
Almond Raspberry Bars

I came upon my baking talent by sheer chance, having accumulated a bunch of unrelated degrees that nonetheless left me confused about my future. I was also very educated in dessert consumption, having indulged way more than I should have until college, when my love for boys overcame my love for food (momentarily). When I graduated from the Boston Museum School (this was *after* college, and *after* graduate school), I still had no idea of how to earn money until, one day, I created some very elegantly decorated sugar cookies to be sold as objets d'art at local galleries and boutiques, which aroused the interest of one Harvard Square bakery owner who insisted I go home and bake more goodies for him.

What followed was an amazing period of self-discovery during which I unearthed my hidden baking talents, tempting the Harvard Square crowd and, eventually, the inhabitants of Boston and the surrounding areas with reincarnations of my favorite childhood desserts. There is no question that my mother's savvy dessert choices, the genes I inherited from my great-grandmother, and my own lust for desserts all burst forth and gave me that needed focus.

Almond paste and raspberry preserves—in combination with a rich pastry crust—was such a memory-rich flavor combination that it begged to be among the first of my creations. I remembered it from Jewish holiday fare, and perhaps it was popular at Éclair, a bakery in our old neighborhood. Both memories combined to inspire this recipe, which is easy to make and yet sophisticated. Although I have also reworked this recipe to make a whole tart, this version makes an elegant dessert that you can slice into small bits to accompany your afternoon tea or tuck into a tin and bring along to a bake sale.

Judy Rosenberg's Rosie Pies, her own version of Whoopie Pies®,
appears on page 166.

Almond Raspberry Bars

Makes one 8 x 8-inch pan or 18 bars

For the crust

1½ cups all-purpose flour

6 tablespoons confectioners' sugar

12 tablespoons (1½ sticks) unsalted butter, cold

For the topping

7 ounces almond paste (available at larger supermarkets and specialty stores)

¼ cup sugar

2 tablespoons plus 2 teaspoons unsalted butter, softened

3 large eggs, beaten

1 teaspoon pure almond extract

1 teaspoon lemon zest

Pinch of salt

⅛ teaspoon baking powder

½ cup raspberry preserves

1. Preheat the oven to 350°F. Lightly mist an 8 x 8 inch baking pan with nonstick cooking spray.

2. In a food processor fitted with the steel blade, combine the ingredients for the crust and pulse the machine for 30 seconds, or until the dough comes together. Remove the dough and press it into the prepared pan. Bake on the middle rack of the oven for 30 to 35 minutes, or until the crust is a light golden brown.

3. Place the pan in the refrigerator to cool quickly.

4. In the food processor, place the almond paste and sugar and blend for 25 seconds, or until the mixture looks like coarse sand. Stop the processor and add the butter, eggs, almond extract, zest, salt, and baking powder and process for 20 seconds, or until the mixture looks smooth.

5. Transfer the filling to the bowl of an electric mixer fitted with the paddle attachment and mix on medium-high speed for 2 to 3 minutes, or until the mixture is pale yellow and very thick.

6. Remove the crust from the refrigerator and spread the jam carefully over the crust, leaving ½ inch of crust around the edges. Gently pour the almond filling over the jam, taking care not to mix the two. Tip the pan from side to side to distribute the almond filling evenly.

7. Return the pan to the oven and bake for 35 to 40 minutes, or until the topping is set and a light golden brown. Cool the pan completely before cutting into bars or squares.

Judy Rosenberg resides in the Boston area with her husband, three children, her mother, and her dog. She is the proprietor of four award-winning Rosie's Bakeries. She is the author of Rosie's All-Butter, Fresh Cream, Sugar-Packed, No-Holds-Barred-Baking Book *and* Rosie's Bakery Chocolate-Packed, Jam-Filled, Butter-Rich, No-Holds-Barred Cookie Book. *Her products can be purchased over the Internet at www.rosiesbakery.com.*

Greg Patent's

Apricot-Cherry Coconut Bars
and his mom's
Walnut Fudge Brownies

I started baking when I was eleven, shortly after we immigrated to San Francisco from Shanghai. My expatriate parents (mom from Iraq, dad from Russia) met, fell in love, and married in China. But fearing Mao's regime, they left for America. Shortly after arriving in our new country, my father bought a television; this was 1950, and programming was limited. But a daily live cooking show, hosted by Edith Green on KRON-TV, really got my attention. There she was, this tiny, kindly lady, making and baking all sorts of things. And it looked so easy, I decided to give it a try. Armed with the one cookbook we had at the time, *Betty Crocker's Picture Cook Book,* I found something I thought I could make with no trouble: baking-powder biscuits. They turned out hard as rocks. And I cried. Our landlady, Mrs. Brown, came to console me, suggesting that maybe I had kneaded the dough too much. "Be gentle," she said. "Biscuits need tender loving care." So I gave it another shot. When the biscuits turned out high and light, I was hooked.

I moved on to cookies, pies, and cakes. By my late teens, I felt confident enough to enter the Pillsbury Bake-Off, but I wasn't sure what dessert to enter. I loved an oatmeal date bar cookie at our neighborhood bake shop, The Sugar Bowl. It reminded me of my Iraqi grandmother and of the date-filled pastry she'd made us back in Shanghai.

Oatmeal was new to me, and though dates were delicious, dried apricots were my real favorites. So I took Betty Crocker's date bar recipe as a guide, but substituted dried apricots for the dates, and walnuts and coconut for the oatmeal. Then I served up large portions of my new bar and topped each with whipped cream. Voilà! My entry for the 10th Betty Crocker Bake-Off was born.

As a minor, I had to be chaperoned at the Bake-Off. My mom and I flew to New York City—we'd never been there before—where we were put up at the luxurious Waldorf-Astoria. We were given a formal tour of the city, some spending money for our own informal sightseeing, as well as lavish evening meals. The morning of the event, we were even served breakfast in bed, though a bad case of jitters killed my appetite. All I could think of was, how could I possibly bake in front of all those people?

Along with ninety-eight other contestants (one lady couldn't make it because she'd just had a baby), I marched into the Grand Ballroom to strains of "When the Saints Come Marching In." We each took our cooking stations. The moment I started cooking, I was calm, in a world of my own. I baked two batches of Apricot Dessert Bars, one for the judges and one for display. The next day, at the awards luncheon emceed by Art Linkletter, we were seated at a table with Ronald Reagan, who was then a movie actor. When the announcement came that I'd won the $1,000 second prize in the junior division, I jumped up and kissed the check Art Linkletter handed me. This was 1958. I was nineteen years old.

I continue to enjoy this now age-old winner, and for this book, I've shared a new version that includes dried cherries and pecans.

Ever since I won that prize, my mother resolved to become a Bake-Off finalist herself. For forty years, she entered recipes. At first, she sent in her versions of my granny's date pastries, sponge cake, and hamantaschen. Later on, she sent in main dishes, usually stir-fries based on what we had enjoyed in Shanghai. As an example of sheer determination, at the ripe young age of eighty-three, she finally made it to the 39th Pillsbury Bake-Off in 2000, with her Walnut Fudge Bars.

There's no longer a "made from scratch" baking category in today's streamlined-for-speed Bake-Off, so Mom's only option was to use a brownie mix. Her submitted recipe took less than fifteen minutes of prep time, the maximum allowed in the Bake-Off's "Fast and Fabulous Treats" category. I've adapted her recipe (Mom, forgive me!) and made it from scratch, which takes only five minutes more!

My mother didn't win any cash at that Bake-Off, so she continues to enter the biennial contest in quest of the big bucks. We talk often on the phone, especially at Bake-Off time, when she calls to ask my opinion of a recipe idea. "Go for it, Mom," I say. "It's always worth a try."

Apricot-Cherry Coconut Bars

Makes one 9 x 13-inch pan or 15 large bars

For the filling

½ **pound dried apricots**

½ **pound dried unsweetened sour cherries**

1 cup plus 2 tablespoons sugar

For the crust

1¾ **cups unbleached all-purpose flour**

½ **teaspoon baking soda**

¼ **teaspoon salt**

½ **teaspoon freshly grated nutmeg**

12 tablespoons (1½ sticks) unsalted butter, softened

1 cup sugar

1 cup chopped pecans

1 cup sweetened shredded coconut

Sweetened Whipped Cream, optional, for serving

1. Combine the apricots, cherries, and 2 cups water in a heavy 2- to 3-quart saucepan. Cook over medium-high heat until the mixture comes to a boil and then reduce the heat to low. Cover the pan and cook slowly, stirring occasionally, until the fruit is very tender, 40 to 45 minutes. Strain over a bowl and reserve ¼ cup juice.

2. Return the fruit to the pan. With a potato masher, smash the fruit until it is almost smooth. Stir in the reserved juice and 1 cup plus the 2 tablespoons sugar. Bring the puree to a boil over medium-high heat, stirring occasionally. Then cook, stirring con-

stantly, for 5 minutes. Transfer the puree to a plate and cool to room temperature.

3. To make the crust, preheat the oven to 400°F. Grease a 9 x 13-inch baking pan with butter or vegetable shortening.

4. In a medium bowl, sift together the flour, baking soda, salt, and nutmeg and whisk to combine.

5. In the bowl of an electric mixer fitted with the paddle attachment, beat the butter on medium speed for 1 minute, or until smooth. Add the sugar and beat on medium speed for 3 to 4 minutes, or until smooth and fluffy. Reduce the speed to low, add the dry ingredients, and mix just to incorporate.

6. Remove the bowl from the mixer and stir in the pecans and coconut to make a crumbly mixture. Press half onto the bottom of the prepared pan. Bake for 10 minutes, or until the crust is lightly browned. Remove from the oven, and spread the cooled fruit filling evenly over the hot crust. Sprinkle the remaining crumb mixture over the fruit and gently pat the crumbs in place. (Do not pack it down.)

7. Bake for 20 to 25 minutes, or until the top is golden brown. Transfer the pan to a wire rack and cool completely before cutting into bars. For serving at home, place each bar on a small plate and top with a dollop of sweetened whipped cream.

❖ Bake Sale Tip

Wrap each individual bar in clear cellophane or wax paper and seal with a sticker.

Walnut Fudge Brownies

Makes one 9 x 13-inch pan or 32 brownies

16 tablespoons (2 sticks) unsalted butter

3 tablespoons Dutch-process cocoa powder

4 ounces unsweetened chocolate, coarsely chopped

2 cups sugar

4 large eggs

1 tablespoon pure vanilla extract

¼ teaspoon salt

1 cup unbleached all-purpose flour

2 cups old-fashioned rolled oats

2 cups chopped walnuts

12 ounces (2 cups) semisweet chocolate chips

One 14-ounce can sweetened condensed milk

1. Preheat the oven to 350°F. Grease a 9 x 13-inch nonstick baking pan with vegetable shortening. (Do not use nonstick cooking spray; you want the batter to adhere to the pan as you spread it.)

2. In a heavy 3- to 4-quart saucepan, melt the butter over low heat. Whisk in the cocoa and cook, stirring occasionally, for 3 minutes. (Cooking the butter with the cocoa intensifies the cocoa flavor.) Though the mixture will not look smooth, do not allow it to boil.

3. Add the unsweetened chocolate and stir occasionally with a whisk until melted.

Sweetened Whipped Cream

2 cups heavy cream
¼ cup confectioners' sugar
1 teaspoon pure vanilla extract

In the bowl of an electric mixer fitted with the whisk attachment, beat together the cream, confectioners' sugar, and vanilla on medium-high speed until the cream is thick and holds a shape. Refrigerate until ready to use.

The mixture will smooth out as the chocolate melts. Remove from the heat. Whisk in the sugar. Continue to whisk, and add the eggs one at a time, incorporating each one thoroughly before adding the next. Mix in the vanilla and salt. Slowly whisk in the flour. Stir in the rolled oats and walnuts.

4. Evenly spread 3 cups of this mixture on the bottom of the prepared pan and set aside.

5. In a medium-size, microwave-safe bowl, combine the chocolate chips and sweetened condensed milk and microwave on low power for 1 to 1½ minutes. Stir the mixture well. If the chocolate has not all melted, microwave a few seconds longer until the mixture is smooth. (Alternatively, you can do this in a heavy 2-quart saucepan over low heat, stirring occasionally until the mixture is smooth.)

6. Scrape the fudge mixture over the brownie base in the pan and spread to form an even layer. Scrape the remaining brownie mixture on top of the fudge layer and gently spread to form a thin, even layer.

7. Place the pan on the middle rack of the oven and bake for 28 to 32 minutes, or until the top feels dry and the edges just begin to pull away from the sides of the pan. Do not overbake. Transfer the brownies to a wire rack to cool for 1 hour.

8. Run the tip of a knife around the sides of the pan to release the brownies. Cover the pan with a board or cookie sheet and invert to drop the block of brownies from the pan. Remove the pan and refrigerate the brownies, uncovered, for 2 to 3 hours, or until the block is firm enough to cut into pieces.

Cut and wrap individual brownies in wax paper or cellophane and store in an airtight container in the refrigerator or at room temperature.

Greg Patent lives and bakes in Missoula, Montana. His book Baking in America *won the 2003 James Beard Award for best baking book of the year.*

Joanne Chang's
Homemade Oreos®

--------------------- ◇◆◇ ---------------------

rowing up in a Chinese household does have its advantages: For example, you get red envelopes filled with money at every holiday, and burping at the table is actually considered good manners. However, a major drawback for me as a kid was that we never seemed to have "normal" food in the house. When friends would come over after school, we had oranges for snacks. Or I'd eat these candied kumquats or sour, salty dried plums or *bao* (steamed buns) that my mother would buy at the Chinese bakery near our house in Houston. (I took the ones filled with red-bean paste while my brother opted for the pork-filled buns.)

My mom shopped only in Chinese grocery stores and she refused to buy American junk food. I learned about Doritos, Twinkies, Devil Dogs, and Snickers by visiting friends' houses. I often tried to get Mom to buy me Oreos because they were one of my favorite cookies, but she scoffed, "Burned cookies, they are just selling you the bad ones. You can't eat these—they are too black!" She wouldn't even taste them.

When I opened my own bakery, Flour, I was determined to make an Oreo-like cookie that would blow Nabisco out of the water—and maybe convince Mom that just because they were black didn't mean they were burned or bad.

Now, when I send her cookies from my bakery to her home in Dallas, she specifically asks for these Oreos.

Joanne Chang's Apple Snacking Spice Cake and
her biography appear on page 220.

Homemade Oreos®

Makes 50 sandwich cookies

For the cookies

2 cups all-purpose flour

2 cups Dutch-process cocoa powder

1 teaspoon baking soda

10½ ounces semisweet chocolate,
    coarsely chopped

14 tablespoons (1¾ sticks) unsalted butter

¾ cup sugar

1 large egg

½ cup light corn syrup

For the filling

16 tablespoons (2 sticks) unsalted butter,
    softened

5½ cups confectioners' sugar

¼ teaspoon pure vanilla extract

1. In a large bowl, sift together the flour, cocoa, and baking soda.

2. In a small heavy saucepan, melt the chocolate over low heat, stirring the entire time. Remove from the heat and cool slightly. (You may also melt the chocolate using a microwave-safe bowl, setting the microwave at half power for 1 minute; remove the chocolate, stir, and return to the microwave for another burst, if needed. When the chocolate is half melted, stirring will complete the process.)

3. In a medium saucepan, over medium heat, melt the butter with the sugar, stirring to dissolve the sugar. Remove from the heat and add the melted chocolate, egg, and corn syrup; mix thoroughly. Pour the chocolate mixture into the dry ingredients and mix well to blend all of the ingredients.

4. Divide the dough into 3 equal pieces. Roll each piece into a 9-inch log. Seal each log in plastic wrap and refrigerate for 6 hours or overnight.

5. Preheat the oven to 350°F and line two or three cookie sheets with parchment paper or silicone mats.

6. Slice the cookies into ¼-inch-thick disks and arrange them on the prepared pan, leaving 1 inch between each cookie. Place the pan on the middle rack of the oven and bake for 10 to 12 minutes, until the cookies are firm. (They won't be perceptibly darker or crispy.) Transfer the baked cookies to a wire rack to cool completely.

7. To make the filling, put the butter in the bowl of an electric mixer fitted with the paddle attachment. Mix on medium speed for 2 minutes, or until creamy. Reduce the speed to low, gradually add the confectioners' sugar, and mix until creamy and smooth. Add the vanilla and mix briefly.

8. Divide the filling in half. Roll each half into a log just a bit smaller than the diameter of the finished cookies. Slice the logs into ⅓-inch disks, and sandwich each between two of the baked cookies. Store the cookies in airtight containers.

❖ Bake Sale Tip

Offer the cookies in bundles of three or four, wrapped in a tube of clear cellophane with each end twisted, and then tied with a colorful ribbon.

Choco–Peanut Butter Oatmeal Chipsters

Not so long ago, my son, Josh, and I baked these cookies together. I wish I could tell you that this was a family tradition, started when the kid was just a tyke, but, in fact, I could never interest him in doing much beyond making tuna salad sandwiches—and then, only when he was really, really hungry and there was nothing immediately munchable in the fridge. But last year things changed. At the age of twenty-three, he began working in a hyper-hip club in downtown Manhattan, and he decided to make the last Tuesday of the month the night he'd bring homemade cookies to the clubsters. Forget that he'd never baked before, all of a sudden he was ready, and anything as common as back-of-the-package Tollhouse Cookies just wouldn't do.

Although Josh's desire to bake was new, the way he went about it wasn't. Just as he had when he was younger and had to do his homework (always rushing into my office with an urgent plea for hurry-up help), he left cookie-making to the last minute. Of course, I wasn't about to turn him down: What mother of an only child, who will soon be on his own, probably living someplace far away, would give up the chance to have a little time with the kid in the kitchen? But he'd waited just too long. I measured out the ingredients with him and then had to leave. By the time I came back, the dough was made and chilled and he'd begun rolling it between his palms to make the little rounds the recipe indicated. I joined in for a little hand-dirtying rolling, but ducked out for a couple of phone calls.

When I returned, the second batch of cookies was already in the oven and the first was cooling on racks. I walked into the room just in time to see Josh's six-foot frame bent over the counter. He had this sweet little smile on his face as he drew in the make-you-happy smell of the chocolate and—I'm sure he had no idea he was doing this—he was gently patting one of the cookies, giving it a little love tap that conveyed both pleasure and tremendous pride.

It was the small pat that so warmed my heart and reminded me of an experience I'd had decades ago. I'd made a few jars of lemon marmalade, covered the lids with fabric, and set the jars on the windowsill to cool overnight. The following morning, when I saw the sun hitting the golden-yellow lineup of jams, I had a rush of almost giddy happiness: In an instant, I fell in love with the marmalade and the satisfaction that I had made something so beautiful with my own hands.

In many ways, this is what makes baking so vibrant and so important. Of course, there is the taste of what's been baked—without that, the work that goes into making anything in the kitchen would be a waste. But the sensory enjoyment of baking, the extraordinary sense of accomplishment that comes from having baked, and the pleasure of sharing your sweets with others—that should never be minimized.

I've known this pleasure for years. And now I've had the thrill of seeing my son know it, too.

Choco–Peanut Butter Oatmeal Chipsters

Makes 5 dozen 2-inch cookies

¾ cup all-purpose flour

½ cup Dutch-process cocoa powder

1 teaspoon ground cinnamon

1 teaspoon baking soda

¼ teaspoon salt

3 cups old-fashioned oats

2 sticks unsalted butter, softened

1 cup chunky peanut butter

1 cup light brown sugar (packed)

1 cup granulated sugar

2 large eggs

1 teaspoon pure vanilla extract

1½ cups chocolate chips or chunks

1 cup raisins, optional (steeped in hot
   water for 5 minutes if not plump, then
   drained)

1. Preheat the oven to 350°F. Line two or three baking sheets with parchment paper, silicone mats, or aluminum foil.

2. In a large bowl, sift together the flour, cocoa, cinnamon, baking soda, and salt. Add the oats and stir to blend.

3. In the bowl of an electric mixer fitted with the paddle attachment, combine the butter, peanut butter, brown sugar, and granulated sugar and beat on medium speed for 3 minutes, until very creamy. Scrape down the surface of the bowl. Add the eggs one at a time, incorporating each one thoroughly before adding the next. Add the vanilla and mix for 30 seconds.

4. Reduce the speed to low and add the dry ingredients, mixing just until the ingredients are incorporated. Stir in the chocolate chips and the raisins, if using. The dough can be prepared to this point and refrigerated for up to 2 days. (You may also freeze this dough for up to 1 month. The dough will take less time to defrost prior to baking if you roll it into ready-to-bake balls before freezing.)

5. Drop rounded tablespoons of dough 2 inches apart onto the prepared baking sheets. (If the dough is very cold, scoop out rounded tablespoons, roll the balls between your palms, and gently flatten each ball with the heel of your hand to create a ½-inch-thick cookie.)

6. Bake 13 to 15 minutes, or until the cookies are firm around the edges. Allow the cookies to cool slightly before placing them on wire racks to cool. The cookies can be stored in airtight containers for 4 days or sealed and frozen for up to 1 month.

Dorie Greenspan, a contributing editor to Bon Appétit *magazine, is the author of* Baking with Julia, *the book that accompanied Julia Child's PBS television series of the same name, and two books written with Pierre Hermé:* Desserts by Pierre Hermé, *an IACP Cookbook of the Year, and* Chocolate Desserts, *which won the 2001 Prix La Mazille for best book in the world. Her latest book,* Paris Sweets: Great Desserts from the City's Best Pastry Shops, *includes recipes and stories from her part-time hometown.*

Lemon Marmalade

Makes 1 quart or eight ½-pint jars

6 large lemons, scrubbed
4 cups sugar

1.   Place the lemons in a large pot, cover completely with cold water, and bring to a boil. Lower the heat and gently simmer for 20 minutes. Drain the lemons and cool them quickly under cold running water. When the lemons are cool, drain and dry them.

2.   While the lemons are cooking, sterilize the jars and lids you will be using to store the marmalade. Place them in a stockpot, cover with cold water, bring to a boil, and heat for 3 minutes. Turn off the heat and leave the jars in the water until ready to be filled.

3.   Working over a bowl to catch the juice, cut the lemons into thick slices and remove the seeds. Coarsely chop the lemons by hand. Drain the lemons, reserving this juice as well.

4.   In a 3- or 4-quart nonreactive saucepan, combine the sugar and ¾ cup water and bring to a boil. Stir until the sugar dissolves. Clip a candy thermometer to the inside of the pan while the syrup cooks. If the sugar coats the sides of the pan, wash down the crystals with a pastry brush dipped in cold water. Cook the syrup for 17 to 20 minutes, until it reaches 240°F and the syrup is thick enough to set when a small spoonful is ladled onto a chilled plate. Add the reserved lemon juice and heat until the temperature is 230°F and the syrup, once again, is thick enough to set when a small spoonful is ladled onto a chilled plate. Stir in the chopped lemon and cook for about 5 minutes or until the marmalade is 220°F. Remove the pan from the heat.

5.   Immediately fill the hot jars with marmalade. Take extra care: The jars and the preserves are extremely hot. Cover the jars tightly and invert them on a kitchen towel for 30 minutes, then turn the jars right side up and allow them to cool to room temperature. Stored in the refrigerator, the marmalade will thicken, and keep for several months.

❖ **Bake Sale Tip**

Cover the lids of the cooled jars with pieces of fabric and tie in place with string or raffia. Place a sticker on the front of the jar stating its contents and the month and year it was made, as well as instructions to store the marmalade in the refrigerator.

François Payard's
Flourless, Butterless Chocolate Cookies

T hese crisp-on-the-outside, chewy-on-the-inside cookies are the result of a quest that I undertook with my baker Chris Hereghty to create an exquisite chocolate cookie that skirts the obligation to include butter and even flour. The walnuts provide the flour and the shortening, as well as a subtle nutty flavor that enhances the chocolate intensity. So while these cookies can certainly provide a treat for Passover holidays or for people who are dieting or who have allergies to wheat, they are just right for daily treats as well.

François Payard's Apricot Cake and his biography appear on page 225.

Flourless, Butterless Chocolate Cookies

Makes 10 large cookies;
an easy recipe to double

- ¾ cup Dutch-process cocoa powder
- 2½ cups confectioners' sugar
- Pinch of salt
- 2 cups walnuts, roughly chopped
- 1 tablespoon pure vanilla extract
- 4 large egg whites

1. Preheat the oven to 350°F. Line two baking sheets with silicone mats or use nonstick baking pans.

2. In the bowl of an electric mixer fitted with the paddle attachment, combine the cocoa powder, sugar, salt, and walnuts, and mix for 1 minute on low speed.

3. In another bowl, briefly whisk together the vanilla and egg whites.

4. Increase the mixer's speed to medium and slowly add the whites to the dry ingredients. Mix for 2 minutes. Scrape down the inside of the bowl.

5. Scoop 2 ounces of the cookie batter

(use a 2-ounce ice cream scoop or a ⅛-cup measuring cup) onto the prepared pan, leaving 3 inches between the cookies, which will spread and flatten as they bake.

6. Place the baking sheet on the middle rack of the oven and immediately reduce the temperature to 320°F. Bake for 14 minutes, or until small, thin cracks appear on the surface and the cookies are firm to the touch. Allow the cookies to cool slightly and then transfer them to a wire rack to finish cooling. Store the cookies in an airtight container.

Susan and Cassandra Purdy's
Apricot Crumb Bars

This tender buttery bar cookie has the melt-in-your-mouth quality of rich shortbread—which it's based upon—combined with layers of semisweet chocolate and tart apricots. The recipe was developed by my daughter, Cassandra Purdy, a food writer, chef, and caterer based in Paris and Connecticut, who learned to mix shortbread even before she could read. She's suggested a few variations as well, since these bars fare beautifully at both casual picnics and elegant buffets.

Susan Purdy's Chocolate Chip Streusel Bundt Cake and her biography begin on page 241.

Apricot Crumb Bars

Makes one 9 x 13-inch pan
or twenty 2 x 2¼-inch bars

8 ounces (1¼ cups, packed) moist, dried apricots

32 tablespoons (4 sticks) unsalted butter, softened

1 cup sifted confectioners' sugar, plus 2 tablespoons for finishing the bars

4 cups all-purpose flour

1 teaspoon salt

½ cup semisweet chocolate chips, or finely chopped semisweet chocolate

1½ cups apricot preserves

1 cup old-fashioned oats

1 cup chopped walnuts

1. In a medium saucepan, cover the apricots with water (1 to 2 cups) and bring to a boil over high heat. Reduce the heat to low and simmer for 5 minutes. Strain the apricots (discard the liquid or reserve it for another use) and place them in a food processor. Pulse the apricots to form small bits. You should have 1½ cups chopped apricots.

2. Preheat the oven to 375°F. Lightly mist a 9 x 13-inch pan with nonstick cooking spray.

3. In the bowl of an electric mixer fitted with the paddle attachment, combine the butter and confectioners' sugar and mix on medium speed for 2 to 3 minutes, or until the butter is creamy. Sift the flour with the salt and add it to the creamed butter. Reduce the speed to low and mix until the dough forms into a ball.

4. Divide the dough into thirds. Crumble one-third of the dough into a bowl and set aside. Press the remaining two-thirds of the dough into an even layer across the bottom of the prepared pan. Place the pan on the lower rack of the oven and bake for 15 minutes, or until the crust turns golden brown. Remove the pan from the oven and, while the crust is hot, scatter the chocolate over the top. Let the chips melt for 2 to 3 minutes and then spread them into an even layer over the crust. Top the chocolate with the apricot preserves and scatter the chopped apricot over the preserves.

5. Add the oats and nuts to the reserved portion of the dough. With your fingertips, pinch the mixture to form a crumbly dough. Gently press the crumbs in a coarse layer on top of the apricots.

6. Return the pan to the oven and bake for 20 to 25 minutes, or until the crumble top is a golden brown.

7. Transfer the pan to a wire rack and cool for 15 to 20 minutes. While still warm, cut into bars. Cool completely (the warm bars are very fragile). Sift a very light dusting of confectioners' sugar over the bars, then lift them out of the pan to a serving plate. Store the bars in an airtight container at room temperature for 3 to 4 days or freeze for up to 1 month.

Variations

Substitute 1½ cups raspberry, strawberry, or cherry preserves for the apricot preserves. You can also drizzle thin lines of melted semisweet chocolate over the baked and cooled bars.

Judy Zeidler's

Korjas

(Crisp Poppy Seed Thins)

and

Poppy Seed Hamantaschen

My passion for baking began when I was just nine years old and made Nestlé's Toll House chocolate chip cookies. I remember following the directions on the package, and the pleasure it gave me when my father raved about how delicious they were. I'm sure this inspired me to experiment with making lemon meringue and apple pies—of course, all this with help from my mother.

She was a fantastic baker, especially when it came to baking for the holidays. One of her specialties was hamantaschen, triangular pastries (based on the shape of the hat worn by the villain Haman in the story of Purim) filled with poppy seeds, prune jam, or fruit preserves, that are always served during Purim. I think what I especially enjoy is the sugar-cookie dough combined with the slightly sweet, crunchy poppy seed filling. I still use my mother's basic recipe, but over the years I have added poppy seeds to the dough for extra texture. At Purim I always make hamantaschen for my family, and now my grandchildren look forward to them when they come to visit. They love to help me roll out the dough, spoon on the filling, fold them into three-corner pastries, and eat them hot from the oven.

I still remember watching my mother making *korjas*, these ever-so-thin poppy seed cookies. She would take a fistful of the dough, and using an heirloom rolling pin, roll it until the pastry was so thin that it looked like a hole would appear at any moment—but she stopped just in time. Then she sprinkled cinnamon-sugar over the top, cut them in uneven diamond-shaped pieces, and baked them until they were golden brown. I understand that the original poppy seed cookies were not that thin, but as each generation rolled out the dough, they would see how thin and crisp they could make them. I make them wafer thin and serve them on a platter piled so high that they almost spill over. The recipe makes hundreds of cookies, about the texture of potato chips. I never cut the recipe in half, since the dough stores well in the refrigerator or freezer and is ready to bake at any time. Simply seal the dough tightly in plastic wrap, store it in a plastic bag, and refrigerate up to four days, or put in the freezer for future use.

I always wondered where my mother's marvelous recipes came from, but I never asked. I know that she never wrote down any recipes, but many years later I met with an older cousin who I hadn't seen in years and we reminisced about past family get-togethers. That was when I found out that many of the dishes were actually my grandmother Eva's. My cousin told me that she was a fabulous cook and baker, and when she became a widow, she supported her three sons by cooking part time for a wealthy family. He was sure that she brought the recipes with her when she came from Eastern Europe. There were tears in his eyes when he told me that he was so happy to see that my passion for cooking and baking was so much like my grandmother's, and that her legacy would continue on in our family.

Korjas
(Crisp Poppy Seed Thins)

Makes about 200 cookies

For the dough

6 cups all-purpose flour, plus extra for
   rolling the dough
3 teaspoons baking powder
¼ teaspoon salt
1 cup vegetable oil
1½ cups sugar
2 large eggs
1½ cups whole milk
2 ounces (scant ½ cup) poppy seeds

For the topping

1 teaspoon ground cinnamon
½ cup sugar

1. Preheat the oven to 350°F. Line three
or four cookie sheets with aluminum foil
and lightly grease the foil.

2. In a bowl, sift together the flour, baking powder, and salt and set aside.

3. In the bowl of an electric mixer fitted
with the paddle attachment, combine the oil
and sugar and mix on medium-high speed
until fluffy. Lower the speed to medium, add
the eggs, and mix for 30 to 60 seconds, until
the batter is smooth. Alternately add one-
third of the flour mixture and half of the
milk, blending until smooth after each addition; begin and end with the dry ingredients. Scrape the inside of the bowl. Stir in
the poppy seeds.

4. For the topping, combine the sugar
and cinnamon in a small bowl.

5. Scoop out a heaping tablespoon of the
dough onto a generously floured work surface and roll out the dough as thin as you
can. (A single spoonful should make one
8 x 11-inch rectangle). Sprinkle a teaspoon
of the cinnamon-sugar mixture over the
dough. Cut the dough into diamond shapes
and place them on the prepared cookie
sheet. Continue to roll out as much dough
as you'd like and fill the other cookie
sheets.

6. Bake for 8 to 10 minutes, or until
golden brown. Transfer the cookies to wire
racks to cool. Store the cookies in airtight
containers.

❖ Bake Sale Tip

Since these are small cookies, package
them in groups of a dozen or so in
small wax or cellophane bags, tied
with a colorful ribbon.

Poppy Seed Hamantaschen

Makes 5 dozen pastries

8 tablespoons (1 stick) unsalted butter, softened

½ cup sugar

3 large eggs

Zest of 1 orange, finely chopped

2 cups all-purpose flour, plus extra for rolling the dough

1½ teaspoons baking powder

¼ teaspoon salt

1 tablespoon poppy seeds

Two 8-ounce cans poppy seed filling (see Note), or 1 recipe Mohn (Homemade Poppy Seed Filling)

1. Preheat the oven to 375°F, line two cookie sheets with aluminum foil, and lightly mist them with nonstick cooking spray.

2. In the bowl of an electric mixer fitted with the paddle attachment, beat the butter and sugar on medium speed until well blended. Reduce the speed to low and add 2 of the eggs and the orange zest, blending thoroughly. Add the flour, baking powder, salt, and poppy seeds and blend until the dough is smooth.

3. Transfer the dough to a lightly floured work surface and divide it into 4 portions for easier handling. Working with one piece at a time, flatten the dough with the palm of your hand, then roll it out to a thickness of ¼ inch. With a scalloped or plain cookie cutter, cut it into 2½-inch rounds. Place 1 heaping teaspoon of poppy seed filling in the center of each round. Cover all but the very center of the filling by folding three flaps of the dough circle inward, toward the center. This will form a triangle with a small center hole. Pinch the three seams to seal them.

4. Place the hamantaschen ½ inch apart on the prepared pans. In a small bowl, lightly beat the remaining egg and brush the dough with the egg glaze. Bake for 10 minutes, or until golden brown. Transfer the cookies to wire racks to cool. Stored in an airtight container, they will last for several days.

Note: Poppy seed filling (crushed and sweetened poppy seeds) is available in the baking or canned fruit section of most supermarkets. The Solo brand is a familiar favorite

Judy Zeidler is a well-known food authority, co-author of Michel Richard's Home Cooking with a French Accent, *and author of the widely acclaimed* The Gourmet Jewish Cook *and* Judy Zeidler's International Deli Cookbook, 30-Minute Kosher Cook, *and* Master Chefs Cook Kosher, *based on her show* Judy's Kitchen *on the Jewish Television Network. She and her husband are founders of the popular Citrus restaurant in Los Angeles, the Broadway Deli and Capo restaurants in Santa Monica, and the new Brentwood Restaurant in Brentwood, California.*

Lora Brody's grandmother's
Mohn Kickle
(Poppy Seed Cookies)

Before my mother went the retirement community route, she was a fearless cook with a flair for the truly unusual. She bravely went where no suburban housewife would dream, making Senegalese peanut soup while the rest of the crowd opened a can of Campbell's, and trying her hand at flambé while my brother and I stood by with the fire extinguisher in case the curtains got in the way. She grew and used fresh herbs when the rest of the country was shaking seasoned salt and MSG over everything. She was a truly marvelous and inventive baker and you'd better believe that no store-bought white-sugar-and-Crisco-iced birthday cakes ever graced our table.

In fact, I never had birthday cakes at all. Who would choose that if you could have made-from-scratch, this-will-make-you-weak-at-the-knees-and-bring-tears-to-your-eyes chocolate banana cream pie?

On the other side of the equation, my father came from the "Raging Bull" School of Culinary Arts in that he raged and bullied my mother into making three plain, unthreatening, boring square meals a day featuring bottled salad dressing and desserts of fruit cocktail suspended in red Jell-O. Even twice-cooked roast was no joke in our house: If the meat wasn't gray inside and black outside, if any rosy juices leaked out, the "small talk" at the table would be a terse order to put it back in the oven.

Likewise, when my father would brag about what a great cook *his* mother was, I assumed that meant she boiled green beans for forty minutes and roasted chicken until it could be drop-kicked from the kitchen into the dining room.

But the one thing my grandmother made that everyone loved—my father, most of all—were plain-looking, but wonderful-tasting, *mohn kickle*, a poppy seed cookie that's perfect for dunking into a cup of hot tea. Rough and rustic, they contained a symphony of flavors and textures rarely found in other cookies.

After my grandmother died, my mother bravely took up the gauntlet and made attempt after futile and fruitless attempt to duplicate my dad's favorite cookie. Each try was criticized and then rejected; none matched the memory of his mother's mohn kickle. Where I would have given up, my mother persevered. One day she got involved in something else (I like to think she was whipping up a plateful of steak tartare), and forgot that she had mohn kickle in the oven. When my father tasted the overbaked (actually, burned) cookies, he pronounced them "Perfect! Exactly the way my mother made them."

I made a video of my mother (over)baking these beloved cookies and gave copies to my three sons, so when the inevitable happens and Millie's not around to make them, the tradition of mohn kickle will live on.

Lora Brody's Ginger Cheesecake appears on page 114.

Mohn Kickle
(Poppy Seed Cookies)

Makes twenty 3-inch cookies

3½ cups unbleached flour, plus extra for
forming and rolling the dough

1 tablespoon baking powder

½ teaspoon salt

1¼ cups granulated sugar

½ cup dark brown sugar (packed)

Scant 1 cup poppy seeds

3 extra-large eggs

1 cup vegetable oil

3 tablespoons freshly squeezed orange
juice

Zest of 1 thick-skinned orange (such as
navel), finely grated

1 tablespoon pure vanilla extract

½ teaspoon ground cinnamon

1. Preheat the oven to 350°F and line two heavy-duty baking sheets with parchment, aluminum foil, or silicone mats. (If using foil, butter and flour the surface, and knock off any excess flour.)

2. In a large bowl, whisk together the flour, baking powder, salt, 1 cup of the granulated sugar, the brown sugar, and poppy seeds. Make sure there are no lumps of brown sugar.

3. In a small bowl, whisk together the eggs, oil, orange juice, zest, and vanilla and pour the wet ingredients into the dry. Mix together with a spatula until an oily dough forms. (If the dough is dry, add water, 1 tablespoon at a time; if it's too wet to form a ball, add flour, 1 tablespoon at a time.)

4. Place the dough on a lightly floured work surface, dust the top lightly with flour, and roll out to a thickness of ¼ inch.

5. Dip a 2½- or 3-inch cookie cutter, or the rim of a similar size drinking glass, into flour. (This will keep the dough from sticking.) Cut circles from the dough, placing them 1 inch apart on the prepared baking sheets. Gather together the scraps, knead again briefly, and continue to cut out as many circles as possible. In a small bowl, combine the remaining ¼ cup granulated sugar with the cinnamon and sprinkle the tops of the cookies with it.

6. Place the cookies on the middle rack of the oven and bake for 25 to 35 minutes. The longer you bake them, the drier and crisper they will be in texture. (And the more Lora's father would have approved of the cookies!) Transfer the cookies to a wire rack to cool completely. Store in an airtight container for a month, or freeze for up to 6 months.

Lora Brody is the author of more than twenty cookbooks, including The Cape Cod Table, Indulgences: One Cook's Quest for the Delicious Things in Life, *and* The Kitchen Survival Guide. *Her own line of baking products may be found at www.lorabrody.com.*

Blueberry Dame Blanche

ne of my earliest memories is making Dame Blanche cookies with my mom at our home in southern France. It took most of the day, since she would also make the jam that goes between the two layers.

Now that I live in America, I see my mom only about once a year—though she's always on my mind. At Mother's Day, I bake a big batch of these cookies and I send them to her. This Labor Day, my wife and partner, Kris, and I will travel to Provence to see her. We will be carrying more than our usual provisions: I will surprise her with some vacuum-packed blueberry puree that I made from berries we picked in August. Together, my mom and I will make the Dame Blanche cookies, filling them with fresh blueberry jam.

They are a traditional shortbread-like cookie with a windowpane in one half that shows the jam filling inside, like small Linzer tortes. Display the finished cookies on a platter for a simple, elegant finish to any meal.

I've come to prize blueberries as much as Kris does. She spent her childhood in Michigan, which is already well known for great cherries. Blueberries are also one of this state's great treasures. A friend of Kris's family owned a blueberry farm. One of Kris's favorite childhood memories is of her annual family blueberry outing. Blueberries are easy to pick: They don't have stickers or thorns and the fruit is within reach, whether you're a little kid or a grownup.

I remember the first time I saw a "U Pick" sign. We were on a back-country road during a visit to Michigan. I asked Kris, "What does that mean?" She explained that the sign was an invitation to visit the farm and pick our own fruit. I couldn't wait! The next summer, the blueberries were late. Every day, I rode past the blueberry fields with my collecting pail tied to my bicycle in anticipation of ripe berries. Finally the "U Pick" sign was posted on the usual corner. I peddled in and picked but rarely did the berries make it back home. I usually perched on the farm's picnic table and enjoyed the fruits of my labor before I left the grounds!

Many of my Michigan mornings begin with fresh berries. I grab my morning coffee and walk to the wild raspberry and blackberry bushes behind our house. Sip, pick, eat. Sip, pick, eat. This is my early morning mantra. I am often standing at the bushes before the dew has dried. If I get there early enough, I can beat the birds and the deer to the ripest, largest berries. There is also competition from our local black bear but he doesn't usually come by when we are there.

This year, the blueberry crop was plentiful. Kris and I had a great time picking and eating berries. We gathered enough to make several tarts. We also picked some extra berries to take to my mom. I hope you will create your own tradition of sharing with the recipe.

Blueberry Dame Blanche

Makes 26 sandwich cookies

----

1 vanilla bean
14 tablespoons (1¾ sticks) unsalted
    butter, cold, cubed
½ cup almond flour
¾ cup plus 2 tablespoons confectioners'
    sugar, plus additional for dusting
2 large eggs

1 cup pastry flour
1 cup all-purpose flour, plus extra for
    rolling the dough
Pinch of salt
½ cup Blueberry Jam

1. Split open the vanilla bean lengthwise and scrape free the seeds; set the pods and seeds aside.

2. In the bowl of an electric mixer fitted with the paddle attachment, combine the butter, almond flour, sugar, and eggs and mix on

medium speed for 2 minutes. There should be no visible pieces of butter; the mixture will resemble scrambled eggs. Add the vanilla bean seeds, pastry flour, all-purpose flour, and salt and mix on low speed for 1 minute, or just until everything is incorporated. (Overworking the dough will make it tough.)

3. Gather the dough and form it into a disk. Seal it in plastic wrap and chill for a minimum of 30 minutes or overnight. (Dough that's chilled overnight should sit at room temperature for 5 to 10 minutes before being rolled.)

4. Preheat the oven to 350°F and line two baking sheets with parchment paper. Place the dough on a lightly floured work surface and roll it into a ⅛-inch-thick rectangle. Lightly flour the rolling pin or the work

Blueberry Jam

Makes six 8-ounce jars

Six 8-ounce canning jars
4 cups fresh blueberries
One 1.75-ounce box powdered pectin
4 cups sugar
1½ tablespoons unsalted butter

1. Sterilize the jars and lids you will be using to store the jam. Place them in a stockpot, cover with cold water, bring to a boil, and heat for 3 minutes. Turn off the heat and leave the jars in the water until ready to be filled.

2. In a large, heavy-bottomed enamel or stainless-steel pan, crush the berries, using a potato masher. Start with 1 cup blueberries, gently crush these, then add each subsequent cup, gently pressing them on top of the previous layers.

3. Add the pectin and bring the berries to a full boil over high heat, stirring constantly with a wooden spoon. Add the sugar and butter and stir until the mixture will not resume a full rolling boil after you stir with the spoon. Stirring constantly, boil the mixture for 1 additional minute, then remove from the heat.

4. Skim and discard any foam or scum that may have formed on the surface.

5. Immediately fill the hot, sterilized jars with the jam, leaving ¼-inch head room in each jar. Process the jars according to the manufacturer's instructions. Seal the jars tightly and invert them on a kitchen towel for 30 minutes, then turn the jars right side up and allow them to cool to room temperature. Any unsealed jars can be refrigerated and used within a month. Properly sealed jam jars can be stored for up to 1 year.

❖ Bake Sale Tip

Label the jars with decorative stickers, and include the date the jam was prepared. You might cover the lids with swatches of fabric, cinching them at the jar's neck with raffia, string, or ribbon.

surface if either gets sticky. (The thinner you roll the dough, the stickier it is likely to become.)

5.   Use a 2-inch-wide cookie cutter, either fluted or plain, to form the cookies. Cut the cookies and place them about 1 inch apart on the prepared pan. Pat together any leftover dough, gently roll it out, and form more cookies.

6.   Use the base of a 1-inch plain decorating tip to cut the centers from half of the cookies on the baking sheet. (As a simpler variation, you may leave all of the cookies whole and simply sandwich them together without the cutout window in which the jam shows. Dust the tops with confectioners' sugar as directed below.)

7.   Place the cookies on the middle rack of the oven and bake for 10 minutes, or until the cookies have turned light brown. Transfer the baking sheet to a wire rack and cool for a few minutes before transferring the cookies directly onto the wire rack to finish cooling.

8.   To assemble the cookies, spread blueberry jam on each whole cookie; leave ¼ inch of the entire outside edge free of jam. Place the extra confectioners' sugar in a fine-mesh sieve and liberally sprinkle the cookies with the cutout centers. Sandwich the sugared tops and the jam-covered bottoms together. The cookies will keep for up to 5 days in an airtight container at room temperature.

Jacques Torres is a recipient of a James Beard award in pastry. He donates his time to many national charitable efforts, including the American Red Cross, Meals on Wheels, God's Love We Deliver, New York's Hard of Hearing Association, Sloan-Kettering Cancer Research Center, and the Association to Benefit Children. He serves as Dean of Pastry Studies at New York's French Culinary Institute. His latest television series, Chocolate with Jacques Torres, *appears on television's Food Network. In 2000, Jacques opened his own chocolate factory. Jacques Torres Chocolate (www.mrchocolate.com) specializes in fresh, hand-crafted chocolates, free of preservatives and artificial flavors. His own Web site is www.jacquestorres.com.*

Nicole Kaplan's
Most Favorite Cheesecake Brownies and Best-Ever Hot Fudge Sundaes

I grew up in Spring Valley, half an hour north of Manhattan. We ate steak pretty much every night when I was a child, and for dessert, we bought Entenmann's or Ring Dings, except at birthdays, when we'd always order a Carvel ice cream cake: layers of ice cream, crunchy cookies, and whipped topping. Carvel was also where my mother would take me for our own special getaway. My dad and my brother would stay home, and just Mom and I would run over in the car. I'd order a hot fudge sundae with bananas and black cherries and marshmallow sauce.

In fact, my first job was working at Carvel for a couple of summers. I earned a little money and ate all the ice cream I could ever want (balancing this by drinking all the Diet Coke I could ever want).

At SUNY Potsdam, I caught a second glimpse into my future, working as the steward at my sorority. I ordered the foods and figured out the menus each week with the cook who came and actually did the cooking. But then I transferred to school in Manhattan and began to miss my friends terribly. I started to send them little treats from my new apartment just to stay in touch. I started very, very simply—Toll House cookies or brownies from the recipe on the back of the flour bag—and I'd mail these with my letters. Then I remember discovering

Maida Heatter's Palm Beach Brownies in one of the two cookbooks I owned, and my ambitiousness increased a bit.

Shortly thereafter, I made sixteen pounds of her cheesecake brownies. And when my parents came to visit me in the city on their anniversary, I decided to undertake a dessert that I'd found in an issue of *Gourmet:* cherries baked in a triangular terrine.

Eventually, I began taking classes at Peter Kump's Cooking School, where I found that you could take one free class for every two you agreed to work, helping the instructor with preparation and cleanup. With that training, and my increasing involvement at the school, I began a little catering on the side and eventually enrolled in the professional chef program, which led me into work at the Sign of the Dove and then Eleven Madison Park.

Even though I appreciate and practice the artistry of fancy desserts, what I'd want someone to bake for me is a brownie. Give me a great version of something I know and love, and I couldn't be happier. I suspect most people feel this way as well, since so much of what we love about food is the comfort it brings, the connection to happier times. Give me a sundae, give me buttercrunch, rocky road ice ream, chocolate peanut crunch—give me that any day over a lemon-thyme sorbet or a lavender–sea salt panna cotta.

Thinking of this book prompted me to share with you how I make the best sundae I can imagine, looking at every component so that it will explode with flavor. It begins with a great cheesecake brownie, which is perfect for a bake sale all by itself. But then, in case you want to offer a made-to-order sundae, in case you have an ice cream social or a slumber party coming up, you can take those brownies and use them as the base for layer after layer of familiar but reinvigorated flavors—everything from a *fresh* cherry garnish to a rich chocolate fudge sauce, from a luscious vanilla ice cream to a fresh topping of whipped cream. This is a fantasy food, in a way, a best-ever sundae inspired by those early memories of what was most special, most rewarding to me, when a sundae really was all it took to make my day.

Most Favorite Cheesecake Brownies

Makes two 8 x 8-inch pans
or 16 large brownies

For the brownie layer

8 tablespoons (1 stick) unsalted butter

½ cup light brown sugar (packed)

8 ounces semisweet chocolate, coarsely chopped

2 ounces unsweetened chocolate, coarsely chopped

¾ cup granulated sugar

4 large eggs

½ cup cake flour

For the cream cheese layer

Six 8-ounce packages cream cheese

1 cup granulated sugar

4 large eggs

2 ounces semisweet chocolate, melted

1. Lightly grease two 8 x 8-inch baking pans and line the bottoms with a piece of parchment paper.

2. To make the brownie layer, combine the butter, brown sugar, semisweet choco-late, and unsweetened chocolate in a double boiler. Over medium heat, stir occasionally until the chocolate has melted and the mixture is smooth. Add the granulated sugar, eggs, and cake flour; mix with a wooden spoon just until incorporated.

3. Scrape the batter into the prepared pan and spread into an even layer. Cover the pan with plastic wrap and place in the freezer for at least 1 hour or overnight.

4. When ready to bake the brownies, preheat the oven to 350°F.

5. To make the cream cheese layer, combine the cream cheese and sugar in the bowl of an electric mixer fitted with the paddle attachment and mix on medium speed for 1 minute, or until smooth. Scrape the inside of the bowl. Add the eggs one at a time, thoroughly incorporating each one before adding the next. Pour the cream cheese batter on top of the brownie layer and spread into an even layer. Using a spoon, decorate the surface of the brownies by drizzling the semisweet chocolate in a loose design.

6. Place the pans on the middle rack of the oven and bake for 40 to 45 minutes, or until the cream cheese layer is golden brown and set. Cool for a few minutes and then place in the freezer for 1 hour. Remove

the brownies from the pan and cut into serving pieces. Eat right away or place on a plate, cover with plastic wrap, and refrigerate.

❖ Bake Sale Tip

Wrap individual brownies in wax paper or clear cellophane and seal with a sticker. Because of the cheesecake layer, they need to be transported in a cooler filled with ice packs to remain cool the entire time.

Best-Ever Hot Fudge Sundaes

Serves 8

For the cherries

1 cup fresh cherries, pitted and halved

2 tablespoons sugar

For the bananas

4 ripe bananas

2 tablespoons unsalted butter, cold, cut into bits

4 tablespoons dark brown sugar

2 tablespoons dark rum

½ recipe (one 8 x 8-inch pan) Most Favorite Cheesecake Brownies, cut into eight 2 x 4-inch pieces

1 recipe Vanilla Ice Cream

1 recipe Sweetened Whipped Cream

1 recipe Chocolate Fudge Sauce

1. Combine the cherries and sugar in a small bowl. Cover and allow them to macerate at room temperature for 1 hour.

2. Preheat the oven to 350°F. Slice the unpeeled bananas in half lengthwise. Place the halves, skin side down, on a baking sheet and sprinkle evenly with the butter, brown sugar, and rum. Place the pan on the middle rack of the oven and roast for 20 minutes, or until the skins blacken. Let cool.

3. To assemble the sundae, place 1 brownie in each dish. Top with half of a roasted banana and a scoop of ice cream. Spoon whipped cream around the brownie and spoon cherries on the top. Ladle the warm fudge sauce over the sundae and serve.

❖ Bake Sale Tip

Pack disposable bowls and plastic spoons, an ice cream scoop, and a Thermos filled with hot fudge sauce. Nestle the ice cream's container, along with a container of each fruit and a container of whipped cream, in a cooler packed with dry ice.

Nicole Kaplan is pastry chef at Eleven Madison Park in New York City. She was selected as one of the Top Ten Pastry Chefs in America for 2003 by Pastry Art and Design, *and her recipes have been featured in the* New York Times, Art Culinaire, *and* Chocolatier *magazine. She strives to combine traditional French cuisine with the New York style to create dessert masterpieces that tempt even the most discriminating diner.*

Chocolate Fudge Sauce

Makes 2 cups

1 cup whole milk
½ cup heavy cream
¼ cup plus 2 tablespoons sugar
1 tablespoon unsalted butter
10 ounces semisweet chocolate

1.   In a medium saucepan, bring the milk, cream, and sugar to a boil over medium-high heat. Add the butter and chocolate. Stirring continuously, bring the mixture back to a boil, then remove the pan from the heat.

2.   Cool the sauce slightly before serving or cool completely and store in an airtight container in the refrigerator.

Sweetened Whipped Cream

Makes 3 cups

½ small vanilla bean
1½ cups heavy cream
2 tablespoons confectioners' sugar

Split the vanilla bean in half. Scrape the seeds into the bowl of an electric mixer fitted with the whisk attachment. (Reserve the vanilla bean pod for another use.) Add the cream and sugar, and whip the cream on medium-high speed to form soft peaks. Cover the bowl with plastic wrap and refrigerate until ready to use.

Vanilla Ice Cream

Makes 1 generous quart

½ vanilla bean
2 cups whole milk
1 cup heavy cream
¾ cup sugar
5 egg yolks

1.   Split the vanilla bean in half and scrape free the seeds; add both the pod and seeds to a medium saucepan. Add the milk, cream, and ¼ cup plus 2 tablespoons of the sugar. Bring to a boil over medium-high heat and then immediately remove the pot from the stove.

2.   In a bowl, whisk together the yolks and the remaining half of the sugar. Slowly pour the hot milk into the egg mixture, whisking the entire time.

3.   Return the mixture to the pan and continue to cook over medium-high heat, until the custard thickens and coats the back of a spoon.

4.   Pour the custard through a fine strainer into a bowl, cover with plastic wrap, and refrigerate. Freeze the custard in an ice cream machine, following the manufacturer's instructions. Place the ice cream in airtight containers and freeze until hardened.

Lindsey Shere and Kathleen Stewart's
Gingersnap Ice Cream Sandwiches with Wild Plum Ice Cream

Lindsey and I met at Chez Panisse, where she was working with Alice Waters on the desserts and pastries at that landmark restaurant. It's funny to think of myself working at that culinary mecca: Having grown up in southern California, I had been so clueless, spending my days at the beach, that I thought we had pumpkins at Thanksgiving because, well, we *needed* pumpkins at that time. And watermelons were around in summer because we *needed* them for picnics. I had no idea there were seasons when fruits and vegetables were ripe for the market. Lindsey, on the other hand, being a country girl, grew up learning how to be incredibly thrifty with whatever foods and goods were locally available.

Then, in 1987, I had the good fortune to open Downtown Bakery and Creamery with Lindsey. A few years later, for Chez Panisse's twentieth birthday party in 1991, Alice managed to get the city of Berkeley to close Shattuck Avenue for a street fair. She prevailed upon all these chefs on the West Coast—and even the East Coast—to come and donate their food and time for this carnival of gourmet tastes. Although food extravaganzas may be common now, this was one of the first outdoor tastings with chefs and foodies lining both sides of the street.

So Lindsey and I set about deciding what we'd offer from Downtown Bakery. This was August, and one of our summer treasures had just been delivered to the restaurant: wild plum puree. Lindsey's mother, Agnes, who passed away several years ago, had a marvelous wild plum tree in her yard. It's a very common tree. It grows here in California, in the Midwest, all over, probably: dark leaves, tiny white flowers that are spicy and fragrant, and tiny plums that ripen in midsummer. The fruit, hardly bigger than a cherry, is sometimes yellow, sometimes a dark garnet red. If you pick one from the tree and bite into it, the taste is bitter and tart. And the pits are almost as big as the fruit. But if you do as Agnes did, baking them in the oven for about 20 minutes (or you can just simmer them in a saucepan with a little water), you can put the softened fruit through a food mill and have a wonderful puree that you can sweeten to taste.

Agnes had a real social life and belonged to five or six senior citizens' groups. To supplement her own cache of cottage cheese and sour cream containers, she'd gather up all the plastic yogurt cups from senior lunches, wash and dry them, and fill them at home with her plum puree. Then she'd deliver boxes with something like seventy-five little plastic containers filled with this fragrant, beautiful plum puree. (Remember, Agnes was "country people," and she'd no sooner go out and buy Tupperware than she would a pair of designer shoes.) These containers of puree would line the freezer shelves at the bakery. People were always asking, "Why do you have so much store-bought yogurt in your freezer?" or thinking, "What on earth do they make with low-fat cottage cheese?"

Our favorite thing to do was to flavor ice cream with the plums, which are sweet and tart like rhubarb, only more so, with that slight sourness that gets you in the back of your throat.

So every August, we were lucky that Lindsey's mother would pick the plums from her backyard (the trees are loaded with fruit, close to the ground), and even puree it for us and pack it in the hilarious hodge-podge of "to go" containers she'd accumulated. And people just clamored for a taste of the wild plums.

For the street fair, we served the ice cream between two gingersnaps, which made the ice cream easy to eat. The bakery cases at Chez Panisse always featured gingersnaps—they're just a classic treat. I think we could have made 25 million wild plum ice cream sandwiches, and it wouldn't have been enough for that festival. Don't underestimate how many your family and friends might want, either.

Another virtue of the sandwiches, besides their unusual, bright taste, is that they are perfect for a summer picnic or for keeping stacked in your freezer for an impromptu get-together.

Gingersnap Ice Cream Sandwiches

Makes 30 ice cream sandwiches

----

2 quarts Wild Plum Ice Cream
   (recipe follows)
60 Gingersnaps (recipe follows)

Sandwich a scoop of ice cream between two cookies. Place on a tray lined with parchment paper and refreeze for 10 minutes, or until firm. Wrap each sandwich in a piece of wax paper and twist or fold under each end to seal. Return the sandwiches to the freezer. Allow the sandwiches to thaw for several minutes before serving.

❖ Bake Sale Tip

Place the wrapped sandwiches in a cooler filled with ice packs or dry ice.

Wild Plum Ice Cream

Makes 2 quarts

For the plum puree

2 pounds plums (preferably wild)
1 to 1½ cups sugar (depending on the tartness of the plums)

For the ice cream base

5 large egg yolks
1½ cups whole milk
¾ cup sugar
2 cups heavy cream

1. To make the fruit puree, remove the pits but leave the plums in large pieces. (If using wild plums, do not bother to remove the small pits. It will be easier to remove them after pureeing.) Place the plums in a wide heavy-bottomed pot or skillet and cook over medium heat, stirring occasionally, for 5 to 7 minutes, or until the fruit becomes too hot to touch.

2. Transfer the plums to a food mill and puree, which will remove the skin (as well as the wild plums' pits). Measure the puree and reserve 4 cups for the ice cream. (Use any leftover puree, sweetened to taste, as a topping for scones or pound cake. The puree also freezes well.)

3. Add about 1 cup of the sugar to the 4 cups of warm plum puree. Taste and add sugar until the plums just begin to taste sweet. Retain a little tartness to counter the sweet custard that you will mix with the puree. The amount of sugar can vary widely: Wild plums require more, as do other tart varieties of plums.

4. To make the ice cream base, place the egg yolks in a small bowl and set aside. Add the milk and sugar to a large heavy-bottomed saucepan. Bring the milk to the point of boiling. Immediately whisk a small amount of the hot milk into the yolks to temper them. Then whisk the yolks into the hot milk and sugar, and remove from heat. Strain into a bowl and whisk in the cream.

5. Add the sweetened puree to the custard and mix well. Chill the mixture thoroughly, and then freeze in an ice cream maker according to the manufacturer's instructions.

Gingersnaps

Makes about 60 cookies

2 tablespoons ground ginger
2 teaspoons ground cinnamon
4 cups all-purpose flour
1½ teaspoons baking powder
1 tablespoon baking soda
½ teaspoon salt
16 tablespoons (2 sticks) unsalted butter, at room temperature, cut into 2-inch pieces
1½ cups sugar, plus additional for sprinkling
2 large eggs
½ teaspoon pure vanilla extract
⅓ cup light molasses

1. In a large bowl, sift together the ginger, cinnamon, flour, baking powder, baking soda, and salt.

2. In the bowl of an electric mixer fitted with the paddle attachment, combine the butter and sugar and mix on medium-low speed for 4 minutes, or until the butter is pale and creamy. Add the eggs one at a time, mixing briefly between each addition. Add the vanilla. Scrape the inside of the bowl. Add the molasses and mix well, scraping the inside of the bowl.

3. Reduce the speed to low, mix in a quarter of the dry ingredients, combine thoroughly, and repeat, adding another quarter of the dry ingredients three times.

4. Cover the top of the bowl with plastic wrap and refrigerate the dough for 1 hour, or until well chilled but not solid.

5. Preheat the oven to 350°F.

6. Divide the chilled dough into 2 pieces; each will weigh just over 1 pound. Roll each piece into an 8-inch log. At this point you can slice and bake the cookies, or securely wrap the logs and refrigerate or freeze them. (Frozen dough should stand at room temperature about 10 minutes, until softened just enough to slice.)

7. Slice the log into ¼-inch slices and place them 1 inch apart on ungreased baking sheets. (You can line the sheets with parchment paper). Lightly sprinkle each cookie with sugar and bake for 10 minutes, or until the cookies have puffed and fallen and the tops have cracked. Transfer the cookies to wire racks and cool completely. Store the cookies in an airtight container for up to 3 days or freeze for up to 1 month.

Lindsey Shere was a founding partner and longtime pastry chef at Chez Panisse restaurant in Berkeley. The author of Chez Panisse Desserts, *she opened the Downtown Bakery and Creamery in Healdsburg, California, with partner Kathleen Stewart. After many years there, Lindsey retired, and now spends her time gardening and enjoying her wine-country home. Kathleen Stewart was a longtime employee at Chez Panisse until 1987, when she opened Downtown Bakery and Creamery with Lindsey. Since her partner's retirement, Kathleen has continued to operate the bakery in this beautiful wine-country village. In addition to contributing to* The Baker's Dozen Cookbook, *Kathleen is a frequent contributor to* Fine Cooking *magazine.*

Candies

Karen DeMasco's grandmother's Cashew Brittle and
her own Caramel Corn and Chewy Caramels

Bill Yosses's Pecan Pralines

David Lebovitz's Peppermint Patty Brownies and Peppermint Patties

Mandy Groom Givler's Earl Grey Truffles

Claire Archibald's Bittersweet Chocolate Truffles
with Tequila and De Árbol Chile

Alice Medrich's Five Fudges

Karen DeMasco's grandmother's
Cashew Brittle
and her own Caramel Corn
and Chewy Caramels

Grandma Rankin is the biggest baker in our family. I *mean* biggest, because she doesn't do anything halfway, whether it's preserves or pickles or cashew brittle. This cashew brittle recipe was passed down from her mother, and now it's something I make all the time at Craft with one kind of nut or another. But even in my professional kitchen, I don't come up to my grandmother's production level.

What I hadn't realized, until I called Grandma Rankin to tell her I was sharing her recipe in this cookbook, is that she made 150 pounds of cashew brittle every Christmas. That's seventy-five pounds of nuts and seventy-five pounds of sugar alone! She sent my grandfather to the nut factory to buy bulk cans of cashews. She would start one batch, and while it hardened, she would get another one under way. And then another would be ready to break into bits and wrap up. And her kitchen is so little, with a standard stove and hardly any counter space. I figure if each batch makes about 2¼ pounds, she was making some sixty batches.

She donated twenty-five pounds to the Deaconess Hospital for their holiday bazaar and fifty pounds for her church fundraiser (where she sold it for . . . ready? a dollar per pound), and then she gave the rest to family and friends.

Her cashew brittle is an essential at the holidays. When I was younger, after opening Christmas presents at our various houses, fifteen or twenty of her children and grandchildren would gather at her house for brunch. She'd make rugelach, pecan puffs, cut-out cookies in the shape of reindeer and Santas and trees, and, on occasion, she would even make a big baked Alaska, too. Oh, and there was her fruitcake.

The cashew brittle was always a gift for the grownups, which she would tuck under her tree: individual cellophane bags tied with a ribbon and a gift tag. Now that we have all moved away from her home in Cleveland, she sends the brittle through the mail to New York, Portland, Chicago, San Francisco, Atlanta. I'll always remember the first time I found a bag of the brittle with my own name on the gift tag. I was about thirteen, and that little bag was there as if to say, "You don't need so many toys anymore." It was a sign that I was growing up.

So my guess is that it's her annual treat of caramelized sugar that has made me something of a caramel-loving chef. I feature caramel in ice cream, in my brown sugar cake, and in so many desserts because it has the unique ability to be both sweet and a little salty, which is how I like it. Salt makes caramel less cloying, creating a more sophisticated flavor.

Here are three caramel treats that are ideal bake sale offerings. And the good news is, unless you're Grandma Rankin, you really *can* get away with making less than 150 pounds of each.

Cashew Brittle

Makes 3½ pounds

----

4 cups sugar

16 tablespoons (2 sticks) unsalted butter

⅔ cup light corn syrup

1 teaspoon baking soda

3 tablespoons salt

1½ pounds salted, roasted cashews

1. Lightly mist two large cookie sheets with nonstick cooking spray. Alternatively, you can use a large marble slab.

2. In a 5-quart (or larger) heavy-bottomed saucepan, combine the sugar, butter, corn syrup, and 1¼ cups water and mix together until all the sugar is moistened.

3. Clip a candy thermometer to the pan. After the mixture comes to a boil, continue to cook over high heat, stirring occasionally, for 17 to 22 minutes, until the mixture is an amber color and the candy thermometer reads between 290° and 300°F. Remove from the heat.

4. Carefully whisk in the baking soda and salt; the caramel will rise and bubble. Fold in the cashews with a spatula or wooden spoon. Pour the brittle onto the prepared pan or the marble; spread the brittle into a thin layer. Allow it to cool for several minutes, and, using two forks, pull and stretch the edges of the brittle to create a thinner candy about ⅜ inch thick.

5. Once the brittle is completely cool, break it into bite-size pieces, using the back of a knife or other blunt object. Store the candy in an airtight container for up to 2 weeks.

❖ Bake Sale Tips

Fill small Chinese carryout containers with the brittle and label the containers. Set out small samples in miniature paper cups.

For making twice the amount, complete the recipe two separate times.

Caramel Corn

Makes 12 cups

----

2 tablespoons vegetable oil

½ cup popcorn kernels

2 cups sugar

1 tablespoon salt

2 tablespoons unsalted butter

1 tablespoon baking soda

1. Lightly mist a sheet pan with nonstick cooking spray.

2. In a large pot, heat the oil over medium-high heat and add the popcorn kernels. Cover the pot with a tight-fitting lid and gently shuffle the pot over the flame until all of the kernels have popped.

3. Mist a large bowl with nonstick cooking spray and pour all of the popped popcorn into it, removing any unpopped kernels.

4. In a heavy-bottomed pan, combine the sugar, salt, butter, and ½ cup water and cook

over medium heat to create a light-golden caramel. Add the baking soda and whisk it into the sugar mixture; be careful, since the mixture will bubble up the sides of the pan. Pour the caramel over the popcorn and use a spatula or wooden spoon (not your fingers) to coat the popcorn evenly. Pour the popcorn onto the prepared sheet pan and flatten, separating pieces with two forks while the popcorn is still warm. Cool completely and store in an airtight container.

❖ Bake Sale Tip

Package the caramel corn in individual wax bags, or have a large, covered bowl of the popcorn at the bake sale and scoop out the desired portion into paper cones.

Chewy Caramels

Makes one 8 x 8-inch pan or 3 to 4 dozen pieces

- -

1½ cups heavy cream
1 cup granulated sugar
1 cup light brown sugar (packed)
2 teaspoons kosher salt
2 teaspoons pure vanilla extract

1. Butter an 8 x 8-inch pan and set aside.

2. In a medium heavy-bottomed pot, stir together the cream, granulated sugar, brown sugar, and salt. Dip a clean pastry brush into water and use to wash down any sugar crystals that cling to the pan's sides. Clip a candy thermometer onto the pot and cook the mixture over medium-high heat without stirring until the temperature reaches 245°F. Remove the pot from the heat and whisk in the vanilla.

3. Pour the caramel into the prepared pan and let cool, undisturbed, overnight. Cut the caramel into pieces of the desired size and wrap individually in wax paper. Store in an airtight container at room temperature; this is particularly key during humid weather, when moist air can make the caramels damp and sticky.

❖ Bake Sale Tip

Place a dozen wrapped caramels in cellophane bags and tie them with colorful ribbons. You can also cut the pan of caramels into a few large pieces, and sell the caramel in large blocks that can be cut, like a fudge, into smaller pieces when served.

- -

Karen DeMasco is the pastry chef at Craft Restaurant, Craftbar, and 'Wichcraft in New York City. She was nominated in 2003 for the James Beard Outstanding Pastry Chef award and is featured in Tom Colicchio's book The Craft of Cooking. *She was born and raised in Cleveland, Ohio.*

- -

Bill Yosses's
Pecan Pralines

ou don't need to hail from New Orleans to like these pralines, you just need to have a generous neighbor, as I did growing up in Toledo, who made the best pralines imaginable. And you must learn to pronounce them "prah-leens," as Mrs. Phillips did in her marvelous South Carolina accent, which she hasn't lost to this day, thank the stars. She specialized in all things Southern, and she would have us over for dinner once in a while, where we would savor her chicken and biscuits and sweet potatoes. She also had a great garden, which didn't interest us kids at all, although it was another example of how fully she relished good food.

Halloween was particularly special in our neighborhood, where trick-or-treating lasted for hours, well into the dark. (My friends and I were probably the only "unsafe" things out there!) Instead of store-bought candies, Mrs. Phillips made pralines. She tucked each one inside a wax paper sandwich bag, folded down the top, and put one into the sack of each costumed kid who came to her door. Now pralines were not what anyone expected, but they surprised us by being even better than a Mars bar or a Three Musketeers.

It's also worth noting that her sidewalks got shoveled and her lawn got mowed before anyone else's in the neighborhood. So while these are perfectly suited for selling at bake sales or for serving as one final postdessert treat at home, you might also consider bartering with them, as Mrs. Phillips did.

*Bill Yosses's Bananas Foster Cake, a caramelized banana and
pecan tart, and his biography begin on page 135.*

Pecan Pralines

Makes 2 dozen 2-inch candies

----

8 tablespoons (1 stick) unsalted butter

1¾ cups granulated sugar

1¼ cups light brown sugar (lightly packed)

1 cup evaporated milk

2 tablespoons dark corn syrup or molasses

4 cups small pecan halves

1. Line a baking sheet with parchment or wax paper.

2. In a large heavy-bottomed pot over medium-high heat, combine the butter, granulated sugar, brown sugar, evaporated milk, and corn syrup. Bring to a boil and clip a candy thermometer to the inside of the pan. Cook for 8 to 10 minutes, stirring constantly, until the mixture reaches 236°F. Remove from the heat, add the pecans, and continue to stir for 1 minute, or until the mixture just begins to look creamy.

3. Using a large tablespoon, quickly drop the candies onto the prepared pan. Cool completely. The pralines can be stored in an airtight container for 1 week.

❖ Baking Sale Tip

To make twice the number of pralines, complete the recipe two separate times.

David Lebovitz's
Peppermint Patty Brownies
and
Peppermint Patties

My mother's brownies were from *The Settlement Cookbook*. That recipe doesn't specify what kind of chocolate you should use. It just says "1 square melted chocolate," and that's because all you could really find in the early 1900s was Baker's chocolate, in squares. But today, you can find as many baking chocolate choices as you can recipes for brownies.

Polvorones con Canela, page 24

Coconut Cream Pie, page 104

Pineapple Strudel, page 129

Plum Crumble Tart, page 137

My mother, who was an artist, cooked pretty simple things. She did them very well and we were happy kids. (It's funny, but I didn't know *how* well we ate, how happy we were as eaters, until I got older and started hearing about other families and their dinner table ordeals.) But we were pretty independent, we four kids. So when we stayed alone, instead of heating up Swanson TV dinners, I'd make chocolate soufflés and chocolate brownies. Truthfully, they were pretty easy, and my mother always had the staples for baking in the house: butter, flour, and sugar. And of all the kids, I was the one who loved to experiment in the kitchen.

And what kid, poking among the cabinets looking for something to snack on, didn't take a sample bite of the Baker's unsweetened chocolate—and then groaned, spitting it out or trying to swallow it. (Oddly, I actually love that taste now.) And what kid didn't sample the vanilla extract? It smells so sweet and fabulous, but how deceptive that is if you try a sip!

Two of my childhood favorites were the annual Girl Scout Thin Mints and York Peppermint Patties—I loved chocolate with mint, and I wish they had made *chocolate*-mint toothpaste. Now, as an adult, I use mint in so many desserts, from crème anglaise with chopped fresh mint stirred into it to melon slices in Chartreuse syrup with ripped mint leaves.

But when I enrolled in the Callebaut School of Chocolate in Belgium, my passion for this combination led me to a new discovery. While learning to mix flavors into chocolate, I saw how I could perfect the mint-chocolate union: Drops of mint oil can be successfully swirled into melted chocolate, while a water-based mint extract makes the chocolate seize up. This led me to reinvent that zingy blend of cool peppermint and rich, dark bittersweet chocolate that's one of life's perfect partnerships.

If I saw little sacks of homemade peppermint patties at a bake sale, I would nab as many of them as possible. Maybe I would buy all of them, and then eat a lot of them on the way home, but then crumble the rest of the patties into a really great brownie batter so I could have an even bigger treat—that might, might last long enough to share with a few friends the next day. I'm guessing these Peppermint Patty Brownies will create quite a buying frenzy at your next bake sale.

Peppermint Patty Brownies

Makes one 8 x 8-inch pan or 12 brownies

----

8 tablespoons (1 stick) unsalted butter, cut into 1-tablespoon pieces

4 ounces bittersweet or semisweet chocolate, coarsely chopped

1 cup sugar

2 large eggs

½ teaspoon pure vanilla extract

½ cup all-purpose flour

¼ teaspoon salt

12 Peppermint Patties

½ coarsely chopped Pralined Almonds (page 75), optional

1. Preheat the oven to 350°F and butter an 8 x 8-inch pan. Line the bottom of the pan with parchment or wax paper and butter it. Dust the inside with flour and tap out the excess.

2. In a medium saucepan, melt the butter with the chocolate over low heat, stirring frequently, until melted.

3. Remove from the heat and stir in the sugar. Add the eggs one at a time, incorporating each one thoroughly before adding the next. Add the vanilla and then stir in the flour and salt. Crumble the Peppermint Patties and pralined almonds, if using, into the brownie batter in large, irregular chunks and gently fold them into the batter.

4. Scrape the batter into the prepared pan and bake for 45 to 50 minutes, until a toothpick inserted into the center comes out clean.

5. Cool the brownies to room temperature. Run a knife around the edge of the pan to loosen the brownies, invert the pan on a cutting board, and cut into squares.

Peppermint Patties

Makes 20 patties; an easy recipe to double

2½ cups confectioners' sugar, plus additional for shaping the patties and dusting the work surfaces

¼ cup light corn syrup

¼ teaspoon peppermint oil (available at most pharmacies; do not substitute peppermint extract, which is not an oil)

8 ounces semisweet or bittersweet chocolate, coarsely chopped

1. Line two baking sheets with plastic wrap or parchment paper and sparingly dust one of them with confectioners' sugar. Spoon a few tablespoons of confectioners' sugar into a small bowl and set aside.

2. In a medium bowl, combine 1 tablespoon water, the corn syrup, and mint oil. Gradually mix in the 2½ cups confectioners' sugar until the mixture forms a smooth ball, kneading with your hands, as necessary.

3. Dust your hands lightly with confec-

Pralined Almonds

Makes about 3½ cups

"Pralined" is another word for "sugared," while "almonds," once they are glazed and caramelized like this, is another word for "irresistible." They're perfect alongside adult cocktails or tucked in lunch boxes. And while it may be compounding indulgences, I even like to add a handful of these nuts to the Peppermint Patty Brownies.

1 cup sugar

2 cup whole untoasted almonds

1. In a large heavy-bottomed skillet, combine ⅓ cup water, the sugar, and the almonds and place over medium heat. Cook, stirring constantly with a wooden spoon, until the sugar is dissolved and the liquid boils. Continue to cook and stir until the liquid crystallizes and becomes sandy, 8 to 10 minutes. As the sugar turns sandy, it will also begin to liquefy at the bottom. Stir the dark syrup that forms at the bottom of the pan and fold it over the nuts. (Most of the sugar will be grainy and crystallized; make certain it does not burn.) Continue to cook until most of the sugar liquefies and coats the nuts with a lovely, dark amber coating.

2. Quickly spread the nuts on an ungreased baking sheet and allow to cool. The cooled nuts can be stored in an airtight container for at least 1 week.

❖ Bake Sale Tips

Place the candied almonds in parchment paper cones or disposable cone-shaped drinking cups; tuck or staple the top closed. You can also stand these filled cups in a large bowl filled with marbles, rock sugar, or sand.

To make twice the number of pralined almonds, complete the recipe two separate times.

tioners' sugar. Pinch off 1 tablespoon of the sugar mixture. Roll it into a ball with the palms of your hands, then lightly flatten it into a disk. Place it on one of the sugar-dusted baking sheets. Repeat, dusting your hands with sugar as necessary, to keep the filling from sticking to your hands.

4. Let the patties stand at room temperature for 4 to 6 hours, or until they are dry to the touch.

5. Place the chocolate in a dry heatproof bowl. Set the bowl over a saucepan of barely simmering water and stir occasionally, until the chocolate is smooth and melted. (The bowl should fit snugly into the pan so no water or steam comes in contact with the chocolate, which will cause it to seize and thicken. You may also melt the chocolate in the microwave; see page 16.)

6. Gently shake any excess confectioners' sugar from the dried peppermint disks. Use two forks to lift and dip each peppermint in the chocolate. Flip the patty to enrobe it completely in chocolate. Slide the disk against the rim of the bowl to remove excess chocolate from the bottom.

7. Slip the dipped patty off the forks onto the second prepared pan and continue to dip the remaining disks. Chill in the refrigerator until the chocolate is firm, then place the patties in an airtight container and keep chilled. To prevent untempered chocolate from streaking (a harmless discoloration), keep cold and eat the patties within 2 days.

❖ Bake Sale Tip

Package several patties in clear cellophane bags and tie with colorful ribbons.

David Lebovitz is the author of Ripe for Dessert *and* Room for Dessert, *which was nominated for an IACP/KitchenAid award. He spent over a decade in the pastry department at Alice Waters's famed Chez Panisse restaurant. Named one of the Top Five Pastry Chefs in the Bay Area by the* San Francisco Chronicle, *David has been featured in such national publications as* Bon Appétit, *the* New York Times, People, *and* Gourmet. *He currently lives in Paris.*

Mandy Groom Givler's
Earl Grey Truffles

◆ ◆ ◆

T hough my mother's family is from Portland, where it always rains, I grew up in San Diego, where rain was always something special—at least, it was to me, as a child. And on those rare days, my mother would make a pot of tea and set it out on the "kiddie table" along with a bowl of those large, colored-sugar crystals and a small plate of egg salad sandwiches. I'd sit in a bright little chair and my mother would pull up a regular chair (her knees couldn't fit under my table, of course), and while my older brother and sister were off doing something they thought was important, we'd have our tea party. So I have always loved tea, not just for its taste, but for the special event of sharing a pot. I even have a collection of teapots, and in Portland, where I live now, there's often time for rainy-day teas, snuggled in bed with my husband and Gus and Lily, our two tabby cats.

Earl Grey tea's bergamot flavor—so floral, so full of romance—combined with the dark chocolate creates a divine truffle. I've also used Earl Grey to make a fragrant crème brûlée—simply steep the hot cream with the tea (as in this recipe), top the custard with thinly sliced orange segments, and sprinkle with sugar to caramelize the top. You don't need a rainy day for either of these indulgences.

Mandy Groom Givler's Rhubarb Sour Cream Coffee Cake
and her biography begin on page 244.

Earl Grey Truffles

Makes 60 pieces

---

4 ounces high-quality bittersweet
   chocolate, finely chopped
8 tablespoons (1 stick) unsalted butter
⅔ cup heavy cream
Pinch of salt
2 tablespoons loose Earl Grey tea leaves
¼ cup Dutch-process cocoa powder

1. Line a 9-inch loaf pan with aluminum foil. Place the chocolate in a medium stainless-steel bowl.

2. In a heavy saucepan, combine the butter, cream, and salt and cook over medium heat just until the butter is melted. Do not allow the cream to come to a boil. Add the tea and steep for 15 minutes. Strain the cream mixture to remove the tea leaves, pressing on the solids. Pour the hot cream mixture over the chocolate and stir until the chocolate is smooth. Pour the mixture into the prepared pan, cover with plastic wrap, and refrigerate for 4 hours, or until firm.

3. To form the truffles, allow the mixture to sit at room temperature for 20 minutes. Place the cocoa powder in a small bowl. Line a baking sheet with another sheet of foil onto which you can place the finished truffles.

4. Using the foil, lift the chocolate from the pan. Slice the block into a grid of ½-inch squares. Roll each square between your palms with as few strokes as necessary to create a crude, dime-size sphere. (The goal is *not* to create symmetrical globes; the heat of your hands will melt the chocolate.) Roll each truffle in the cocoa, coating lightly. Set the finished truffles on the foil-lined baking sheet. Chill for 1 hour before storing the truffles between sheets of wax paper in an airtight container in the refrigerator. They can be frozen for up to 1 month. For the best flavor, allow the truffles to come to room temperature before serving.

Variation

Espresso Truffles

To offer a coffee-flavored truffle alongside the tea version, replace the Earl Grey leaves with ¼ cup crushed espresso-roast beans. Pulverize the beans by pressing them with a rolling pin between sheets of parchment. Steep as in the directions for the tea truffles and garnish each finished truffle by pressing one whole bean on top.

❖ Bake Sale Tips

Transport the truffles in an airtight container tucked inside a cooler with ice.

Present them in small cellophane bags tied with ribbons, in cupcake liners, or in small white cardboard boxes, often found in craft or housewares departments.

Bittersweet Chocolate Truffles with Tequila and De Árbol Chile

I had been cooking for fifteen years—Mediterranean, southern French, and Italian cuisines—when I first visited Oaxaca, and I had no concept of the range and depth of Mexico's regional cuisines. (In the United States, we mostly know northern Mexican food, which is just a fraction of Mexico's many cuisines.) But that stay, and a chance to cook intensively with Diana Kennedy at her home, changed my passions entirely; Mexican foods now form the center of my cooking life.

I used a chile powder in the truffles I made at Chez Panisse. At that time, Lindsey Shere had created a crispy black cookie with cayenne and cinnamon that was incredibly popular. I'm sure these spicy sweets convinced me of the winning combination of chocolate and chile.

In these truffles, I've added tequila, but other Mexican or traditional Mayan liqueurs are also terrific: a mescal, for instance, with almond or orange or anise flavor. And home-toasted chile powder adds a subtle smoky heat that comes through as the truffle warms in your mouth; it glows in the back of your throat. (The powder is also great in various soups, or in a salad made of julienned jicama and orange slices dressed with lime juice. Corn on the cob is fantastic with unsalted butter, lime, and a sprinkling of the De Árbol Chile Powder and coarse salt.)

Keep the truffles cold, and then, just before serving, lift each one with a toothpick and dust it with cocoa powder. To make them even more durable for a bake sale, you can leave off the cocoa and dip them again in a bowl of your favorite melted bittersweet chocolate.

Claire Archibald's Quince Empanadas and her
biography begin on page 147.

Bittersweet Chocolate Truffles with Tequila and De Árbol Chile

Makes sixty ¾-inch truffles

----

1 pound bittersweet chocolate, finely
    chopped

2 cups heavy cream

⅓ cup sugar

3 ounces tequila

½ teaspoon De Árbol Chile Powder

2 cups Dutch-process cocoa powder

1. Place the chocolate in a large non-reactive, heat-resistant bowl.

2. In a medium heavy-bottomed saucepan, combine the cream and sugar and bring to a simmer; do not boil. Pour the hot cream mixture over the chocolate, pressing the chocolate bits into the cream. Allow the chocolate to rest for 1 minute without stirring, then stir until the chocolate and cream are completely blended and smooth. Add the tequila and de árbol chile powder; mix until smooth.

3. Pour the mixture into an airtight container and refrigerate overnight.

4. Scoop individual truffles from the chilled mixture, using a ¾-inch melon baller; set each ball on a tray lined with parchment paper. Quickly roll each truffle between your palms to make it smooth and round. Return the truffle to the tray, and then refrigerate the entire tray for 30 minutes, or until the truffles are firm.

5. Place the cocoa powder in a shallow bowl and roll each truffle in the powder to coat the entire surface. Place the finished truffles in an airtight container and refrigerate; you may also freeze the truffles for up to 1 week. Remove the truffles from the refrigerator 10 minutes before serving.

❖ Bake Sale Tip

Although the truffles need to be kept chilled, you can offer these unusual treats in small boxes lined with wax or parchment paper and sealed with a sticker.

De Árbol Chile Powder

Makes 2 tablespoons

12 dried De Árbol chiles

De Árbol chiles, widely available in the Latino section of larger grocery stores, are usually packaged and sold alongside other dried chiles. To make a powder of the chiles, remove the stems and place the chiles in a dry frying pan. Toast them over medium heat, stirring and turning each chile until the skin is golden brown on both sides. Cool the chiles, crumble them into 3 or 4 pieces, and grind to a powder in a spice or coffee grinder. Store in an airtight container.

Alice Medrich's
Five Fudges

My devotion to bittersweet chocolate began in a darkened movie theater. I might have been ten years old when I slid the paper sleeve back an inch or so and peeled thin foil neatly from the end of my first bar of semisweet chocolate. This child of Hershey Bar–loving parents inhaled the mingled aroma of foil and dark chocolate and devoured the bar slowly, nibbling through one section at a time. I don't remember the movie but I will never forget the sweet-yet-bitter chocolate melting on my tongue in waves of intense earthy flavor. In due course, and quite naturally, semisweet led to bittersweet—and the more bitter the better.

How, then, does a hardcore bittersweet girl explain an adult weakness for sweet creamy fudge?

When we were kids in the fifties, my mother sometimes brought home a particularly toothsome three-layer chocolate cake, filled and lavishly slathered with glossy swirls of fudge frosting. The cake was kept on the sideboard in the dining room on a heavy cut-glass cake plate under a shiny metal dome with a black knob on top. The dome rested in a narrow groove around the edge of the plate to keep it from slipping around. But that didn't keep me or my brother Michael from slipping around! Our one-story house in suburban Los Angeles was long and narrow. My parents' bedroom and bathroom were at one end, just off the dining room. My two brothers and my grandmother and I lived at the opposite end of the house beyond the den and the living room, which was smack in the middle of the whole lineup. To snitch a slice of fudge cake—say on Sunday morning when the parents were still in bed—we had to cross the dining room, pass their door, and get the dome off the plate without a sound. Now, a chrome cake dome is capable of "ringing" if it isn't removed from its base with just the right touch. Like seasoned jewel thieves, we each had our own technique for the heist. I tipped one edge of the dome up as though the opposite side was hinged before my careful liftoff. Mikey (who became an actor in his teens) raised the whole thing in one daring flourish. Either way, the dome had to be set aside with excruciating care, while pieces of cake—very small ones lest their absence be noted—were carved and removed. We kept an ear cocked for movement in the bedroom. It took nerves of steel (no giggling or fighting) to replace the dome without its literally singing out an alarm.

"Sneaking" is what we called this Sunday morning ritual and it made chocolate cake taste great. If we had asked, we might have been given a piece. But forbidden cake and the thrill of imaginary danger was just too delicious. Even the memory makes me smile. And so I still eat fudge, usually in private, and always with just a little frisson of that old naughty pleasure.

Bittersweet Fudge

Makes 3 pounds
or sixty-four 1-inch pieces

1½ cups half-and-half

3½ cups sugar

¼ cup light corn syrup

10 ounces semisweet or bittersweet
   chocolate, coarsely chopped

2 ounces unsweetened chocolate,
   coarsely chopped

½ teaspoon salt

2 tablespoons unsalted butter

2 teaspoons pure vanilla extract

1½ cups toasted skinned hazelnuts,
   coarsely chopped, optional

1. Line an 8 x 8-inch pan with aluminum foil or parchment or wax paper.

2. Combine the half-and-half, sugar, corn
syrup, chocolate, and salt in a 3- to 4-quart
heavy-bottomed saucepan. Stir very gently
over low heat for 10 to 12 minutes, or until
the chocolate is completely melted. Raise the
heat to medium and, without stirring, bring
the mixture to a medium boil. Wipe the sides
of the pot with a wet pastry brush to remove
any sugar crystals that form. Clip a candy
thermometer to the inside of the pot and
cook without stirring until the temperature
reaches 235°F, 35 to 45 minutes.

3. Pour the mixture onto a marble surface. (Alternatively, you can use a large heatproof bowl, such as a mixer bowl, if you plan
to beat with an electric mixer.) Add the butter
and the vanilla to the surface of the fudge,
but do not stir them in. Cool the mixture to
110°F, without stirring. (This may take up to
90 minutes if cooling in a mixing bowl.)

4. When the fudge is adequately cooled,
work it back and forth over the marble with
a scraper (or beat it in the bowl by hand or
with an electric mixer) until it begins to
thicken. Add the hazelnuts and continue to
scrape or beat until the fudge begins to lose
its gloss. (Excess beating will cause the fudge
to tighten and become difficult to spread.)

5. Spread the fudge into the prepared
pan. Cover and allow the fudge to mellow
overnight at room temperature. Lift the
ends of the pan liner and transfer the fudge
to a cutting board. Cut into sixty four 1 inch
squares, or as desired.

❖ Bake Sale Tip

   To make twice the amount of fudge,
complete the recipe two separate times.

Variations

Bittersweet Mocha Fudge
Dissolve 2 to 3 tablespoons espresso powder in 1 to 1½ tablespoons water. Add this
to the fudge after it has cooled to 110°F,
when you begin to mix the fudge.

Aztec Fudge
This unusual fudge includes some of the
spices these early chocoholics used when
preparing their chocolate beverages. The
two peppers are not meant to create real
heat, but rather a heightened sensation
in your mouth. You can adjust the
amount of both peppers to taste.

Combine 1 teaspoon ground cinnamon, ¼ teaspoon freshly ground white pepper, and ¼ teaspoon cayenne pepper (or to taste) in a small bowl and mix.

Add this spice mix to the fudge after it has cooled to 110°F, when you begin to mix the fudge.

Bianco "Fudge" with Cranberries, Orange, and Pecans

Makes 1¼ pounds or 64 thin 1-inch pieces

- -

9 ounces best-quality white chocolate, coarsely chopped

1½ teaspoons grated orange zest

1 tablespoon freshly squeezed orange juice

¼ cup heavy cream

1 tablespoon light corn syrup

1 cup dried cranberries

1 cup coarsely chopped pecans

1. Line an 8 x 8-inch pan with aluminum foil or parchment or wax paper.

2. In a food processor, pulverize the chocolate until the largest pieces are no larger than lentils. Add the orange zest and juice; pulse briefly.

3. In a medium saucepan, combine the cream and corn syrup and bring to a boil over medium heat. Pour the hot cream over the chocolate in the food processor and pulse just until the mixture is smooth and the chocolate is entirely melted.

4. Scrape the chocolate base into a bowl and stir in the cranberries and pecans. Spread the mixture into a thin layer across the prepared pan and cool at room temperature for at least 1 hour, or until firm. Lift the ends of the pan liner and transfer the fudge to a cutting board. Cut into 64 thin 1-inch squares, or as desired.

Variation

Eggnog Fudge

Substitute 1¼ teaspoons freshly grated nutmeg and 2 tablespoons brandy or dark rum for the orange juice, orange zest, cranberries, and pecans. This version will be particularly thin.

❖ Bake Sale Tips

Package one or a combination of these fudges in small, fluted paper cups or in little cardboard boxes lined with vellum.

To make twice the amount of fudge, complete the recipe two separate times.

- -

Alice Medrich, the author of five cookbooks, is a pastry chef, teacher, and a two-time winner of the James Beard Cookbook of the Year Award for Cocolat: Extraordinary Chocolate Desserts *and* Chocolate and the Art of Low-Fat Desserts. *Her latest book is* Bittersweet: Recipes and Tales from a Life in Chocolate. *Alice won the prestigious Wine and Food Achievement Award from the American Institute of Wine and Food in 1991. She lives in Berkeley with her daughter, Lucy.*

- -

Pies and Cheesecakes

Jim Dodge's Lattice-Top Sour Cream Peach Pie and
Fresh Sour Cherry Pie

Flo Braker's Super Peach Dumpling with Butterscotch Sauce

Elizabeth Falkner's Rhubarb-Strawberry-Rose Pie

Sara Foster's Chocolate Raspberry Chess Pie and
Old-Fashioned Sweet Potato Pie

Emily Luchetti's Coconut Cream Pie

Rick Rodgers's Chocolate-Banana Cream Pie
with Almond Crust

Karen Barker's Brown Sugar Cheesecake
with Bourbon Peach Sauce

Lora Brody's Ginger Cheesecake

Michel Richard's Basque Custard Cookie Cake

Nick Malgieri's Pizza Dolce di Ricotta (Sweet Ricotta Cheesecake)
and Biscotti di Pasta Frolla (Biscotti with Almonds)

Jim Dodge's
Lattice-Top Sour Cream Peach Pie
and
Fresh Sour Cherry Pie

My childhood was spent in the beautiful Lakes Region of New Hampshire. The first ten years were divided between my family's mountaintop resort and our nearby home, a two-hundred-year-old family farm. Both properties had expansive views of the lake below and its surrounding mountains: a spectacular beauty that you noticed and appreciated every day.

The resort and farm offered my siblings and me the formal privileged world of an exclusive small hotel, which pampered its guests, and the simple country life of an old farm. Although both profoundly influenced my life, it was the farm where I developed my appreciation of seasonal ingredients. Unlike a commercial farm with its one or two crops, a family farm is structured to harvest a crop as well as to supply the family with most of its food. While our home was no longer a working farm, we still had the benefits of seasonal fruits several generations of farmers had planted. Each spring began with gathering and boiling maple syrup, which was used in the hotel's kitchens and sold to the guests. Then the tiny perfumed wild field strawberries would appear, and, in August, blueberries, blackberries, and raspberries lined our old stone walls. Later came the tree fruit, mostly apples and pears.

We had two small peach trees that struggled in our northern climate to bear fruit each year. Yet fighting these climatic odds made our small crop of peaches sweet and delicious. We monitored the peaches daily to calculate when we would have our first bite of the sun-ripened fruit. When you grow up on a farm you see that allowing the fruit to mature on the tree will ensure its full flavor.

When selecting peaches for this pie, choose delicate, juicy, yet still meaty fruit. Lift the peach and sniff; its seductive aroma should fill your nostrils with pleasure. If it doesn't, move on to another market—or better yet, your local farmstand.

Lattice-Top Sour Cream Peach Pie

Makes one 9-inch pie, serving 8

For the dough

3 cups all-purpose flour, plus extra for rolling the dough

½ teaspoon salt

16 tablespoons (2 sticks) unsalted butter, cold, cut into ½-inch pieces

6 tablespoons ice water

For the filling

4 large ripe peaches

1 extra-large egg yolk (reserve the white for the glaze)

½ cup sugar

2 tablespoons all-purpose flour

1 cup sour cream

½ teaspoon ground ginger

½ teaspoon freshly grated nutmeg

1 teaspoon pure vanilla extract

For the glaze

1 extra-large egg white

1 tablespoon sugar

1 recipe Berry Puree, optional, for serving

1. Combine the flour and salt in a food processor and pulse a few times. Add the butter and process until the mixture forms a coarse meal. Add the ice water and continue processing for a few seconds, just until the dough forms into a ball. Do not overwork the dough.

2. Turn out the dough onto a lightly floured work surface. Divide the dough in half and shape each half into a ball. Seal each ball in plastic wrap, lightly flatten into a disk, and chill the disks for at least 30 minutes.

3. For the filling, gently wash the peaches in cold water and dry with a towel. If the peaches feel fuzzy, peel them. (You may do this with your fingers, a paring

knife, or see page 95). Cut each peach into 6 wedges, then halve each wedge. Place the peach chunks in a bowl and set aside.

4. In a bowl, combine the egg yolk, sugar, and flour and mix until smooth and pale yellow. Whisk in the sour cream, ginger, nutmeg, and vanilla. Fold in the peaches and set aside.

5. Preheat the oven to 375°F and adjust the oven rack to the lowest position.

6. Lightly flour a work surface. Unwrap one piece of the dough, dust it lightly with flour, and roll the disk into a 13-inch circle, dusting with flour as needed to keep the dough from sticking. With a soft brush, remove any extra flour from the dough. Fold the dough in half and unfold over a deep 9-inch pie pan. Gently press the dough against the sides of the pan to eliminate air pockets. Tuck any extra dough under the outside edge, forming a thicker lip.

7. Spoon the peach filling into the pan and set aside.

8. Flour the work surface, if necessary, then roll out the second disk of dough into a 10 x 16-inch oval. (The shorter strips will be used for the sides of the pie, while the longer strips will be used in the center.)

Berry Puree

Makes about 2 cups

This sauce is fast and easy to make. I normally avoid using frozen ingredients, since the flavor and quality is usually compromised, but berries are the exception. For a sauce they are often a better choice than the unripe and bland berries many supermarkets carry. IQF stands for "individually quick frozen," and these berries are picked fully ripe, which is why they are often a better choice for a fruit sauce. When choosing frozen berries, pick up the bag and make sure you can feel the individual berries and not a solid brick (which means an inferior taste, since the berries were probably defrosted and refrozen).

One 16-ounce bag IQF frozen raspberries or boysenberries
2 tablespoons sugar
1 teaspoon freshly squeezed lemon juice

Defrost the berries in a bowl; save all of the juice. Pour into a blender and add the sugar and lemon juice. Blend at high speed until completely pureed. To remove the seeds, place a fine-mesh sieve over the top of a medium bowl and pour the puree into the sieve, pressing it with a rubber spatula or kitchen spoon. Refrigerate the strained puree in an airtight container, where it will last for 3 days; discard the seeds.

Transfer the dough to a cookie sheet covered with parchment paper or aluminum foil. Cut the dough into sixteen 1-inch strips. Place the cookie sheet in the freezer for 10 minutes, or until the strips of dough are slightly firm. To create a lattice, place 8 strips, about 1 inch apart, horizontally across the filling; use the longest pieces in the middle of the pie. Alternately draw every other strip to the right side of the pie, add a vertical strip across the middle of the pie, and then switch the positioning (unfolding and folding) of the horizontal strips. Add 3 more vertical strips, weaving the vertical strips over and under half of the horizontal strips as before. Repeat this same process across the left side of the pie with the 4 remaining strips.

9.   Pinch the end of each strip to the bottom crust to secure a seal. Crimp or flute the top edge of the pie.

10.   For the glaze, beat the egg white until smooth and lightly brush the top of the lattice. Sprinkle the top with the sugar.

11.   Place the pie in the oven and bake for 20 minutes. Rotate the pie 180 degrees and continue baking for another 20 to 30 minutes, or until the center has slightly risen and the top is golden brown. Take care not to overbake this pie (the filling can break down and curdle).

12.   Cool on a wire rack. The pie is particularly delicious served with a puree of fresh raspberries or boysenberries. The pie is best eaten that day; however, the leftover portion can be stored in the refrigerator for up to 2 days. Allow the pie to come to room temperature before serving.

Fresh Sour Cherry Pie

Makes one 9-inch pie, serving 8

My appreciation and love of sour cherries began in the summer of 1978, when I was the pastry chef at the Grand Hotel on Mackinac Island, Michigan. This magical resort sits on a high bluff above Lake Huron. The same family has been its devoted owner and caretaker for three generations. Their dedication to local ingredients ensured that our kitchens were supplied with the seasonal harvest of Michigan farms. This was not as easy as you might think, given that delicate ripe fruit came to us via a combination of nineteenth- and twentieth-century modes of transportation. All hotel supplies were trucked to the lakeshore docks and loaded onto the ferries for the ten-mile trip over to the island. Once unloaded onto the island's docks, they were loaded onto horse-drawn wagons for the trip up the hill to the hotel's kitchens.

One of the finest ways to understand the range and complexity of cooking ingredients is to immerse yourself totally in a single ingredient, and that is just what I did with local cherries. I pushed the limits by exploring different flavor combinations. Some worked. Others failed. In the end, this simple pie is my favorite recipe for sour cherries.

That fall when I left Mackinac Island for a new job in San Francisco, I didn't know that I wouldn't set eyes on another fresh sour cherry for twenty years.

Though I searched in vain and regularly pestered the very patient GreenLeaf Produce Company, sour cherries were not to found. Twenty years later, I moved to Boston to take over the restaurants at the Museum of Fine Arts and once when I was shopping in my local grocery store, there they were! Sour cherries! These cherries were from a small orchard in New York's Hudson Valley, but what I soon learned was that their crop lasted only two weeks. So each year I wait patiently until early June for the year's crop of sour cherries to make this pie.

Many recipes will have you add a few drops of almond oil to bring out the flavor of the cherries. When you have fresh cherries there's no need. Here's another tip: Always let a fruit pie cool after baking so that the juices thicken and set. Otherwise the hot filling will flood out and away from the crust. Unless you plan to eat the entire pie at once, you'll have to be a little patient.

1 recipe Flaky Crust Dough, plus flour
   for rolling the dough
¾ cup plus 1 teaspoon sugar
3 tablespoons tapioca flour or
   cornstarch
3 pints fresh sour cherries, washed,
   dried, stems and pits removed
   (see Note)
1 large egg white, well beaten

Pistachio ice cream or heavy cream,
   optional, for serving

1. Preheat the oven to 400°F.
2. On a lightly floured surface, roll half of the dough into a 12-inch circle. Line a 9-inch pie pan with it, gently pressing the dough to the sides of the pan to prevent air bubbles.
3. In a small bowl, combine the ¾ cup sugar and the tapioca flour or cornstarch. Sprinkle the sugar mixture over the cherries and toss to coat the fruit. Heap the cherries into the pie shell, piling them higher in the center. Scrape any liquid left in the bowl over the fruit.
4. Roll the other half of the dough into a 13-inch circle. Lightly brush the edge of the pie shell with beaten egg white. Lay the second circle of dough over the pie, pressing it to the bottom crust, then fold and crimp the edges to form a fluted rim. Brush the top of the pie (but not the fluting) with the egg white and sprinkle on the remaining 1 teaspoon sugar. Cut 6 small steam-holes around the very center of the pie.
5. Place the pie on the bottom rack of the oven and bake for 20 minutes. Rotate the pie, slip a cookie sheet under it, and lower the oven temperature to 375°F. Continue baking until the crust is golden brown and the fruit is bubbling, about 40 more minutes, for a total baking time of 60 minutes. Transfer the pie to a wire rack and cool.
6. Serve the pie at room temperature with pistachio ice cream or unsweetened

heavy cream (lightly whipped to the consistency of yogurt). Set a slice of pie in a soup plate to catch all of the juices.

❖ Bake Sale Tip

To make two pies, complete the recipe two separate times.

Note: Fresh sour cherries are generally available only a few weeks each year, so pre-pare this pie when you have the chance. To substitute frozen sour cherries, defrost the cherries once the pie plate is lined with the bottom crust. (You may keep the crust refrigerated.) When the frozen cherries have partially thawed, toss them with the sugar and tapioca flour or cornstarch, and immediately fill the pie. A pie made with frozen fruit will still be juicier than one made with fresh fruit.

Flaky Crust Dough

Makes 2 piecrusts

This untraditional method of rolling out dough uses the rolling pin, rather than a pastry cutter or your fingertips, to distribute the butter in the flour. You ensure a flaky crust by stretching the butter into long strands and then folding the dough repeatedly as if it were a very informal puff-pastry dough.

> 2¼ cups unbleached all-purpose flour, plus additional for dusting
> 1 teaspoon sugar
> ¼ teaspoon salt
> 16 tablespoons (2 sticks) unsalted butter, cold, cut into ½-inch pieces

1. In a large bowl, combine the flour, sugar, and salt. Add the butter chunks and toss in the flour to coat. Turn out onto a work surface and roll the mixture with a heavy rolling pin until the butter forms long thin flakes. If the flour spreads out too far, scrape it back into the center.

2. Scrape up the dough into a mound with a pastry scraper or flat spatula. Return the mixture to the bowl and fold in 6 tablespoons cold water.

3. Lightly flour the work surface and turn out the dough once again. Begin rolling the dough with a rolling pin. When the mixture gets wide, fold the two ends over into the center. Continue rolling to form a flaky dough by folding the sides back into the center of the dough, thereby increasing the layers of flour and butter. Lightly flour the top and bottom of the dough as needed to prevent the dough from sticking. Once the dough comes together in one piece, divide it in half, wrap each half in plastic, and chill for 1 hour or overnight.

Jim Dodge, a renowned pastry chef and author, is included in almost everyone's short list of those who have had the greatest influence on American cuisine in the past twenty years. Dodge's hospitality "pedigree" originated in the White Mountains of New Hampshire, where his ancestors were innkeepers for seven generations. He is currently Director of Specialty Programs for Bon Appétit Management Company and is based at the Getty Center in Los Angeles.

Flo Braker's

Super Peach Dumpling with Butterscotch Sauce

The first peach I came to love, growing up in Evansville, Indiana, was the Elberta peach, a freestone that was fabulous for just eating out of hand. When you'd slice the peach open, the flesh near the pit was a vivid red. Each summer, my mother would fill the counter with these peaches, canning halves so that we could have them all year long. I was too young to help with the hot jars and simmered fruit, but I loved watching. What I can picture, even now, is how she would slide those glistening, bright-orange halves into the jars, all of them shining and gorgeous, facing outward in their even rows. And there were peach pies, too, that I would watch through the oven's window.

We didn't have a peach orchard and there wasn't one nearby where we could go and pick peaches, but the father of the wonderful woman who worked for my mother for close to twenty years had a farm, and for several summers running I'd spend two weeks at their home in a rural area that didn't even have electricity. This family butchered their own chickens and pigs, pasteurized their own milk, and even pressed their clothing with irons they heated on a fire. They owned gardens, fields of corn, fruit trees from which we all gathered bushels of most everything, and a storm cellar you'd enter by lifting a long wooden door on the side of the house and walking down a few stairs into a room filled with canned goods.

It was a prolific farm, typical of that region of Indiana, and I was lucky to be a part of their large family for those weeks. I'm sure that this was where I gained a greater respect for the food we eat, having seen the effort it takes to grow plants and nurture animals, to preserve or prepare anything that comes to the table.

When I got married, I finally began to cook myself. I honestly hadn't baked much, or cooked much, until then. The only mealtime contribution I'd made during my adolescent years was helping to crank ice cream in the summer. We had a White Mountain ice cream maker, and we'd bring that, along with a crate of peaches, a heavy bag of ice, and a box of coarse salt we never used for anything else, to a park near our home.

My younger brother and I would take turns cranking, waiting for the ice cream to get so hard we could barely budge the handle. Then Mom would add some small chunks of peaches and, with a few more turns, the ice cream would be ready: a wonderful vanilla cream with lovely bits of bright fresh peaches.

These days, one of my most appealing peach desserts is this double-crusted, freeform peach tart. You could call this a galette, but it reminds me of a colossal fruit dumpling, which seems just right, since baking a dessert that stars fresh peaches guarantees an old-fashioned deliciousness.

Super Peach Dumpling

Makes one 12-inch, double-crusted pie,
serving 10 to 12; an easy recipe to double

For the dough

2 cups all-purpose flour, plus extra for
 rolling the dough

½ teaspoon salt

6 tablespoons (¾ stick) unsalted butter,
 cold, cut into ½-inch pieces

⅔ cup solid vegetable shortening, cold

6 to 8 tablespoons whole milk, cold

For the filling

2½ pounds ripe, firm-fleshed peaches,
 such as Red Top or Glamorous Lady
 (6 to 7 medium peaches)

½ cup sugar

½ cup freshly squeezed orange juice

1-inch piece fresh ginger, peeled and
 grated

2 teaspoons finely grated lemon zest

¼ teaspoon freshly ground black pepper

4 teaspoons reserved peach juice

½ cup confectioners' sugar

Butterscotch Sauce, optional, for serving

1. In a large bowl, combine the flour and
salt. Cut in the butter and shortening with a
pastry blender until the crumbs are no
larger than peas. Sprinkle the milk, 1 tablespoon at a time, over the mixture, stirring
with a fork until a cohesive dough forms.
Divide the dough into 2 portions: two-thirds

and one-third of the dough. Wrap each
piece in plastic, press it into a disk, and refrigerate for at least 2 hours. (This dough
makes one double-crusted pie but is also
enough for two standard single-crust pies.)

2. For the filling, place the peaches in a
large heat-resistant bowl and pour enough
boiling water over the peaches to cover
them. After 30 to 45 seconds, lift out the
peaches with a slotted spoon and plunge
them into an ice water bath.

3. Slip off each peach's skin by pulling it
away from the flesh. Return each peeled
peach to the icy water. (This activates an en-
zyme in the fruit that prevents it from dis-
coloring.) You may notice a slight
deepening of the flesh's yellow color.

4. Cut each peach into 6 to 7 slices and
transfer the pieces to a large bowl. Sprinkle
with sugar and orange juice and toss gently.
Set aside for 2 hours or cover the mixture
with plastic wrap and refrigerate overnight.

5. Strain the juice from the peaches. You
should have 1 cup juice; reserve 4 teaspoons
for the peach glaze. (The remaining juice
makes a delicious peach sparkler, diluted
with soda water to taste.)

6. Preheat the oven to 450°F and adjust
one rack so that it rests in the lower third of
the oven. Line a baking sheet with parchment paper.

7. On a lightly floured work surface, roll
the larger portion of dough into a 13-inch
circle. Carefully transfer the pastry to the
baking sheet.

8. Pile the drained peach slices in the
center of the pastry, leaving 2 inches of

dough around the edges. Sprinkle the peaches with the ginger, lemon zest, and black pepper. Roll the smaller portion of dough into a 12-inch round. Center it on top of the peach filling.

9. With a pastry wheel or scissors, trim the bottom layer so that 1 inch extends beyond the edge of the top pastry layer. To form a border, lift the exposed bottom layer of pastry, and, incorporating the top crust, seal the two layers by rolling both crusts toward the filling. Continue rolling all sides of the dumpling to completely seal the pastry.

10. Make 6 small slits with the tip of a knife near the center of the pastry to allow steam to escape. Bake for 10 minutes, reduce the heat to 400°F, and bake for 20 to 25 minutes more, or until golden brown.

11. Cool the pan on a wire rack.

12. In a small bowl, combine the reserved peach juice and confectioners' sugar and brush the glaze over the crust while it's still warm. Serve warm or at room temperature. This dumpling is best eaten the same day it is baked, accompanied by the Butterscotch Sauce, if desired.

❖ **Bake Sale Tips**

Transfer the dumpling to a disposable platter, cover with plastic wrap or clear cellophane, and label. Sell as a whole.

The Butterscotch Sauce can be poured into sterilized jars, kept chilled, and sold as a refrigerated (not a pantry) item.

Flo Braker is the author of the classic and newly revised The Simple Art of Perfect Baking, *as well as* Sweet Miniatures. *She has written "The Baker" column for the* San Francisco Chronicle *since 1989. In 1997, she was inducted into the James Beard Foundation Who's Who of Food and Beverages in America for sharing her baking techniques and trademark sweet miniatures in classes, columns, and books for almost thirty years.*

Elizabeth Falkner's
Rhubarb-Strawberry-Rose Pie

 long time ago, I made a batch of strawberry-rhubarb jam at home and added fresh rose petals from a friend's garden on a whim. After I made the jam, and loved it, I remembered the popularity of rose petal jam in France. Later, I learned about the tradition of using roses in some Mediterranean cuisines. Rosewater, too, became a favorite ingredient. In fact, next time you make a crème brûlée, try flavoring the custard with some rosewater just before you take it off the stovetop.

I suppose I've long loved rhubarb because of my grandmother's rhubarb pies. She grew several kinds of fruits that provided her with the ingredients for gooseberry or blackberry pie, as well as a cupboardful of jams that she would send home with us after a visit with her in Missouri. While she liked the taste of her own jams, putting up the jars was simply another chore: something that had to be done with fruit, or it would go to waste. "Homemade" was not a culinary quest for her; it was the way you held up your end of the deal when nature provided such wonderful things to eat.

You can use any rose petals in this recipe, as long as they haven't been sprayed with fertilizers or pesticides. You may be surprised at how well strawberries and roses go together. The peppery taste of the roses adds to the perfume of the ripe berries. And then the rhubarb contributes its unique tartness.

Elizabeth Falkner's Browned Butter–Walnut Tea Cakes
appear on page 26.

Rhubarb-Strawberry-Rose Pie

Makes one 9-inch pie, serving 8 to 10

----

5 cups (1½ pounds) chopped rhubarb

2 cups (8 ounces) quartered strawberries

1¼ cups sugar, plus extra for sprinkling

12 fresh organic rose petals

⅓ cup tapioca flour or all-purpose flour

1 recipe Cream Pie Shell (below)

Organic heavy cream, optional, for
   serving

1. In a large bowl, combine the rhubarb, strawberries, and ¾ cup of the sugar and set aside for 1 to 2 hours to allow the liquid to drain from the fruit.

2. Preheat the oven to 375°F and place a baking sheet on a rack positioned in the bottom third of the oven.

3. Strain the fruit mixture and add the remaining ½ cup sugar, the rose petals, and up to ⅓ cup flour to the fruit. (Discard or save the fruit juice for another use.)

4. Fill the dough-lined pie tin with the fruit mixture and fold up any overhanging crust to give the pie a rustic or homey ap-

Cream Pie Shell

*Makes one 9-inch piecrust;
an easy recipe to double*

½ cup pastry flour

½ cup all-purpose flour, plus extra for
   rolling the dough

Pinch of salt

8 tablespoons (1 stick) unsalted butter,
   cold, diced

¼ cup ice water

2 tablespoons heavy cream

1. Combine the pastry and all-purpose flours with the salt in a bowl of an electric mixer fitted with the paddle attachment. Add the butter and mix on the lowest speed for 1 to 2 minutes.

Bits of butter should be visible in the dough.

2. Combine the ice water and cream and add to the dry ingredients, mixing only until incorporated.

3. Transfer the mixture to a lightly floured work surface, fold the dough over onto itself to form a rough disk, then seal it in plastic wrap. Press the dough gently to form the disk and chill for at least 1 hour.

4. Transfer the dough to a lightly floured work surface and roll it into a 12-inch circle that's ¼ inch thick. Carefully transfer the dough to a pie tin, allowing the extra crust to hang over the pie's lip; when folded over the fruit, this will create the pie's rustic top crust.

pearance. Some of the filling will show in the center where the dough does not meet. Sprinkle with sugar and transfer the pie to the baking sheet in the oven. Bake for 45 to 55 minutes, or until the crust is lightly browned and the fruit juices are thick and bubbling. Transfer the pie to a wire rack to cool. At home, serve cooled slices of the pie in a pool of cold organic heavy cream.

❖ Bake Sale Tip

This is a pie to sell as a whole. Wrap it in a sheet of tulle that's cinched above the pie with a colorful ribbon.

Elizabeth Falkner is the owner/executive chef of Citizen Cake, located in San Francisco. Before opening her own restaurant, Elizabeth worked for three years at Drew Nieporent's Rubicon, as well as with chefs Traci Des Jardins, Julian Serrano, and Elka Gilmore. A San Francisco Chronicle "Rising Star Chef," Elizabeth's pastries have been featured in Pastry Art and Design, Gourmet, Food & Wine, *and* Travel and Leisure.

Sara Foster's
Chocolate Raspberry Chess Pie
and
Old-Fashioned Sweet Potato Pie

Spending summers on my grandparent's farm in Tennessee was a part of my childhood that I looked forward to every year. For three months, we'd go back and forth from their house in the country to our house in the city. I got to do things I never did at home: One was cooking and baking—pies always signaled a family gathering and the importance of those meals—and the other was working in the garden.

Grandma had a huge vegetable garden, and with its yield, we'd help her put up jars of jams, pickles and relishes, tomato sauce, and chili sauce (like a sweet salsa that we'd have on eggs or black-eyed peas), and we'd can tomatoes and lima beans. We'd also do the particularly time-consuming job of shelling peas and green beans (sitting on the front porch, snapping off both the stem and the pointy ends, making sure that all the beans would be an even four inches long).

From the time I was old enough to climb up on a stool, I would help my grandmother make chess pies, breaking the eggs and mixing the sugar. (And chess pies are a good dessert to do with kids because you can't really go wrong in all that many ways.) This pie originated during the Depression because even then a homemaker would have had butter, sugar, milk, and eggs on hand. That's certainly one reason my grandmother continued to appreciate the pie. And today, I, too, always have the ingredients on hand.

This variation, which is a little more extravagant with the chocolate, is great with coffee or as a rich, yet simple, finish to a great meal. There are endless other chess pie variations: lemon, buttermilk, buttermilk with rum or maple syrup—you can even add a layer of fresh berries to the custard.

My grandmother kept a recipe book, which my sister and I have now. It's a little three-ring binder bought at the five-and-dime, and there must be sixty years of recipes in that book. She clipped recipes from the food section of the *Jackson Sun*, the *Commercial Appeal*, or *Woman's Day*, 1947, where she found "Caramel Fudge Pecan Cake," which I have yet to try. She exchanged recipes with her friends; they're handwritten on old checks, index cards, pieces of brown paper bags, and backs of envelopes, with the date or notes on the back: "Judy's favorite," or "Sara Jane likes this one."

Just reading the names tells a history of who we are and who we knew: Irene's Potato Cake, Mrs. Anderson's Fresh Apple Cake, Margaret's Jam Cake,

Leslie Hinton's Chocolate Pie ("Jimmy's favorite"—my dad), Eula's Golden Fruit Cake, Helen's Lemon Rub Pie, Prune Cake, Miss Brownie's Pumpkin Bread . . .

But if I were to pick one other special pie from those summers, it would be the sweet potato pie: Sweet potatoes are more flavorful than pumpkin, and nearly always available. This pie is so good you won't want to reserve it just for holiday time.

Chocolate Raspberry Chess Pie

Makes one 9-inch pie, serving 8 to 10; an easy recipe to double

----

2 cups sugar

½ cup Dutch-process cocoa powder

2 tablespoons all-purpose flour

3 large eggs, lightly beaten

4 tablespoons (½ stick) unsalted butter, melted and cooled

1 cup half-and-half

2 teaspoons pure vanilla extract

½ cup fresh raspberries

1 unbaked pie crust (see page 141 or use your favorite pie crust)

1. Preheat the oven to 350°F degrees.

2. In a bowl, combine the sugar, cocoa, and flour and stir until well blended (there should be no lumps of cocoa).

3. In a separate bowl, whisk together the eggs, butter, half-and-half, and vanilla until well blended. Add the egg mixture to the sugar mixture and stir until well blended. Place the raspberries in the bottom of the unbaked pie shell and pour the batter over the raspberries.

4. Place the pie on a rack in the middle of the oven and bake for 50 to 55 minutes, or until the pie is firm around the edges and slightly loose in the center. Cool completely on a wire rack before slicing.

Variations

Chocolate Chess Pie
Make the pie as directed, leaving out the fresh raspberries.

Buttermilk Chess Pie
Replace the half-and-half with buttermilk and add 2 tablespoons of either maple syrup or dark rum. Leave out the cocoa powder. You could also include the raspberries—or blueberries or blackberries—to create further variations.

Old-Fashioned Sweet Potato Pie

Makes one 9-inch pie, serving 8 to 10;
an easy recipe to double

2½ cups mashed sweet potatoes (from
    about 2 pounds raw sweet potatoes)
1 cup heavy cream
3 large eggs, lightly beaten
1 cup sugar
2 tablespoons all-purpose flour
½ teaspoon ground ginger
¼ teaspoon ground cardamom
¼ teaspoon ground cloves
¼ teaspoon ground nutmeg
¼ teaspoon finely ground black pepper
¼ teaspoon salt
1 unbaked pie crust, chilled (see page 141
    or use your favorite pie crust)
Lightly sweetened whipped cream or
    eggnog, optional, for serving

1. Preheat the oven to 350°F.

2. In a large bowl, combine the sweet potatoes, cream, and eggs and whisk to blend.

3. In a small bowl, combine the sugar, flour, ginger, cardamom, cloves, nutmeg, pepper, and salt. Add the sugar mixture to the sweet potato mixture and stir until smooth and well blended.

4. Pour the mixture in the chilled unbaked pie shell and bake for 50 to 55 minutes, until a toothpick inserted in the center of the pie comes out clean.

5. Transfer the pie to a wire rack and cool completely. At home, serve slices with a dollop of lightly sweetened whipped cream or in a pool of eggnog.

❖ Bake Sale Tips

Transport whole pies in a cooler filled with ice packs. Keep the pie chilled the entire time. Sell the chess pie as a whole.

The sweet potato pie can be sold in slices: Place individual wedges on small plates and cover in plastic wrap.

Sara Foster is the founder and owner of Foster's Markets, two café takeout shops in Durham and Chapel Hill, North Carolina, and the author of The Foster's Market Cookbook. *She has worked as a chef for Martha Stewart's catering company, as well as for several well-known New York chefs and caterers. Sara has been featured in* Martha Stewart Living, House Beautiful, Country Home, *and* Southern Living. *She lives on a farm outside of Durham.*

Emily Luchetti's
Coconut Cream Pie

Dessert recipes are not just sweets to make but a link to others. All truly passionate bakers share recipes, which only expands their passion. Why keep secrets when a particular dessert can bring others so much pleasure? When I eat a Toll House cookie, I think of how my mother timed it so the kitchen counters would be covered with warm cookies just as we walked in the door from school. I have given her recipe to many friends so that they and their kids can have that same experience.

Baking helps to keep the memories of people and special occasions in the present. Making a cream pie, for instance, reminds me of my parents, both of whom have passed away. Coconut cream pie was my father's favorite dessert. And while we didn't really have desserts except for special occasions, when my father had a particularly trying day—he edited our local newspaper—my mother would take that as a special occasion and make him a coconut cream pie to cheer him up.

My parents had subscribed to *Gourmet* magazine since 1953, the year they were married; they loved cooking and dining out. After my father retired, they moved from Corning, New York, to Sanibel Island, Florida, and opened The Unpressured Cooker, a cooking store, in 1975. This was the moment that gourmet emporiums were just appearing in America.

When I was working on my first dessert cookbook, *Stars Desserts*, I gave it to my dad to edit. My mother told him to be nice, but like a true editor, he said he'd tell it like it is. He made plenty of comments, but they were all very constructive and he was gentle in the tone of his critique, something I, as a new writer, greatly appreciated. He died six months after the book came out, but he did get to see it, and I did get to serve him my version of his favorite dessert at Stars, where the dessert became a feature on the menu.

Recipes for cream pies haven't changed much over the years. They haven't needed to. What made a great coconut cream pie a generation ago is the same today.

Emily Luchetti's Espresso Chocolate Chip Angelfood Cake and
her biography begin on page 222.

Coconut Cream Pie

Makes one 9-inch pie, serving 8 to 10;
an easy recipe to double

----

2 cups sweetened coconut flakes

½ vanilla bean

2½ cups whole milk

8 large egg yolks

½ cup sugar

Pinch of salt

3 tablespoons cornstarch

2 tablespoons unsalted butter, softened

1 Pre-baked Pie Shell (recipe follows)

1 recipe Sweetened Whipped Cream,
   for serving

1. Preheat the oven to 350°F. Place the coconut on a baking sheet and toast for 5 to 7 minutes, or until golden brown. Cool.

2. Split the vanilla bean and scrape out the seeds. Add both to a heavy-bottomed saucepan along with the milk. Heat just to a simmer, then remove the pan from the heat and stir in 1½ cups of the toasted coconut.

3. Put the egg yolks in a nonreactive heavy-bottomed saucepan and then quickly whisk in the sugar. Mix in the salt and cornstarch. Whisk the hot coconut milk into the egg mixture and cook over medium heat for 5 to 7 minutes, stirring the entire time, until the mixture is thick. Remove from the heat, stir in the butter, and remove the vanilla bean.

4. Scrape the coconut cream into a nonreactive bowl, place a sheet of plastic wrap directly on the surface of the cream, and place the bowl in an ice water bath to cool.

5. Spread the coconut cream into the baked pie shell, top with the Sweetened Whipped Cream, and sprinkle with the remaining ½ cup toasted coconut. Keep chilled.

❖ Bake Sale Tip

This dessert is best sold as a whole pie, brought from the refrigerator or cooler at the last minute.

Pre-baked Pie Shell

Makes one 9-inch pie shell; an easy recipe to double

1⅔ cups all-purpose flour, plus extra for rolling the dough

1 tablespoon sugar

Pinch of salt

14 tablespoons (1¾ sticks) unsalted butter, cold, cut into 1-inch pieces

2 tablespoons ice water

1. To make the dough by hand, combine the flour, sugar, salt, and butter in a large bowl. Cut the butter into the dry ingredients with a pastry blender or two forks until the mixture resembles small peas. Pour the ice water into the flour and mix just until the dough comes together.

2. If using a food processor, combine the flour, sugar, salt, and butter and pulse about thirty times, until the mixture resembles small peas. With the machine on, quickly pour in the ice water and process just until the dough starts to come together. (This will happen very quickly. Do not overwork the dough.)

3. Remove the dough from the bowl and press it together to form a disk. Seal it in plastic wrap and refrigerate for at least 30 minutes. You may also freeze it for up to 1 month; allow frozen dough to thaw before rolling.

4. Lightly flour a work surface and roll the dough into an 11-inch circle that's slightly thicker than ¼ inch. Line the pie pan with the dough, folding the excess dough along the top edge of the pie pan to form a decorative border.

5. Refrigerate the shell for at least 30 minutes.

6. Preheat the oven to 400°F. Cover the pie dough with a circle of parchment paper or aluminum foil and fill with pie weights, dried beans, or rice. Bake for 20 minutes, or until the edges are golden brown. Remove the liner and weights, and bake for an additional 5 to 7 minutes, or until the bottom of the shell is a light golden brown.

Sweetened Whipped Cream

Makes 1¼ cups

¾ cup heavy cream

2 tablespoons sugar

In the chilled bowl of an electric mixer fitted with the whisk attachment, combine the cream and sugar and whip until soft peaks form. You may also whip the cream by hand, using a whisk and a chilled bowl.

Rick Rodgers's
Chocolate-Banana Cream Pie with Almond Crust

 nutty crust, almond-flavored whipped cream, and the addition of chocolate to the pie filling make for an unexpected and entirely delicious version of this American classic.

Rick Rodgers's Chocolate-Cherry Fudge Torte with Kirsch Whipped Cream and his biography begin on page 210.

Chocolate-Banana Cream Pie with Almond Crust

Makes one 9-inch pie, serving 8 to 10; an easy recipe to double

For the chocolate-banana cream

2¼ cups half-and-half

⅓ cup plus 1 tablespoon sugar

Pinch of salt

2 tablespoons plus 1 teaspoon cornstarch

3 large egg yolks

4 ounces high-quality bittersweet or semisweet chocolate, finely chopped

1½ tablespoons unsalted butter, cut into bits

½ teaspoon pure vanilla extract

2 large ripe bananas

1 recipe Almond Crust, baked

For the topping

1 cup heavy cream

2 tablespoons confectioners' sugar

½ teaspoon pure vanilla extract

¼ teaspoon almond extract

¼ cup sliced almonds, natural or blanched

1. In a medium saucepan, combine 1¾ cups of the half-and-half, the sugar, and salt. Over medium heat, stir until the sugar dis-

Almond Crust

Makes one 9-inch pie crust;
an easy recipe to double

1¼ cups all-purpose flour, plus extra
    for rolling the dough
¼ cup sliced almonds, natural or
    blanched
1 tablespoon sugar
½ teaspoon salt
6 tablespoons vegetable shortening,
    cold, cut into ½-inch cubes
3 tablespoons unsalted butter, cold,
    cut into ½-inch cubes
1 large egg yolk
3 tablespoons ice water
½ teaspoon cider vinegar
¼ teaspoon almond extract

1. In a food processor, combine the flour, almonds, sugar, and salt and process until the almonds are ground into a fine powder. Transfer to a medium bowl. Using a pastry blender or two forks, cut in the shortening and butter until the mixture resembles very coarse meal with a few pea-size bits.

2. In a small bowl, mix the egg, ice water, vinegar, and almond extract. Gradually stir just enough liquid into the flour mixture to make the dough begin to clump together. (You may not need all the liquid.) Form the dough into a ball (it will feel softer than traditional pie dough) and press it into a thick disk. Wrap it in wax paper and refrigerate until chilled, but not hard—about 1 hour.

3. Lightly flour a work surface and dust the top of the dough with flour. Roll out the dough into a 12-inch circle that's about ⅛ inch thick. Line a 9-inch pie pan with the dough, fold the excess dough on top of the edge of the pan, and form a decorative lip. Repeatedly prick the bottom and sides of the dough with a fork. Freeze the shell for 20 to 30 minutes.

4. Preheat the oven to 375°F. Position a rack in the lower third of the oven and place a baking sheet on the rack.

5. Line the pastry shell with a piece of aluminum foil lightly misted with non-stick cooking spray and fill with pie weights, dried beans, or rice. Bake on the hot baking sheet for 12 to 15 minutes or until the pastry is set; it will not have browned. Carefully lift up and remove the liner and the weights. Continue baking for 15 to 20 minutes, or until the pastry shell is crisp and golden brown. If the crust bubbles up during baking, pierce it with a fork. Transfer the pan to a wire rack and cool completely before filling.

solves and tiny bubbles appear around the edges. Remove from the heat.

2. In a medium bowl, sprinkle the corn-starch over the remaining ½ cup half-and-half and whisk to dissolve. Whisk in the yolks and gradually whisk in the hot half-and-half mixture. Rinse the saucepan and return the mixture to the pan. Cook over medium heat, whisking constantly, until the custard comes to a boil. Reduce the heat to medium-low and stir for 1 minute as the custard simmers. Remove from the heat, add the chocolate, butter, and vanilla, and whisk until the chocolate and butter melt completely.

3. Transfer the cream to a medium bowl and set this bowl in a larger bowl of ice. Let stand for 10 minutes, stirring occasionally, until the custard has cooled. (Do not allow it to set completely or you will not be able to pour it into the shell.)

4. Thinly slice the bananas and spread them evenly across the bottom of the pastry shell. Spread the filling over the bananas and smooth the surface. To keep a skin from forming on the filling, place a piece of buttered plastic wrap directly on the filling. Cool completely, then refrigerate for 4 hours or overnight.

5. To make the cream topping, combine the cream, confectioners' sugar, and vanilla and almond extracts in the bowl of an electric mixer fitted with the whisk attachment. Whip on high speed until the cream is stiff. Spread the whipped cream over the filling. (Alternatively, you may spoon the whipped cream into a large pastry bag fitted with an open star tip, and cover the filling with piped rosettes.) Sprinkle with the almonds. Serve chilled.

❖ Bake Sale Tips

The pie can be prepared up to 1 day ahead without the cream topping, covered tightly with plastic wrap, and refrigerated. Just before serving, prepare the cream and top the pie with it. To transport the whole pie, fill a cooler with cold packs and keep chilled. It's best to sell this pie as a whole.

Karen Barker's
Brown Sugar Cheesecake with Bourbon Peach Sauce

W hen I was a child, cheesecake was *the* company dessert, and we were always entertaining someone at our small apartment. And while assorted Danishes also played a part in my family's steady diet, cheesecake was *the* dessert of that era, especially since we lived in Brooklyn, the very home of Junior's, and Lindy's was right across the river: the two great delis that popularized the big, fat, rich New York–style cheesecake.

One year, my cousin Steve decided he was going to learn how to make his own cheesecakes. He liked to cook from magazines, and for years, he and his wife, Iris, hosted Thanksgiving for the entire family, preparing a huge dinner that never—with the exception of the turkey—*never* repeated a single dish from a previous year. (The turkey was my aunt's, slathered with chicken schmaltz and studded with 140 cloves of garlic, so there was no tinkering with that recipe!) But all the other dishes came from ideas they had borrowed or adapted from the various November issues of the food magazines.

As it turned out, nearly everyone in my family ended up working in the New York public schools and spending their spare time tinkering in the kitchen. My father figured out how to re-create my grandmother's stuffed cabbage with stewed lamb, raisins, and tomatoes. That was his big triumph, and it's the dish I still get each time I visit my parents in Florida.

And it was my father who also began working with—or competing with—

his nephew Steve in inventing cheesecakes. One weekend, my father would bake a cheesecake, and they'd sample it and debrief, and then the next weekend, Steve would fuss with the recipe and bring over a different version. This went on and on for years, adding a crumb crust, adding ground nuts, taking turns finessing their ultimate cheesecake.

When I moved down south, I took this years-old recipe with me, and gradually, I put my own stamp on it, so it's a Brooklyn-childhood cheesecake with a North Carolina touch: brown sugar. That particular flavor plays such a key role in so many Southern desserts: There's brown sugar in pecan pies, in my favorite homemade ice cream, sprinkled on fresh peaches, and substituted for some of the plain sugar in a pound cake.

I, too, have my family's tinkering impulse, and cheesecake really is an exceptionally adaptable dessert. Occasionally, I add bourbon for extra flavor, or I put cornmeal in the crust instead of all the graham crackers. In any case, I often make two cheesecakes at a time, one for eating and one for freezing (simply seal the cooled cheesecake in lots of plastic wrap, and it will keep for a couple of months in the freezer; defrost it overnight in the refrigerator before serving). Company just might be coming.

Brown Sugar Cheesecake

Makes one 8-inch cheesecake, serving 8 to 10

For the crust

¼ cup plus 2 tablespoons graham cracker crumbs (about 5 individual crackers)

¼ cup plus 2 tablespoons finely ground pecans (see Note)

2 tablespoons granulated sugar

2 tablespoons unsalted butter, melted

For the cheesecake

Three 8-ounce packages cream cheese, softened

1 cup light brown sugar (lightly packed)

2 tablespoons molasses

1 cup sour cream

1 teaspoon pure vanilla extract

3 large eggs plus 1 large egg yolk, lightly beaten

1 recipe Bourbon Peach Sauce

1. Preheat the oven to 350°F. Butter an 8-inch seamless cheesecake pan. Line the bottom of the pan with a lightly buttered circle of parchment paper. Make a parchment collar and line the sides of the pan; butter it as well. (Alternatively, you may use a springform pan and tightly wrap the entire pan with a seamless sheet of aluminum foil to prevent water from seeping in while cooking in the water bath.)

2. For the crust, combine the graham cracker crumbs, pecans, sugar, and melted butter in a small bowl. Press the crumb mixture into the bottom of the pan. Press the crumbs at the margin of the pan to form a ¼-inch lip that rises up the side.

3. Bake the crust on the middle rack of the oven for 8 to 10 minutes, or until golden brown. Cool.

4. For the cheesecake, in the bowl of an electric mixer fitted with the paddle attachment, combine the cream cheese and brown sugar and mix for 2 to 3 minutes, or until very smooth, scraping the inside of the bowl several times. Add the molasses, sour cream, and vanilla; mix until just combined. Scrape the bowl again.

5. Add half the egg mixture and mix for 30 seconds or just until incorporated; repeat with the remaining half.

6. Pour the batter into the prepared pan and set it inside a shallow roasting pan. Place the roasting pan on the lowest rack of the oven. Create a water bath by pouring hot water into the roasting pan until half the cake pan is immersed.

7. Bake the cake for 1 hour, then lower the temperature to 325°F and bake for an additional 20 minutes. The cheesecake should be set and puffed up around the edges, while its center should still jiggle slightly. Remove the pan from the water bath and allow the cheesecake to cool completely. Cover and refrigerate for at least 6 hours before serving.

8. To remove the cake, briefly dip the pan in very hot water. Gently pull the parchment collar from the pan. Loosen the cake from the sides of the pan using a knife

with a thin blade. Cover the top of the cake with parchment paper and then a plate. Invert the cake, remove the paper liner adhered to the bottom, and invert the cake again, this time onto a serving platter. Serve with Bourbon Peach Sauce.

❖ **Bake Sale Tip**

To make two cheesecakes, prepare the fillings in two batches unless you have a large-capacity mixer.

Note: Ground graham crackers can be found in the baking section of larger supermarkets. Grinding whole graham crackers (about five 1 x 3-inch squares) along with the pecans in a food processor will help pulverize the pecans and create a more flourlike texture.

Karen Barker, who won the 2003 James Beard Award in Pastry, is owner and chef, along with her husband, Ben, of Magnolia Grill in Durham, North Carolina. Their cookbook, Not Afraid of Flavor, *features the Grill's seasonally based, big-flavored food. They live in Chapel Hill with their son, Gabriel.*

Bourbon Peach Sauce

Makes 2 cups

8 ripe, medium-size freestone peaches
¼ cup sugar, or to taste
2 teaspoons freshly squeezed lemon
    juice
¼ cup bourbon
Pinch of salt
One 500-milligram tablet vitamin C
    (to prevent the peaches from
    darkening)
½ teaspoon pure vanilla extract

1. Bring a medium saucepan of water to a boil. Prepare a large bowl of ice water. Using a small paring knife, draw a long shallow X across the skin of each peach. Gently slide the scored peaches into the saucepan and blanch for 30 to 40 seconds. Using a strainer, remove the peaches from the water and plunge them into the ice bath for a few minutes.

2. Peel the peaches, halve them, and discard the pit. Slice each peach half into several thick wedges.

3. In a medium nonreactive saucepan, combine the peaches, sugar, lemon juice, bourbon, salt, and vitamin C. Cook over medium heat, stirring occasionally, for 10 to 15 minutes, or until the peaches are very soft and the cooking liquid has a syrupy consistency. Remove from the heat and stir in the vanilla.

4. Cool the peach mixture and then puree in a blender. Strain the puree through a fine-mesh strainer. Taste the sauce, adding sugar or lemon juice, if necessary. Cover and refrigerate the sauce; it can made 2 days in advance.

Lora Brody's
Ginger Cheesecake

In the 1970s and 1980s I ran a catering business and wore almost every hat possible, from plumber (when the bridesmaid dropped the ring down the drain) to marriage counselor ("Mr. Greenberg, I think your wife's idea of using the aquarium as a punch bowl warrants some consideration . . ."). Mostly I wore a decidedly unglamorous KP hat while I peeled potatoes and washed dishes. What saved me was a hyperactive fantasy life that allowed me to abandon the hot kitchen and my aching back while I became (at least in my imagination) rich and famous. I was going to accomplish this by inventing a recipe no one had even thought of, marketing it to the world, and sitting back and watching the cash roll in. This goal gave me the liberty to play matchmaker with ingredients (something I can do in my head instead of being able to add or subtract two-digit numbers). Late into the night I would create truly outrageous combinations that (thankfully) never saw the light of day.

One day, after a huge wedding, I looked in the refrigerator to find the following things: eight pounds of cream cheese, enough fresh ginger to open a Thai restaurant, several pounds of smoked salmon, and several dozen eggs. It occurred to me that I could take the lox and cream cheese, throw in some eggs and other stuff, and come up with a savory cheesecake. It also made sense to try an unusual dessert cheesecake with the fresh ginger and some candied ginger I just happened to have. Where other recipes stalled in my head, these leapt right into the oven with delicious results. I made those cheesecakes over and over for my customers, friends, and family. Everyone raved, especially my mother, who shares my devotion to the Sunday *New York Times Magazine.*

"You should send these recipes to Craig Claiborne," she advised me with all the blind confidence only a mother could have in her offspring. And since I was the daughter of an incurably optimistic woman, I did just that. The fact that he paid any attention to this over-the-transom submission is just enough to make you believe in miracles.

When Craig Claiborne ran my recipes in the *New York Times Magazine,* he changed my life. I didn't attain wealth, but the exposure from that one article gave me a foot in an editor's door and ultimately led to my first book, *Growing Up on the Chocolate Diet.* Craig published my recipes in the magazine two additional times and in two of his books, as well. I know I am one of thousands of lucky, and deeply grateful, cooks who were blessed by his mentoring and friendship.

Lora Brody's grandmother's Mohn Kickle (Poppy Seed Cookies)
and her biography appear on page 50.

Ginger Cheesecake

Makes one 8-inch cake, serving 12 to 14

- 6 tablespoons (¾ stick) unsalted butter, melted and slightly cooled, plus 2 teaspoons for the pan
- ½ cup gingersnap crumbs
- ½ cup chocolate wafer crumbs
- 2 pounds cream cheese, softened (see Note)
- ½ cup heavy cream
- 4 extra-large eggs
- 1½ cups sugar
- 1 tablespoon pure vanilla extract
- 2 tablespoons finely chopped fresh ginger
- 1 cup crystallized ginger, cut into ¼-inch pieces (use scissors misted with nonstick cooking spray)

1. Preheat the oven to 300°F. Butter the bottom and sides of an 8-inch springform pan with the 2 teaspoons of butter. (If you do not wish to cut the cake on the springform base, place an 8-inch circle of parchment in the bottom of the pan and coat this with butter as well.) Tightly wrap the entire outside of the pan with aluminum foil to prevent water from seeping in once the pan is immersed.

2. Mix both cookie crumbs together with the 6 tablespoons melted butter and press the mixture over the bottom and

halfway up the sides of the prepared pan.

3. Place the cream cheese and cream in a food processor. (This works better than a regular mixer, which beats air into the batter and causes the cheesecake to rise during baking, and then fall while cooling, cracking the surface.) Process until smooth. Turn off the machine and scrape the inside of the bowl. Add the eggs one at a time, incorporating each one well before adding the next. Add the sugar, vanilla, and the fresh ginger and process for 20 seconds, or until incorporated. Scatter the candied ginger over the batter and pulse two or three times just to mix the ginger into the batter. The candied ginger should remain in distinct pieces.

4. Scrape the batter into the prepared pan and smooth the top. Place the cake pan in a larger roasting pan. Place the roasting pan on the middle rack of the oven and then add enough hot water to form a water bath that reaches halfway up the sides of the cake pan. Bake for 2 hours, checking after 1 hour; replenish the hot water in the roasting pan, if necessary. Turn off the oven, but allow the cake to remain in the closed oven for 1 additional hour.

5. Remove the cheesecake from the oven and transfer the cake pan to a wire rack to cool. Chill completely in the refrigerator.

6. To unmold, run a sharp knife around the sides of the cake to release it from the pan, and remove the collar. If you have lined the pan with parchment, run a long, sharp knife between the parchment and the springform base; use a wide spatula to transfer the cake to a serving plate.

❖ **Bake Sale Tips**

Cheesecake must be kept chilled. Store and transport the cake in a cooler filled with ice packs. Sell the cake as a whole, or slice it into wedges, placing each on a sturdy, disposable plate tucked into a cellophane bag or sealed in plastic wrap.

To make two cheesecakes, you may double the crust recipe, but prepare the filling two separate times unless you have a large capacity mixer.

Note: The best-quality, full-fat cream cheese will make a big difference in the rich taste of this cheesecake. Do not substitute anything like whipped cream cheese or a reduced-fat cream cheese.

Michel Richard's
Basque Custard Cookie Cake

his specialty of France, the gâteau Basque, is a custard cookie cake: a pastry cream encased in two layers of crisp cookie crust. This is the dessert I ordered with a glass of orange juice at our pastry shops from the time I was very small through my teenage years. And I still love a short pastry dough with a burst of cream filling inside.

In France, this was known as a "weekend cake" in the old days, because it was perfect for traveling—not that I had time for traveling! All I had was my bicycle . . . but still, you could pack this cake in a box, or in your suitcase, and wherever you were off to for your holiday, the cake was ready to eat when you got there.

When I had my own pastry shop, years later, my wife used to call me at work and say, "Hey, Michel, please, please, bring me home some dessert." And I'd pack up one of these cakes, and it would sit in a box on the front seat of the car next to me. And then . . . well, it was a long drive and I just couldn't resist. So by the time I arrived at home, I'd throw away the empty box and tell my wife that I'd accidentally forgotten to bring her dessert!

I've learned a bit more restraint in the years since then. Still, this is a traveling cake, so it would be ideal for a bake sale.

Michel Richard's Hazelnut Grahams and his
biography appear on page 22.

Basque Custard Cookie Cake

Makes one 9-inch cake, serving 6 to 8;
an easy recipe to double

For the pastry cream

1 vanilla bean
2 cups milk
Pinch of salt
½ cup sugar
4 large egg yolks, at room temperature
⅓ cup all-purpose flour

For the cookie dough

4 tablespoons (½ stick) unsalted butter, softened
1 cup confectioners' sugar, sifted
3 large egg whites, at room temperature
½ cup plus 1 tablespoon all-purpose flour

1. For the pastry cream, split the vanilla bean lengthwise and scrape the seeds from the halves. In a heavy medium saucepan, combine the vanilla seeds and pod, milk, salt, and ¼ cup of the sugar. Bring to a boil over medium-high heat, then remove the pan from the heat, cover, and allow the vanilla to steep for 1 hour.

2. Strain the milk and pour it into a clean saucepan.

3. In the bowl of an electric mixer fitted with the paddle attachment, beat the yolks and the remaining ¼ cup sugar until the mixture is thick and pale yellow, 2 to 3 minutes. Add the flour, mix thoroughly, then re-move the bowl from the mixer stand. Re-heat the milk mixture over medium heat until it is hot and gradually pour this into the mixing bowl, whisking vigorously. Re-turn the mixture to the saucepan and whisk over medium-high heat until it comes to a boil and becomes very lumpy. Reduce the heat to medium-low and whisk until smooth, 2 to 3 minutes. Scrape the mixture into a bowl and set a sheet of plastic wrap directly on the cream's surface. Place the bowl in the freezer while preparing the cookie dough. The cream can be cooled and refrigerated for up to 1 day in advance.

4. Preheat the oven to 350°F. Gener-ously butter and flour a 9-inch round tart pan with a removable bottom; shake out any excess flour.

5. For the dough, in the bowl of an elec-tric mixer fitted with the paddle attach-ment, combine the butter and sugar and mix on medium speed for 1 minute or until light in color. Add the egg whites one at a time, incorporating each one thoroughly after adding the next. Add the flour, and mix just until the flour is incorporated. You should have a soft batter.

6. Spoon enough of the batter (about ⅓ cup) into the bottom of the prepared pan to form a layer ⅛ inch thick. Bake for 10 to 12 minutes, or until the dough is firm to the touch. The edges may turn a light golden brown.

7. Evenly spread the cold pastry cream over the baked tart; leave a ½-inch border without cream at the tart's outer edge. Spoon the remaining cookie dough over the

pastry cream and the border, spreading evenly to cover the entire pan. Return the pan to the oven and bake for 25 to 35 minutes, or until golden brown. Cool completely on a wire rack.

8. To serve, release the cake from the tart pan and slice into 6 wedges. Cover any remaining pieces with plastic wrap and keep refrigerated. The cake tastes best when allowed to come to room temperature for 1 hour before serving.

❖ **Bake Sale Tips**

Seal this dessert, either as a whole or in wedges, with plastic wrap and keep it stored in a refrigerator or cooler. It can stand at room temperature for an hour or so, but should not be kept in warm conditions for a prolonged period. It "travels" well because the crusts hold in the filling, and in cooler weather the cookie-cake will hold its shape and freshness.

Nick Malgieri's
Pizza Dolce di Ricotta
(Sweet Ricotta Cheesecake)

and

Biscotti di Pasta Frolla
(Biscotti with Almonds)

My maternal grandmother, Clotilde Basile Lo Conte, lived with us in Newark, New Jersey, when I was a child. She was our family's undisputed master of traditional southern Italian specialties such as this sweet ricotta cheese pie. Clotilde had been born in Grottaminarda, an ancient market town in the province of Avellino, settled more than a thousand years ago. Until the last earthquake in 1980, there were many buildings dating from that age. My family emigrated to America not to escape financial hardship or persecution, but because my grandmother was deathly afraid of earthquakes—in 1928, Mount Vesuvius rocked her village, raining ash on everything, and that was enough for her.

This recipe is based on her traditional Easter pie, a dish made in many versions throughout southern Italy, where Easter is the year's major celebratory holiday. (Christmas lags behind in about sixth place, after Saint Joseph's Day, the local town's patron saint's day, and so on.) The flavorings and presentation of the pie may vary, but the essentials are sweetened ricotta bound with eggs and baked in a sweet crust. My grandmother would make five or six varieties and some forty pies each and every Easter. The whole point was to bring an Easter pie to each of your friends and relatives—who would, in turn, have made the same pies to give to all *their* friends and neighbors—so you could take some home as well and make sure yours were better. It was like a pie version of a highly competitive cookie exchange!

After my grandmother was no longer able to bake, my mother didn't exactly pick up her cooking spirit. In fact, she felt that the minute she stopped cleaning up after her mother in the kitchen, she had to start cleaning up after me. Our first attempts to replicate my grandmother's dishes weren't really successful. It got to the point that when we'd see an elderly Italian-looking lady in a supermarket looking at ricotta, we'd cozy up and see if we could get some baking tips from her. But now I'm finally able to recreate some of those desserts of my grandmother's, like this one, that I most love.

I've given this version for an American-style pie pan, which is more common and easier to find than the traditional straight-sided pan.

Pizza Dolce di Ricotta
(Sweet Ricotta Cheesecake)

Makes one 9-inch cheesecake, serving 8;
an easy recipe to double

For the *pasta frolla*
(sweet Italian dough)

- 2 cups all-purpose flour, plus extra for rolling the dough
- ⅓ cup sugar
- ½ teaspoon salt
- 1 teaspoon baking powder
- 8 tablespoons (1 stick) unsalted butter, cold, cut into 10 pieces
- 2 large eggs

For the filling

- 1 pound whole milk ricotta
- ⅓ cup sugar
- 1 tablespoon anisette or ½ teaspoon anise extract
- 1 teaspoon pure vanilla extract
- ¼ teaspoon ground cinnamon, plus more for sprinkling
- 3 large eggs
- 2 tablespoons finely diced citron or candied orange peel, optional

1. Preheat the oven to 350°F and position a rack in the lower third of the oven.

2. For the dough, in a food processor, combine the flour, sugar, salt, and baking powder and pulse several times to mix. Add the butter and pulse repeatedly until the butter is finely mixed in. Add the eggs and continue to pulse until the dough forms a ball. Divide the dough into 2 disks (one should be slightly bigger than the other), wrap both in plastic, and set in the refrigerator to chill.

3. For the filling, in a medium bowl, whisk the ricotta until smooth. Add the sugar, anisette or anise extract, vanilla, and cinnamon and mix just to incorporate. Add the eggs all at once and mix only until the filling is smooth. (Too much mixing incorporates air that will cause the filling to balloon in the oven.) Fold in the citron or candied orange peel.

4. Remove the dough from the refrigerator; it should be thoroughly chilled, but pliable. Dust the larger piece of dough and the work surface with flour. Roll the dough into a 12-inch circle, then fold it in half and transfer it to a 9-inch pie pan. Unfold the dough, gently press it into the pan, and trim off any dough that goes over the edge of the pan.

5. Pour in the filling and sprinkle with cinnamon.

6. For the top crust, flour the work surface and form the second disk of dough into a small square. Dust the dough with a little flour and roll it into a 10-inch square. Use a serrated cutting wheel (also known as a jagger) to cut the dough into ten ¾-inch-wide strips. Arrange 5 of the strips equidistant from each other across the filling, letting the excess dough hang over the lip. Arrange the remaining 5 strips at a 45-degree angle to the others, forming a diagonal lattice. Gently press the ends of the strips against the edge

of the crust and trim off any extra dough that hangs beyond the lip.

7. Bake for 35 to 40 minutes, or until the dough is golden and the filling is slightly puffed but still soft in the center. Transfer the pie to a wire rack and cool completely. The pie can be made in advance, wrapped in plastic, and refrigerated. Bring it back to room temperature before serving and refrigerate any leftovers.

❖ Bake Sale Tip

Offer wedges of the cheesecake on individual plates or white paper liners covered with plastic wrap, or sell the pie as a whole. Transport the cake in a cooler filled with ice packs, and keep cool during the entire sale.

Biscotti di Pasta Frolla

Makes about 50 biscotti

These biscotti were the bonus that came from all the pies undertaken at Easter. They were made from the scraps, trimmings, and all the extra dough that was never used. There wasn't really a recipe for this: Just take a few handfuls of coarsely chopped almonds or other nuts, knead them into the dough, form the dough into logs, and bake it. Sometimes the loaves were given a second baking after slicing. But since you might not want to make forty Easter pies just to have enough leftover dough, this

recipe, which is really the same pasta frolla from above, will give you the same delicious results.

> 3 cups all-purpose flour, plus extra for shaping the dough
> ½ cup sugar
> ½ teaspoon salt
> 1½ teaspoons baking powder
> ½ teaspoon ground cinnamon
> 12 tablespoons (1½ sticks) unsalted butter, cold, cut into 1-tablespoon bits
> 3 large eggs
> 2 teaspoons pure vanilla extract
> 1 cup whole unblanched almonds, coarsely chopped

1. Preheat the oven to 350°F and cover two baking sheets with parchment paper or aluminum foil.

2. In a food processor, combine the flour, sugar, salt, baking powder, and cinnamon and pulse several times to mix. Add the butter and pulse repeatedly until it's finely mixed in. Add the eggs and vanilla and pulse until the dough forms a ball.

3. Scrape the dough onto a floured work surface and press it into a rough rectangle. Scatter the almonds on the dough and quickly knead them into the dough. Cut the dough in half and form it into two 14-inch-long cylinders. Transfer both to one prepared pan, leaving space between the loaves and the edges of the pan. Slightly flatten each log by pressing gently.

4. Place the pan on the middle rack of the oven and bake for 30 to 40 minutes, or

until the loaves are well risen, golden, and firm. Transfer the pan to a wire rack to cool the logs.

5. Move one log to a cutting board. Using a serrated knife, slice it into ½-inch-thick biscotti. Place each biscotti on the pans, cut side down, and readjust the oven racks so that one rests in the upper third and one rests in the lower third of the oven. Fill both baking sheets with the cut biscotti, and then return the cookies to the oven and toast them for 15 to 17 minutes, or until they are a light golden. After 5 minutes, the baking pans should switch racks, and the pans should also be rotated from front to back so that the biscotti color evenly.

6. Transfer the pans to wire racks to cool completely. Store the biscotti in an airtight container.

Nick Malgieri received the James Beard Award for How to Bake *and is the 1998 winner of the IACP/Julia Child Cookbook Award. His recipes have been published in the* New York Times, Ladies' Home Journal, *and* Cuisine, *among other newspapers and magazines.* The Los Angeles Times *syndicates his column "Ask the Baker" throughout the United States. Malgieri is one of the founders and owners of the Total Heaven Baking company and currently serves as the director of the baking program at the Institute of Culinary Education.*

Tarts and Other Fruit Desserts

Stephanie Hall's **Strawberry Shortcake**

Michael Schlow's **Pineapple Strudel**

Jimmy Schmidt's **Blueberry Slump**

Bill Yosses's **Bananas Foster Cake**

Jerome Audureau's **Plum Crumble Tart**

Christopher Kimball's **Maple Walnut Tart**

Miguel Ravago's **Capirotada (Mexican Bread Pudding) and Flan Almendrado (Almond Flan)**

Claire Archibald's **Quince Empanadas**

Sharon Reiss's **mom's Smooshed Apple Pie (page 2)**

Stephanie Hall's
Strawberry Shortcake

◇ ◆ ◇

W hen the fresh strawberries come in, here in Savannah, there is nothing sweeter or better than this cakelike biscuit, this rich vanilla cream, and those perfect fruits. And nothing's better than letting everybody create their own version of the perfect strawberry shortcake. For July Fourth, we set up a "strawberry shortcake bar," and everyone comes up and chooses how many biscuit halves and how much whipped cream and how much custard, and whether to put the strawberries in layers or on top or whatever. It's perfect for parties, and you could even try this idea at a fundraiser. Like at an ice cream social, folks can buy a ticket and then join in the dessert making. Try it with strawberries *and* blueberries, and you can have your red-white-and-blue patriotic colors!

Stephanie Hall's No-Mistake Red Velvet Cake with Pecan Cream Cheese Frosting and her biography begin on page 206.

Strawberry Shortcake

Serves 8; an easy recipe to double

- ⅓ cup sugar
- 2 cups all-purpose flour, plus extra for rolling the dough
- 2½ teaspoons baking powder
- ½ teaspoon kosher salt
- 10 tablespoons (1¼ sticks) unsalted butter, cold, cut into small pieces

1¼ cups heavy cream
1 recipe Marinated Strawberries
1 recipe Pastry Cream
Whipped cream, optional, for serving

1. Preheat the oven to 375°F. Lightly grease a baking sheet.

2. In a large bowl, combine the sugar, flour, baking powder, and salt. Add the butter and cut it in using two forks; the mixture should resemble pea-size crumbs. Stir in the cream and knead the mixture in the bowl

five to ten times, until the dough comes together.

3. Lightly dust a work surface with flour. Pat the dough into a ½-thick disk. Using a 3-inch biscuit cutter, press out 8 circles and place them on the prepared pan.

4. Place the pan on the middle rack of the oven and bake for 10 to 15 minutes, or until the biscuits are a light golden brown. Cool completely.

5. To assemble the shortcakes, split each cake. Place the bottom half on a serving plate and top with a good portion of strawberries. Cover the berries with a generous spoonful of the pastry cream. Top with the top half of the shortcake. Add a few more berries to the base of the plate and serve with whipped cream, if desired.

Pastry Cream

Makes about 4 cups

2¾ cups whole milk
10 large egg yolks
1 cup sugar
¼ cup all-purpose flour
¼ cup cornstarch
1 tablespoon unsalted butter
1 tablespoon pure vanilla extract

1. In a small saucepan over medium-low heat, cook the milk just until it barely simmers.

2. In a heavy nonreactive medium saucepan, quickly whisk together the egg yolks and sugar. Add the flour and cornstarch and mix until smooth. Whisk in the hot milk and cook the pastry cream over medium heat for 5 to 7 minutes, or until it comes to a boil, whisking the entire time. The cream should be very thick. Remove from the heat and stir in the butter and vanilla. Mix until smooth.

3. Scrape the cream into a nonreactive container and place a piece of plastic wrap directly on the surface of the cream. Refrigerate for 2 hours, or until the cream is completely chilled

Marinated Strawberries

Serves 8

2 quarts strawberries, hulled and quartered
4 tablespoons port
1½ teaspoons balsamic vinegar
2 tablespoons turbinado sugar (also known as sugar in the raw or granulated brown sugar)

In a large bowl combine all the ingredients and gently toss the berries. Cover and refrigerate. Prepare the berries several hours before serving for best results.

Michael Schlow's
Pineapple Strudel

I attended high school in Somerville, New Jersey, and once or twice a year our PTA would host a bake sale. The long lunchroom tables were pulled into the hallways or out onto the lawn, skirting was wrapped around the tabletops, and all the mothers brought in their family favorites. Perhaps I remember more than the average number of sales because my mother wrote and organized community cookbooks with her friends throughout the 1960s and 1970s. She was active in all kinds of organizations, and she and her friends would pool their favorite recipes and publish a small book whose proceeds would go to various charities.

One thing about these bake sales I'll always remember is how everyone patrolled the tables, looking to see whose brownies or cupcakes would be the first to sell out. There's nothing more upsetting to a kid than seeing the plate of whatever you brought just sit there while your friend Tommy's or Tammy's treats are vanishing before your eyes.

Each year, my mother would say something like, "Michael, how about if I make some brownies for Thursday's sale," and I'd say, "No, you have to do brownies with *lots* of nuts. And then, cover the whole thing in chocolate frosting." Or she would suggest something else dubious, and I'd make her promise to bake her Hello Dolly Bars (a mysterious sort of brownie with coconut, graham crackers, nuts, and so on) that I figured would sell out fast because when they appeared at our house around the holidays, no one in our family could resist them.

I guess I was a pretty competitive kid. (And I guess there's proof: I gave up a baseball scholarship and ninety-five-mile-per-hour fastball to go to culinary school.) Even today, I want my food to really appeal to people. I could bring out a spiced fig-and-peanut-butter torte for dessert, but how many people would eat it? But offer up a great strudel with rolls of crispy crust and a dense fruit filling: People clamor for that. And while pineapple may not be as common as an apple or cherry filling, it brings an extra crunch and fragrance that makes the familiar all the more enticing, especially with some almond paste to bind the chunks into something almost custard-like. (Still, you should still feel free to substitute other fruits, or even chocolate, since the whole idea is to make this strudel appeal to *your* clan.)

The reality is, we eat what we know, we covet what we like, and the rest . . . we just shove to the side of our plates. But something simple made perfectly: That's what we all love. And here's that strudel. Though really adventurous cooks might want to make strudel dough from scratch, fresh phyllo dough works beautifully, crisping up into a buttery bundle that's easy to slice, and sure to be snatched up as soon as it's set on the table—whether the just-cleared dinner table, or the crowded tables of a bake sale.

Michael Schlow's Great Bay's Great Cinnamon Rolls
appear on page 278.

Pineapple Strudel

Makes 2 strudels, each serving 10;
an easy recipe to double

For the almond filling

4 ounces almond paste

⅓ cup sugar

3 tablespoons unsalted butter,
   softened

¼ teaspoon kosher salt

2 large eggs

⅓ cup all-purpose flour

For the strudel

6 sheets phyllo dough (if frozen, defrost
   overnight in the refrigerator)

8 tablespoons (1 stick) unsalted butter,
   melted

¾ cup sugar

¾ cup almonds, coarsely ground

1 pineapple, peeled, cored, and diced
   into ½-inch pieces

Sweetened whipped cream or
   premium vanilla ice cream, optional,
   for serving

1. For the filling, combine the almond paste and sugar in a food processor and pulse until a grainy mixture forms. Transfer to the bowl of an electric mixer fitted with the paddle attachment. Add the butter and salt and beat on medium speed for 1 minute, or until smooth. Scrape the inside of the bowl. Add the eggs and mix for 30 seconds, or until blended. Scrape the inside of the bowl, add the flour, then mix for 1 minute, or until smooth. Chill the mixture for at least 1 hour.

2. Preheat the oven to 350°F. Lightly mist a baking sheet with nonstick cooking spray.

3. For the strudel, place a rectangular sheet of parchment paper on a work surface and orient it so that it forms a wide rather than tall rectangle in front of you. Remove the phyllo from the refrigerator and place the stack under a clean, dry towel. (Phyllo will dry out instantly, so uncover the phyllo only as long as necessary to take out a single sheet.) Place the first sheet of phyllo on the parchment paper. Brush with melted butter and sprinkle about 2 tablespoons of the sugar and 3 tablespoons of the ground almonds. Cover with the second sheet of phyllo, brush with butter, and sprinkle again with the same amount of sugar and almonds. Place the third layer of phyllo on top; brush this layer with melted butter only.

4. Place half of the almond filling in the center and spread it into an even layer, leaving 6 inches at the top and bottom of the phyllo as well as ½ inch on each of the sides. Place half of the diced pineapple on top of the almond filling. Using the edge of the parchment paper as a handle, flip the 6-inch bottom flap of phyllo over the filling and roll the pastry into a log. End with the seam side down and tuck the sides of the roll underneath to seal the logs. Brush the strudel with melted butter and sprinkle with 1 tablespoon sugar.

5. Transfer the strudel to the prepared pan. (Use a cookie pan as a spatula to move the strudel if it is too difficult to move with your hands.)

6. Repeat this process to assemble the second strudel.

7. Place the pan on the middle rack of the oven and bake for 35 minutes; rotate the pan from front to back after the first 20 minutes. The finished pastry should be golden brown and crisp. At home, serve slices of warm or cooled strudel with sweetened whipped cream or premium vanilla ice cream.

❖ Bake Sale Tip

The strudel can be sold as a whole, or in slices that you might arrange on small disposable plates, covered with plastic wrap.

In 1985, Brooklyn-born Michael Schlow enrolled in the Academy of Culinary Arts in New Jersey. Schlow began his career with renowned New York restaurateur Pino Luongo, then opened Radius in 1999, which has garnered such awards as Best New Restaurant 2000 by Food & Wine. *Michael received the James Beard Award for Best Chef/Northeast, and a place in* Gourmet's *50 Best American Restaurants for 2001. His new book,* It's About . . . Time, *is a cookbook with personal essays.*

Jimmy Schmidt's
Blueberry Slump

When you're the youngest in the family—I'm the fifth of five, and the youngest by a long shot—you're the closest to the ground. So it falls to you to pick the asparagus in the spring, gather the wild blueberries on vacation, and collect the black walnuts from the ditches. And your older brothers and sisters get the job of tormenting you.

Every summer, my family traveled from Illinois to Wisconsin, where we'd rent a cabin on a little lake. It was very rustic, you know, with one light bulb suspended from the ceiling of the outhouse. We'd spend a couple of weeks there—mostly I'd fish, fall out of the canoe, and do all the usual things kids find to do at a little lake. But among my jobs was collecting.

Wild blueberries are pea-size fruit, not big and plump like the cultivated varieties that grow on tall bushes in neat rows and are very easy to harvest. I'd go out with a blueberry rake, which is like a dust pan with teeth along the broad edge, and comb out the berries, which grow very close to the ground. The rake tugs the berries free but leaves the plants rooted in the ground.

True, I did get the first crack at eating them.

Based on how many I gathered, we'd have wild blueberries on top of cereal, or my mother would make a great blueberry pie. But even better was blueberry slump, which is like a cobbler, except midway through the baking, you push the crust into the fruit.

The flavor of wild blueberries is incredibly concentrated—and baking only brings out more flavor. But they require a lot of time and work. It would take me a few days to gather enough for a slump. I'd wander the woods a couple of hours each afternoon, eating almost as many as I'd put into the bucket. True, I was a little tyke back then, but from my point of view, it seemed as if I'd spent the entire week collecting berries and avoiding poison ivy.

I remember one time I was collecting blueberries and feeding myself a few handfuls, when I glanced over to the other end of this patch of berries—not fifteen feet away—and there was a bear feeding himself. This scared the hell out of me! I dropped the whole morning's worth of berries and bolted back to the cabin, shouting, "Bear! There's a bear!" No one believed me.

After I collected the berries, the little stems had to be removed. That was my job, too. If I asked any of my brothers and sisters to help, they'd answer, "*No. We had to do that when we were little.*"

Now they *would* help pick strawberries, which are big and easy to gather. But when it was time for black walnuts, that was left to me, as well. I'd shuffle along in the roadside ditches, collecting the green-shelled nuts, filling a big sack. Invariably, one of my siblings would yell, *"Snake!"* But that's what brothers and sisters are for.

Once I'd stockpiled a couple bushels of the walnuts, I'd lay them out on the country road, and then my dad would get into our light-blue '55 Chevy, and drive back and forth over the yellow-green husks, splitting them.

We'd take all the cracked nuts home, let them cure in the basement for a month, and then each of us—yes, even the older kids—had a quota of nuts we had to crack so that Mom could make her special black walnut bread. It's a pound cake with that unmistakable walnut flavor—a little ashy, maybe a little spicy and pinelike. The cake was so wonderful, we didn't even mind having yellow-stained hands for a few days.

These two desserts prove something to me: The time and the labor of gathering and picking over those wild blueberries or finding and cracking and curing those nutmeats—that creates a flavor you just can't find any other way.

Jimmy Schmidt's Black Walnut Pound Cake with a Ginger–Black Pepper Glaze
appears on page 236.

Blueberry Slump

Serves 8

- 2 pounds wild or cultivated blueberries, rinsed, any stems removed
- 1 cup cranberry juice
- ¾ cup granulated sugar
- ¼ cup bourbon, optional
- 1 cup all-purpose flour
- ¼ cup light brown sugar (lightly packed)
- 1 teaspoon baking soda
- Pinch of salt
- ½ teaspoon ground allspice
- ½ teaspoon ground nutmeg
- 12 tablespoons (1½ sticks) unsalted butter, cold, cut into 1-inch pieces
- ¼ cup buttermilk
- 1 tablespoon pure vanilla extract
- Ice cream or sorbet, optional, for serving
- Confectioners' sugar, for dusting
- Fresh mint springs, for garnish

1. In a 3-inch-deep, 10-inch skillet with a tight-fitting lid, combine the blueberries, juice, ½ cup of the granulated sugar, and bourbon, if using. Bring to a boil over medium heat, then lower to a simmer, cooking for 5 to 10 minutes, until the berries release their juices.

2. Meanwhile, in the bowl of a food processor, combine the remaining ¼ cup granulated sugar, the flour, brown sugar, baking soda, salt, allspice, and nutmeg. Pulse several times to mix. Add the butter and pulse twenty-five to thirty times to cut the butter into the dry mix. The mix should look like cornmeal. Add the buttermilk and vanilla and pulse five to six times, just to combine.

3. Spoon the batter into dumplings over the simmering blueberries. Cover tightly and cook on medium to medium-low heat at a gentle simmer for 15 to 20 minutes. After the first 10 minutes, press the dumplings into the thickening fruit. Remove the pan from the heat and cool, uncovered, for 15 to 20 minutes before serving. Scoop out a generous portion onto a rimmed plate or bowl, top the slump with a scoop of ice cream, and dust generously with confectioners' sugar. Garnish with mint.

❖ Bake Sale Tips

Seal the lidded skillet in foil to transfer this dessert to a bake sale. Bring along disposable bowls and spoons, and scoop out individual portions all at once (seal these in plastic wrap or foil) so that the juicy fruit and "dumplings" are distributed evenly. If desired, bring along a cooler with a tub of ice cream surrounded by ice packs, and finish each, as it's bought, with a small scoop.

To double the recipe, use two separate covered skillets.

Variation

Blackberry-Raspberry Slump
Replace the blueberries with 1½ pounds fresh raspberries and ¾ pound fresh blackberries. Replace the bourbon with crème de cassis, if desired. Increase the granulated sugar in the recipe to 1 cup (¾ cup for the berries.) For the dumplings, use 1 teaspoon cinnamon instead of allspice and nutmeg.

Jimmy Schmidt, a native Midwesterner, opened Detroit's Rattlesnake Club in 1988. In 2002, Schmidt partnered with Donald Trump and opened a Rattlesnake in Palm Springs, California, in the new Trump 29 Casino. Jimmy and his restaurants have received the Ivy Award, the James Beard Award for Best Chef/Midwest, Wine Spectator's *"Award Winning Wine Lists" 1993–2003, and the DiRoNa Award 1993–2003. Schmidt is also CEO of Functional Foods Company, which produces his chocolate bars, SmartChocolate. The author of* Cooking for All Seasons *and* Jimmy Schmidt's Cooking Class, *and co-author of* Heart Healthy Cooking for All Seasons, *Jimmy writes a weekly cooking column that appears in two hundred newspapers nationwide.*

Bill Yosses's
Bananas Foster Cake

B ananas Foster has been one of my favorite desserts, ever since I tasted it for the first time with my Uncle Bob at Dyer's Chop House, a fancy restaurant in Toledo, Ohio, where I grew up. He was our worldly relative who worked in advertising and public relations and often traveled to New York. Uncle Bob spoiled his nieces and nephews rotten, and he gave us kids a Midwestern version of his sophistication, taking us to local gourmet restaurants and to touring companies of Broadway shows at the Valentine Theatre. I remember the first show we saw together was *Damn Yankees*, which followed a prolonged discussion about whether or not an eight-year-old should be able to see a play with a swear word in the title. (Yes, I could see the play; no, I could *not* use that word in the title whenever I felt like it.) We saw *Auntie Mame, Music Man, Oklahoma*—it was a golden age for Broadway shows, and for me.

This particular restaurant served lobster. Now, remember, this was Ohio in the sixties, so I doubt that those lobsters were newly deceased—but no matter. The maître d', the flowers, the linens—I can remember all the restaurant details to this very day. But it's the dessert—Bananas Foster complete with the flambéed explosion at the finale—that taught me how much fun being a grownup could be.

This recipe is a caramelized tart that starts with bananas prepared as in a Bananas Foster, but then adds a pecan-cake batter on top. Then the whole tart is baked and inverted. As much as I love chocolate desserts, I'm always glad to invent one without chocolate, like this banana-pecan-caramel tart, that has the same satisfying depth and intensity as a great chocolate dessert.

Bill Yosses's Pecan Pralines appear on page 72.

Bananas Foster Cake

Makes one 9-inch cake or 1 dozen cupcakes

For the banana layer

⅓ cup sugar

1 tablespoon freshly squeezed lemon
    juice

8 tablespoons (1 stick) unsalted butter

6 medium bananas, sliced ⅛ inch thick

2 tablespoons aged or dark rum

For the cake

10 large egg whites

¼ teaspoon cream of tartar

⅓ cup turbinado sugar (also known
    as sugar in the raw or granulated
    brown sugar)

2 tablespoons all-purpose flour

2 tablespoons almond flour (see Note)

¼ cup confectioners' sugar

½ cup finely chopped pecans

Sweetened whipped cream or vanilla ice
    cream, optional, for serving

1. For the banana-caramel mixture, put
the sugar and lemon juice in a heavy-
bottomed pot over medium heat. Stir occasionally. Use a wet pastry brush to wash
down any sugar crystals that cling to the
side of the pan. When the sugar has
caramelized to a dark amber color, remove
from the heat.

2. Stir in the butter (be careful of spattering). Return the pot to the heat, add 2
tablespoons water, bring to a boil, then remove the pan from the heat and cool the
liquid for a few minutes. Place the bananas
in a bowl and toss with the still-warm
caramel syrup and the rum.

3. Preheat the oven to 350°F. Grease the
bottom and sides of a 9-inch round springform pan and line the bottom of the pan
with a circle of parchment paper. If making
cupcakes, line one 12-cup muffin mold with
paper baking cups.

4. Pour the banana-caramel mixture
into the prepared pan, smoothing it into an
even layer.

5. For the pecan cake, in the bowl of an
electric mixer fitted with the whisk attachment, combine the egg whites, cream of
tartar, and 1 tablespoon of the turbinado
sugar, and whip for 10 minutes at medium
speed, allowing the egg whites to form
firm peaks.

6. Add the remaining sugar and increase
the speed to high for 1 minute, or until the
meringue is fluffy. Combine the flour, almond flour, and confectioners' sugar in a
sieve and sift it into the mixture, folding
the batter halfway through the addition.
Gently fold in the chopped pecans.

7. Ladle the batter onto the banana-
caramel mixture in the prepared pan and
bake for 15 to 20 minutes for the cake (12 to
15 minutes for the cupcakes). Cool for 15
minutes, then place a serving dish over the
pan and carefully invert the cake onto the
serving dish. At home, serve this dense,
gooey cake with sweetened whipped cream
or vanilla ice cream.

❖ Bake Sale Tips

For the most appealing presentation at a bake sale, offer this cake whole, supported on a sturdy plate. Or prepare the cupcakes, placing each one in a cellophane bag, tied with a ribbon or string.

To double this recipe, complete the recipe two separate times.

Note: Almond flour is available at larger groceries or specialty food stores. In a pinch, you can grind whole or sliced almonds in a coffee or spice grinder, using long pulses to pulverize the nuts into a powder. To keep the nuts from turning to a butter, grind a few nuts at a time.

Pastry chef Bill Yosses began his career working at La Foux in Paris. Bill completed his culinary studies at New York City Technical College and quickly found himself in one of the city's most highly regarded kitchens, The Polo at the Westbury Hotel. His pastry apprenticeship included work with his close friend Jean-Pierre LeMasson, the chefs of La Maison du Chocolat, and with Pierre Hermé at the world-renowned Fauchon. In 1985, Bill teamed up with David Bouley at Montrachet and moved with him to his four-star restaurants Bouley and Bouley Bakery. He is now the pastry chef at Citarella.

Jerome Audureau's
Plum Crumble Tart

The south of France supplies fruits for much of the country, and during the summer ripening fruits are so prolific that you can hardly keep up with them. My parents had a garden, and our local markets had such wonderful items—and so cheap at peak season—that we always had more, and bought more, than we could use.

One particular yellow plum, the *quetsch*, perhaps the most famous in that part of France, was always in abundance. When the kitchen was overflowing with the fruit, my mother and I would make plum tarts. Tarts were certainly more fun than cakes, since you got to use the rolling pin, which almost felt like a game. I always took the leftover dough from my mother's tarts—and she often made tarts with tomatoes or other vegetables for lunches or first courses—to fashion my own tart. We had a kid-size tart pan (just an individual tartlet pan), and we'd fill and then bake our two tarts together: my mother's big one, which was to share at the table, and my own small tart, which was decidedly not for sharing!

Tarts continue to be an open door—an *open face*—for creativity. That easy dough can be filled and quickly cooked with all kinds of ingredients, often mixing something savory with something sweet, or traditional garden flavors with some unusual spices. So while I love a leek and celery tart, or a simple tomato tart with herbs, I enjoy creating something like a zucchini curry currant tart.

In fact, it was the tart that began Once Upon a Tart. Beginning in my home, I wanted to offer vegetable tarts—something lighter than a quiche—in Manhattan. And one tart led to another, and here we are today.

Jerome Audureau's Pistachio and Fig Scones appear on page 250.

Plum Crumble Tart

Makes one 7-inch tart, serving 6 to 8;
an easy recipe to double

For the plum filling

1 tablespoon unsalted butter
8 to 10 small damson or Italian plums,
    quartered and left unpeeled
2 tablespoons granulated sugar
½ teaspoon ground cinnamon

For the crumble topping

¼ cup granulated sugar
3 tablespoons light brown sugar
½ teaspoon ground cinnamon
¾ cup all-purpose flour
¾ cup chopped walnuts
5½ tablespoons unsalted butter, cold,
    cut into 10 pieces
1 recipe Flaky Tart Crust, par-baked
    (use a 7-inch pan)

1. Preheat the oven to 375°F and adjust the racks so that one rests in the oven's lowest position.

2. For the filling, heat a large sauté pan over medium heat. Add the butter, let it melt completely, and then add the plums, sugar, and cinnamon. Sauté the mixture for 2 to 3

Flaky Tart Crust

Makes enough for one 7- or 9-inch tart;
an easy recipe to double

> 1¼ cups unbleached all-purpose flour,
> plus extra for rolling the crust
> ½ teaspoon sugar
> ½ teaspoon salt
> 6 tablespoons (¾ stick) unsalted butter,
> cold, cut into 12 pieces
> 6 tablespoons solid vegetable
> shortening, cold, cut into 12 pieces
> ½ cup ice water

1. In a food processor, combine the flour, sugar, and salt and pulse for few seconds. Add the butter and shortening to the flour mixture and pulse until it possesses the texture of a coarse meal.

2. Add the ice water and pulse for few seconds until the dough just forms a ball. Seal the dough in plastic wrap and press it into a disk. Chill the dough in the refrigerator for at least 30 minutes or overnight.

3. Lightly flour a work surface and roll the dough into a circle with a 10-inch diameter. Roll the dough back onto the rolling pin and line the tart pan. Press the dough into the pan. Roll the pin across the tart's rim to trim any excess dough, creating an even edge. Alternatively, you may trim the edge with a knife. Refrigerate the tart shell for 30 minutes so that the pastry dough will relax.

4. Preheat the oven to 400°F.

5. Use a fork to prick holes in the tart dough. Line the tart with parchment paper or aluminum foil and fill it with pie weights, dried beans, or rice.

6. Par-bake the tart shell on the oven's middle shelf for 10 to 15 minutes, or until the dough is a pale tan and just dry to the touch. (For other tart recipes, adjust baking time and temperature according to their instructions.) Remove the weights and proceed with the recipe.

minutes, until the sugar has dissolved and the plums begin to lose their shape. Set aside.

3. For the crumble topping, combine the granulated sugar, brown sugar, cinnamon, flour, and walnuts in a large bowl or in a food processor. Blend the ingredients briefly. Add the butter and blend to create coarse crumbs either using a pastry blender or by pulsing the food processor briefly.

4. To assemble the tart, pour the plum filling into the par-baked Flaky Tart Crust. Cover the filling completely with the crumble topping. Bake on the lowest rack for 20 to 25 minutes, until the crumb mixture is browned and the tart begins to ooze thickened juices. Transfer the tart to a cooling rack. Serve slightly warm or cool.

❖ Bake Sale Tip

Pop the tart out of its pan and slide it onto a disposable plate or tray. Wrap the tart in clear cellophane and tie with a colorful ribbon. To make individual tartlets, cut the plums smaller to fit in the pans, and reduce the baking time by 5 or 10 minutes, depending on the size of your tartlets.

Jerome Audureau began his career in hotel management, and his bakery, in his own kitchen. He is now the master baker and owner of Once Upon a Tart in Manhattan. With Frank Mentesana, he is co-author of a cookbook of the same name. His Web site is www.onceuponatart.com.

Christopher Kimball's
Maple Walnut Tart

Here the maple syrup adds its unique aroma to what is more or less a pecan pie filling baked in a thin layer in a tart shell. The filling is more intense and slightly sweeter, since there is more crust than in a typical tart. Two things will ensure success with this dessert: Don't overbake the tart, and give it at least two hours to set before slicing.

Christopher Kimball's The Best White Cake with Maple Meringue Frosting and his biography appear on page 191.

Maple Walnut Tart

Makes one 9-inch tart, serving 10

----

1 cup walnuts, coarsely chopped

1 recipe Foolproof Tart Pastry, unbaked,
  refrigerated for at least 2 hours, or
  one unbaked 9-inch tart shell

3 large eggs

¼ cup dark brown sugar (packed)

¼ cup pure maple syrup (preferably
  Grade B)

¼ cup light corn syrup

2 tablespoons unsalted butter, melted

½ teaspoon pure vanilla extract

¼ teaspoon salt

1. Preheat the oven to 375°F and set one rack in the middle of the oven and one in the lowest position. Place the nuts on a baking sheet and toast them on the middle rack for 5 minutes, or until aromatic and golden.

2. Poke the chilled crust several times with a fork, place the tart shell on the oven's lowest rack, and par-bake it for 6 to 10 minutes, or until the dough looks and feels dry to the touch. The crust will not be baked completely.

3. In a large bowl, whisk together the eggs, sugar, maple and corn syrups, butter, vanilla, and salt, and then stir in the nuts. Pour the filling into the hot shell.

4. Bake for 15 to 17 minutes, or until the custard edges are firm but the center still quivers when jiggled. Do not overbake. Cool for 2 hours, allowing the filling to set before serving.

❖ Bake Sale Tips

Transfer the tart whole to a bake sale. The tart can be wrapped in clear cellophane and tied with a colorful ribbon. Individual slices (cut carefully with a clean, sharp knife) can be placed on small plates and sealed in plastic wrap.

If making two tarts, complete the filling recipe two separate times.

Foolproof Tart Pastry

Makes one 8- or 9-inch tart crust;
an easy recipe to double

> 1¼ cups all-purpose flour, plus extra
>   for rolling the dough
> ½ teaspoon salt
> ¼ cup sugar
> 4 tablespoons solid all-vegetable
>   shortening, cold, cut into 4 pieces
> 4 tablespoons (½ stick) unsalted butter,
>   cold, cut into small pieces
> 1 large egg yolk, lightly beaten with
>   1 tablespoon cold water

1. In a food processor, combine the flour, salt, and sugar and pulse several times to incorporate the ingredients. Add the shortening and butter, pulse four times, and then run the food processor continuously for 15 seconds, or until the mixture thickens and resembles cornmeal. The mixture will rush up the side of the food processor bowl and slide back down. There should be no visible lumps of butter. Turn the mixture into a medium bowl.

2. Sprinkle the egg yolk–water over the flour mixture. With a large rubber spatula, fold the liquid evenly throughout the dough; this should take less than 1 minute. If the dough needs more moisture, add up to 1 more tablespoon cold water. (It is better to use too much water here than too little; test the dough by pressing it together to form a ball. If it holds together easily, it is ready. If it doesn't, add a bit more water.)

3. Place the dough on a floured work surface and lightly sprinkle flour over the top. Turn the dough over a few times, lightly shaping it into a 4-inch disk. Wrap in plastic and refrigerate for at least 2 hours.

4. Return the chilled dough to the floured work surface and allow it to rest for several minutes. When the dough is still cool, but workable, roll it into a 10- to 11-inch circle. Lift one end of the dough up and over the rolling pin and roll the dough back onto the pin. Unroll the dough into the tart pan and fit the dough into the pan, pressing the dough into the sides of the pan. Roll the pin over the top of the pan to trim off the excess dough, creating a smooth top edge all around. Cover with plastic wrap and refrigerate for at least 2 hours.

Miguel Ravago's
Capirotada
(Mexican Bread Pudding)
and
Flan Almendrado
(Almond Flan)

I must have twenty-eight different recipes for this bread pudding: Every region of Mexico creates a *capirotada*. Most all of them combine the bread with the raw sugar, cinnamon, and, usually, anise—but after that, each area and each chef adds what seems most natural or traditional.

This particular recipe is from my grandmother who lived in the northern part of Mexico, close to Nogales, in Sonora. Her family used to own a chain of bakeries throughout Mexico, so my family would cross the border from Arizona, where my parents had moved us, and we'd drive south through all the towns, visiting each of my grandmother's *panaderias*. We'd end up in the Yucatan. Those trips showed me so much about the variety of cuisines in Mexico.

Her bakery featured the typical Mexican treats: *cornitos,* the little horns, the cinnamon cookies with chocolate, the small breads shaped into pigs or other creatures. But my personal favorite of all that she prepared was this capirotada, which she would make for us throughout the year, not simply at Christmas when it's traditionally served. Every time, it would seem as special as a holiday treat. Often she substituted dried fruits or even candied cactus (which is so sweet and marvelous) to vary her basic recipe.

When people first look at this recipe and see the range of the textures and spices (peanuts, bananas, mint, dried pineapple, spices . . .) and try to imagine how the sweetness can join with scallions and cilantro—well, it's too much for them! (And that's putting their skepticism mildly.) But I have made this capirotada at the Sunday brunches at Fonda San Miguel for many years, and even the tentative newcomers who spoon just a tiny dollop by the rim of their plate come back for a larger serving. You'll simply have to take my word for this—my word, and my grandmother's, and the word of generations of Mexican cooks—and just try it. *And* you'll have to make enough for seconds.

Miguel Ravago's Polvorones con Canela (Mexican Wedding Cookies)
and his biography appear on page 24.

Capirotada
(Mexican Bread Pudding)

Makes one 9 x 13-inch pan, serving 12 to 14

For the syrup

Two 8-ounce *piloncillo* cones (see Note)
1 cup light brown sugar
2 tablespoons anise seeds
6-inch piece cinnamon stick
¼ cup pure vanilla extract
16 tablespoons (2 sticks) unsalted butter

For the bread mixture

1 loaf French bread (12 ounces), sliced
    and lightly toasted
3 cups sliced bananas (3 to 4 large
    bananas)
4 tablespoons ground cinnamon
½ cup fresh cilantro leaves, chopped
1 cup shredded cheddar cheese

1 cup dark raisins
½ cup chopped scallions (about 1 bunch),
    both white and green parts
1 cup dry roasted peanuts, coarsely
    chopped
1 cup dried candied pineapple, chopped
6 large eggs, lightly beaten
Whipped cream, for serving
Fresh mint sprigs, for garnish

1. Preheat the oven to 350°F and butter a 9 x 13-inch baking dish.

2. To create the syrup, pour 4 cups water into a 3-quart saucepan; add the piloncillo, brown sugar, anise seeds, cinnamon stick, vanilla, and butter. Bring to a boil over medium-high heat. Reduce the heat to medium and simmer for 20 minutes.

3. For the bread mixture, tear the toasted bread into bite-size pieces and place in a large bowl. Add the bananas, cinnamon, cilantro, cheddar, raisins, scallions, peanuts,

and pineapple. Toss well. Add the eggs to the mixture and toss gently.

4. Strain the cooked syrup into the bread mixture and fold everything together. Pour the bread pudding into the prepared baking dish, cover in aluminum foil, and bake for 55 minutes.

5. Remove from the oven; let stand for 5 minutes before serving. Spoon into glass cups and top with whipped cream and a fresh mint sprig.

❖ Bake Sale Tip

Transport this unusual bread pudding by spooning individual portions into small clear plastic tumblers; leave off the whipped cream or add it just before selling each piece. Cover each portion with plastic wrap.

Note: Piloncillo cones, a minimally processed raw sugar with a slight molasses flavor, are available at Latin markets or in the Latin section of larger groceries. You may make the recipe without the piloncillo and increase the total amount of brown sugar to 3 cups.

Flan Almendrado
(Almond Flan)

Makes one 9-inch round flan, serving 10 to 12

The flan is very traditional, and it's made all over Mexico. Milk, eggs, and sugar form the basis, but this version has crushed almond slivers, and though this is a simple addition, it adds a unique, but not gratuitously unfamiliar, flavor.

This recipe came to me from a lady who lives in Austin and frequently joined us at Fonda San Miguel. One evening, she shared this recipe, which belonged to her grandmother, who, some twenty-five years ago, was Miss Quintana Roo and competed in the Miss Mexico beauty pageant.

Just thinking of her when I serve this flan gives this dessert a special aura.

¾ cup sugar
One 14-ounce can sweetened
    condensed milk
One 12-ounce can evaporated milk
1 cup whole milk
3 large eggs
3 large egg yolks
1 teaspoon pure vanilla extract
1 cup slivered almonds

1. Preheat the oven to 350°F.

2. Sprinkle the sugar in a 9-inch round cake pan; place over medium heat and caramelize the sugar to a light golden brown. Watch carefully, and as soon as the sugar begins to turn brown—about 4 minutes—remove from the heat, tilting the pan so the syrup creates an even color. Set the pan aside.

3. Place the condensed, evaporated, and whole milks, the eggs, egg yolks, vanilla, and almonds in the jar of a blender. Mix at high speed for 15 seconds.

4. Pour the custard over the caramelized sugar and place the cake pan in a large shal-

low pan. Pour 1 inch hot water around the pan (do not let any water splash onto the flan) and cover the entire cooking bath with aluminum foil. Poke several steam holes in the foil that is not directly over the flan.

5. Carefully slide the sealed flan onto the middle rack of the oven and bake for 55 to 60 minutes, or until a knife inserted near the center of the flan comes out clean. Remove the flan from the bath and allow to cool to room temperature, then refrigerate overnight or for up to 4 days.

6. To serve, run a knife along the inside edge of the pan to loosen the flan. Cover the pan with a large plate and quickly invert. Allow the caramel to drain around the flan. Serve wedges in dessert bowls with a large spoonful of the caramel syrup.

❖ Bake Sale Tips

Although wedges of the larger flan hold up when sliced, you can also bake the flan in individual ramekins. Melt the sugar in the same fashion as directed on page 144. Pour a small amount of the caramel into the bottom of each ramekin and divide the custard among the ramekins. Bake the custards as above for 20 to 22 minutes.

Unmold the custards onto clear plastic disposable plates and wrap each one in clear cellophane. Transport the flans in a cooler filled with ice packs and keep chilled the entire time.

To make 2 flans, complete the recipe two separate times.

Claire Archibald's
Quince Empanadas

My family made pies when I was growing up; it was our idea of dessert. And now, as an adult, I've come to relish a three-course, all-pie dinner: The first pie might be an onion–goat cheese tart with little garden tomatoes; the second a main course savory chicken pie with chipotle chiles, for instance; and then a fruit pie for dessert.

At heart, this empanada is really a sort of pie, which contains two things I'm passionate about: quinces, which I know from my own front yard, and regional

Mexican cooking, which I discovered when my mother and sister and I first visited Oaxaca almost a dozen years ago.

My quince tree was planted in the early 1950s. It's not a quince bush but a pineapple quince tree that's as big as an apple tree. The green fruit are fuzzy on the outside, and you have to cook them quite a long time to soften the flesh and bring out the floral aroma.

When we were younger, my mother would drive around town looking for a yard with a quince tree—they really are quite rare, at least where we lived. She'd go up to the door of the house and ask the owners if they were planning to use all the fruit (hardly anyone said they were), and she'd offer to buy some. She knew where the persimmon trees were, as well, and who grew blueberries in Oregon's Chehalem Valley. In our family, these special fruits were the real treats. This was in the 1960s, and things like mangos were amazingly exotic: We'd peel and eat them over the sink, thinking ourselves extravagant and experimental.

Now I also like to do two other things with quinces: I make quince paste, that traditional Spanish semidried paste of the fruit called *membrillo;* and I roast quinces at Thanksgiving. You just clean and core them (leave the skins on), and roast them with honey and butter at 375°F for about an hour, covering them with foil for the first 30 minutes so they steam, and then roasting them, uncovered, until they're tender. Set these beside a turkey, and you're in business.

Claire Archibald's Bittersweet Chocolate Truffles with Tequila
and De Árbol Chile appear on page 80.

Quince Empanadas

Makes 2 dozen 3-inch pastries

For the pastry

5 cups all-purpose flour, plus extra for
    rolling the dough

1 tablespoon salt

32 tablespoons (4 sticks) unsalted butter,
    cold, cut into 1-inch pieces

1 large egg

1 tablespoon champagne vinegar

For the filling

2 large egg yolks

2 tablespoons heavy cream

12 ounces plain soft goat cheese

8 ounces *membrillo* (quince paste), cut
    into 24 pieces, ¼ x ½ x 1 inch (see
    Note)

Coarse sea salt, for sprinkling

1. For the pastry, in a large bowl, sift together the flour and salt. Using two knives or a pastry blender, cut in the butter so it forms pea-size pieces. Add the egg and vinegar to a 1-cup measuring cup; lightly beat together, then add enough cold water to fill the cup. Add the wet ingredients to the flour mixture and work the pastry lightly until mixed.

2. Alternatively, the dough can be prepared in a food processor. Follow the above directions, and pulse several times to chop the butter into the pea-size pieces. Once the egg mixture is added, pulse just until the dough starts to come together.

3. Turn out the pastry onto a lightly floured work surface or pastry board. Flatten and fold the pastry three times. Cut the dough in half. Form each piece into a disk and seal it in plastic wrap. Refrigerate for at least 1 hour.

4. Roll one disk into a large circle that's ⅛ inch thick. Cut out 12 circles that are 4 inches in diameter. Set each one on its own small sheet of plastic wrap or wax paper. Repeat with the second half of the dough. Stack the circles (interleaved with the paper or wrap) on top of one another and chill the stacks for 15 minutes.

5. For the filling, in a small bowl, make the egg wash by blending together the egg yolks and the cream. Preheat the oven to 350°F. Line two baking sheets with parchment paper.

6. Arrange the circles of dough on a work surface and place 1 teaspoon of goat cheese and a piece of membrillo in the center of each disk. Brush half of each circle's border with the egg wash. Fold the unbrushed edge onto the brushed edge and form a half circle; crimp the edges with a fork. Transfer the pastries to the prepared pans and brush the top surface with the egg wash. Sprinkle lightly with sea salt.

7. Bake for 20 to 30 minutes, or until the pastry turns golden brown. These empanadas can be made up to 6 hours ahead

and reheated in a toaster or oven before serving.

❖ Bake Sale Tips

Package 2 empanadas on a clear plastic plate and wrap with clear cellophane, tied with colorful ribbon. Or place all of the empanadas on a flat basket or tray and sell the pastries individually.

To make more empanadas, complete the recipe two separate times.

Note: Membrillo is available at cheese stores, Latino groceries, and larger specialty food stores. It is often stocked in the cheese or produce department.

Claire Archibald is chef and co-owner of Café Azul in Portland, Oregon, which focuses on the traditional foods of the regions of Mexico, foods that blend the best influences of European and pre-Columbian cuisine. Claire and her sister Shawna, with whom she operates Café Azul, have developed long-term relationships with organic growers to encourage sustainable agriculture in their area.

Iced Cakes
and Cupcakes

◇ ◆ ◇

Michelle Gayer Nicholson's Vanilla Bean Cupcakes
with White Chocolate Mascarpone Frosting

Ann Amernick's "That Baltimore Cake" and
her mother's Hot-Milk Sponge Cake

Kelly Bailey's Chocolate Bonanza Fruitcake
with Mom Bailey's "Sozzled Santa" Raisin and Walnut Sauce

Judy Rosenberg's Rosie Pies

Edna Lewis and Scott Peacock's Gingerbread Cupcakes
with Caramel Glaze

Gale Gand's Marshmallow Heart Throbs and Homemade Marshmallows

Rémy Fünfrock's Chouquettes (Filled or Glazed Pastry Puffs)
and Chocolate Carolines

Dan Dye and Mark Beckloff's Chocolate Cake and Carob Dog Treats

Maida Heatter's Buttermilk Key Lime Cake

Christopher Kimball's The Best White Cake with
Maple Meringue Frosting

Fran Bigelow's Classic Chocolate-Chocolate Icebox Cake

Marcel Desaulniers's Chocolate Sunburst Birthday Cake

Jane and Michael Stern's Cola Cake with Broiled Peanut Butter Frosting
and Milky Way Cake

Stephanie Hall's No-Mistake Red Velvet Cake with
Pecan Cream Cheese Frosting

Rick Rodgers's Chocolate-Cherry Fudge Torte with
Kirsch Whipped Cream

Michelle Gayer Nicholson's

Vanilla Bean Cupcakes with White Chocolate Mascarpone Frosting

A cupcake is a personal cake. It says "just for you." It's a cake-to-go with its own wrapper. And most cupcakes can be as fancy or as simple as you like. Just a little cake batter poured into a few cupcake cup liners can make a special treat for dinner.

And for kids' birthday parties, cupcakes are essential. My mother always made us cupcakes for our birthdays, and now that I have two toddlers, I know I'll bake them, too.

For my daughter Isabelle's second birthday party, the theme was an animal jungle. I made bear cookies, zebra cookies with two colors of frosting, and elephant cookies with marshmallows and colored sugars. We hung a piñata in the shape of the number 2, filled with all kinds of candy treats, and the older kids took turns swatting at it with a broomstick.

I set out paper plates with matching napkins and filled Chinese takeout cartons with animal stickers and plastic animals. In the center of the table was what looked like a giant three-tiered cake. I made these vanilla-bean cupcakes—which are particularly moist and airy with both baking power and egg whites to keep them light—as well as chocolate cupcakes. I arranged a tower of maybe four dozen cupcakes on three cake stands, balancing one stand on top of the next. From a distance it looked like Isabelle had one enormous cake. We had three or four dozen guests at the party—relatives, neighbors, friends, friends' kids (some of whom are Isabelle's age and *might* become her friends, although she's not sure what friends are just yet)—and everyone got his or her own cupcake. So there was no mess from cutting a big cake and no waiting for your slice to be passed hand to hand from across the room.

Not that there wasn't a mess. Isabelle, like most two-year-olds, doesn't really understand the design of the cupcake. She licks and bites the top frosting and then munches into the center of the cake until she's done. She doesn't know about peeling off the paper liner or about trying for a bit of cake and a little icing with each bite. Her hands, her face, the chair, the carpet—all shared her cupcake.

In a few months, I'll be making cupcakes again for my nine-month-old's first birthday. The happy mess continues.

Vanilla Bean Cupcakes

Makes twelve 3¾-inch cakes

----

1 vanilla bean (see Note)

12 tablespoons (1½ sticks) unsalted butter, softened

2 cups plus 5 tablespoons sugar

3½ cups pastry flour

¼ teaspoon salt

1 tablespoon baking powder

6 large egg whites

1 recipe White Chocolate Mascarpone Frosting

6 to 8 ounces white chocolate, peeled into curls, optional, for garnish

1. Preheat the oven to 350°F. Fill twelve 3¾-inch muffin cups with paper baking cups. Split open the vanilla bean and scrape free the seeds.

2. In the bowl of an electric mixer fitted with the paddle attachment, put the butter, 1½ cups plus 3 tablespoons of the sugar, and the vanilla seeds. Mix for 2 minutes on medium speed or until light and fluffy.

3. In a large bowl, sift together the flour, salt, and baking powder. Reduce the mixer

White Chocolate Mascarpone Frosting

Makes enough for 12 to 16 cupcakes; an easy recipe to double

2 cups heavy cream

8 ounces white chocolate, finely chopped

17.6 ounces mascarpone (see Note)

1. In a small saucepan, warm the cream over medium heat until it feels hot but is nowhere near a simmer. Place the chopped chocolate in a heatproof bowl and pour the warm cream over the chocolate. Whisk until the chocolate melts. Set the bowl in an ice bath until the mixture is chilled. Place a piece of plastic wrap directly on the surface of the mixture and a second piece over the bowl and refrigerate for at least 4 hours. You may also make this 1 day ahead.

2. In the bowl of an electric mixer fitted with the whisk attachment, combine the mascarpone and half of the white chocolate mixture and whip for 2 minutes, or until well combined. Add the remaining white chocolate mixture, increase the speed to high, and beat the mixture until the frosting holds stiff peaks.

Note: Mascarpone cheese, which is imported from Italy, is sold in small tubs that are measured in grams. Converting to ounces creates this odd, just-over-one-pound unit.

---

speed to low, and alternately pour into the butter-sugar mixture one-third of the dry ingredients and one-half of the water, mixing well after each addition and scraping the inside of the bowl; begin and end with the dry ingredients. Remove the mixing bowl.

4. Fit the mixer with the whisk attachment. In another mixing bowl, beat the egg whites on medium-high speed for 2 to 3 minutes, or until soft peaks form. Reduce the speed to low and slowly add the remaining ½ cup plus 2 tablespoons sugar. Increase the speed to medium-high and beat until soft peaks form. The egg whites should look glossy. Do not overmix. Gently fold the egg whites into the cake batter in two or three additions, incorporating all the egg whites thoroughly.

5. Spoon the batter into the baking cups, filling each one three-quarters full. Place the pan on the middle rack of the oven and bake for 15 to 20 minutes, or until the centers of the cupcakes spring back. Transfer the pan to a wire rack to cool for 5 minutes. Remove the cupcakes and cool completely.

6. Frost each cake with generous spoonfuls of the mascarpone frosting or another favorite frosting. Use a vegetable peeler to scrape a block of white chocolate to create large curls. Place several on top of each cupcake.

7. Place the cupcakes in an airtight con-

tainer and refrigerate. Allow the cakes to sit at room temperature for 10 minutes before serving.

❖ Bake Sale Tips

Since the chocolate curls are fragile and the frosting needs to be kept cool, transport the cakes in a deep lidded container and keep in an ice chest or refrigerator. You could also wait and add the chocolate curls upon arrival.

To make twice as many cupcakes, complete the recipe two separate times.

Note: It's worth the trouble to seek out the freshest whole vanilla beans you can find. Mail order houses or gourmet emporiums often have Tahitian beans, which have an exceptionally floral quality.

Michelle Gayer Nicholson was educated at the Culinary School of Kendall College in Chicago, trained under Charlie Trotter, served as Nancy Silverton's assistant baker at La Brea Bakery and Campanile, and traveled extensively throughout the country and Europe with Charlie Trotter. Currently she is executive pastry chef at Trotter's To Go, a prepared foods market with an elaborate selection of artisanal pastries and baked goods. Michelle was awarded Bon Appétit's Best Pastry Chef 2003 and was nominated in 2002 for the James Beard Foundation Best Pastry Chef. She coauthored Charlie Trotter's Desserts and has been the featured pastry chef at many culinary expositions and charity benefits.

Ann Amernick's
"That Baltimore Cake"
and her mother's
Hot-Milk Sponge Cake

I had two cakes in the back of my mind when I created "That Baltimore Cake." One is the memory of a tradition my mother began when we were young. For each of her four children's birthdays, she'd bake a hot-milk sponge cake. It often had strawberry or another kind of preserves between the layers, and the frosting was usually white. (I believe it came from the back of the Domino sugar box: a pound of sugar, some butter and some milk, vanilla extract . . .) There's a snapshot of me standing in front of a birthday cake studded with little candles held up by little blue animals—deer, I think.

The other memory was of a rainbow cake from Silber's Bakery near our house in Baltimore. This was a wondrous thing: a dense, rectangular pound cake that was layered green and red and yellow and white (the cake's natural color). They spread raspberry jam between the sections and covered the whole cake with chocolate frosting. Growing up, I thought this cake was splendid, but my very favorite desserts were whatever came from Fisk Caterers, a fancy company that created individual ice creams in tiny molds, wonderful petits fours and petits gâteaux, as well as special occasion cakes. They were much more expensive, but I remember we had their cakes at my bat mitzvah and my sweet sixteen party.

It's curious, but even as a young girl, I had some sense of what was truly delicious. I can remember being about eight, walking home from school with my saved-up money, and stopping into the dairy store to buy a thirty-five-cent chocolate bar. Now this is more than fifty years ago. But I wanted that one, three-ounce bar of chocolate with black script on the white label that tasted so much better than the chocolates kids were supposed to eat. Now I know it was Lindt's dark chocolate.

Today, at our bakery, we create many things that my mother, who is in her eighties, doesn't care for: mousse cakes, buttercream, fancy tortes—it's all too rich, she's decided. She's not alone: People go wild for an old-fashioned, home-made cake with a great frosting, like the birthday cakes my mother used to make us. On the other hand, no one is more proud than my mother when a cake of mine is featured in a magazine. For several years, she helped me make the sugar flowers that adorn my wedding cakes. On Wednesdays, my sister would drive our mother in from Baltimore to my home in Washington. I taught my mother how to shape the buds, and it became her specialty; she was incredibly good at it. When a food magazine had a photograph of one of my cakes, my mother always asked, "Are those my buds?"

For her most recent birthday, I wanted to create the kind of cake that she'd most love. An old-fashioned, buttery pound cake, not unlike her hot-milk sponge cake or that Silber's Bakery cake, but with a really flavorful frosting— lemon came to mind—rather than a buttercream. So I invited her for dinner at our new restaurant, Palena. The birthday cake was to be a surprise, even though she was clearly expecting something. But when the server arrived and asked for her dessert order, my mother just looked at me—she was crestfallen—"You didn't bake me a cake?" I shrugged and told her how busy we'd been . . . and then I suddenly realized that she really was very upset, and that I should never have been teasing her. Just then the staff arrived holding a whole beautiful cake with one lit candle, and we cut her a big slice, and she just cried her eyes out, she was so happy. (But I still felt awful for kidding her.) My mother declared it absolutely the best cake she'd ever eaten.

"It's like *that Baltimore cake!*" she announced, and that's where I found the name for this dessert, which makes ideal cupcakes for a bake sale.

"That Baltimore Cake"

Makes 2 dozen 3-inch cakes

For the cake

3 cups cake flour

¼ teaspoon salt

¾ teaspoon baking soda

16 tablespoons (2 sticks) unsalted butter, softened

2¾ cups sugar

6 large eggs

2 tablespoons finely grated lemon zest

1 cup sour cream

3 tablespoons half-and-half or milk

For the lemon soak

½ cup freshly squeezed lemon juice (from 4 to 5 large lemons)

1¼ cups sugar

1 cup seedless raspberry jam

1 recipe Lemon Frosting

1. Preheat the oven to 350°F. Line two 12-cup, 3-inch-deep muffin pans with paper baking cups.

2. For the cake, in a medium bowl, sift together the flour, salt, and baking soda.

3. In the bowl of an electric mixer fitted with the paddle attachment, cream the butter and sugar on medium speed for 2 minutes, or until light and fluffy. Add the eggs one at a time; beat for 1 minute after each addition. Add the lemon zest and mix to incorporate. On the lowest speed, alternately add one-third of the sifted ingredients and half of the sour cream, mixing well after each addition and scraping the inside of the bowl; begin and end with the dry ingredients. Add the cream or milk. Increase the speed to medium and mix for less than a minute, just until the batter is smooth.

4. Spoon the batter into a large pastry bag with a wide opening (no tip necessary) and pipe each baking cup two-thirds full. Bake on the middle rack of the oven for 15 to 18 minutes, or until the top of the cupcake has risen into a dome and a toothpick inserted into the center comes out clean.

5. While the cakes are baking, assemble the lemon soak by mixing together the lemon

juice and sugar in a small bowl. It is not necessary for all the sugar to be dissolved.

6. As soon as the cakes come out of the oven, brush the tops with the lemon soak, then transfer the cakes from the pans to a wire rack to cool completely.

7. Remove the paper baking cups and slice each cake in half horizontally. Dip both cut surfaces in the lemon soak. Spread one side of the soaked cake with seedless raspberry jam and press the halves together again. Turn the cupcakes upside down in a fresh paper baking cup. Frost the sides and top (which was the bottom) with Lemon Frosting. (If you find it easier, you may hold the split cupcakes in your hand and frost them before inserting them into the paper cups.)

❖ Bake Sale Tip

To make twice as many cupcakes, complete the recipe two separate times.

Hot-Milk Sponge Cake

Makes one 9-inch 2-layer cake, serving 10

1 cup whole milk
6 tablespoons (¾ stick) unsalted butter
2 cups cake flour
2 teaspoons baking powder
4 large eggs
2 cups sugar
2 teaspoons pure vanilla extract
⅓ to ½ cup strawberry jam, optional
1 recipe Vanilla Butter Frosting

1. Preheat the oven to 350°F. Grease two 9-inch round cake pans, line the bottoms with circles of parchment paper, and butter the paper.

2. In a small saucepan, heat the milk and butter just until the butter is melted. Remove from the heat.

Lemon Frosting

Makes 3 cups, enough for 2 dozen cupcakes; an easy recipe to double

12 tablespoons (1½ sticks) unsalted butter, softened
4½ cups confectioners' sugar
6 tablespoons freshly squeezed lemon juice (from 2 to 3 large lemons)

1. In the bowl of an electric mixer fitted with the paddle attachment, beat the butter and sugar on medium speed for 1 minute, or until combined. Add the lemon juice and continue to beat for 3 to 4 minutes, until light and fluffy.

2. Frost the cupcakes immediately, or store the frosting in an airtight container in the refrigerator or freezer until ready to use.

Vanilla Butter Frosting

Frosts one 2-layer cake

16 tablespoons (2 sticks) unsalted butter, softened
1½ pounds (5½ to 6 cups) confectioners' sugar, sifted
1 tablespoon pure vanilla extract
3 tablespoons milk or half-and-half

1. In the bowl of the electric mixer fitted with the paddle attachment, whip the butter on medium-high speed for 2 minutes, or until fluffy. Reduce the speed to low and add the confectioners' sugar, ½ cup at a time; mix thoroughly between each addition. Pour in the vanilla and the milk or half-and-half. Increase the speed to medium-high and beat for five minutes, or until light and very fluffy.

2. Frost the cake immediately or store the frosting in an airtight container in the refrigerator for up to 4 days or place in the freezer.

3. In a medium bowl, sift together the flour and baking powder.

4. In a large bowl, beat the eggs with a wire whisk until the eggs are light, then gradually add the sugar in a stream and continue to beat for 1 minute, or until the sugar is thoroughly incorporated. Fold in the sifted ingredients and mix thoroughly to form a smooth batter. Fold in the hot-milk mixture and the vanilla and form a smooth batter.

5. Divide the batter evenly between the two prepared pans and place them on the middle rack of the oven. Bake for 18 to 20 minutes, or until the cakes have risen nicely and turned golden brown on top. A toothpick inserted into the center of the cake should come out clean.

6. Transfer the cakes to wire racks and allow them to cool for 5 minutes. Invert the pans and carefully peel the paper from the bottom of each cake. Allow the cakes to cool completely.

7. Transfer one layer of cake to a plate and, with a spatula, spread a smooth, even layer of the jam, if using, or the frosting over the top surface of the cake. Place the second cake, right side up, on top of the first layer and gently press into place. Swirl the frosting across the top and around the sides of the two layers.

❖ **Bake Sale Tips**

Wrap individual slices in clear cellophane or wax paper and seal each one with a sticker. Of course, this is a perfect cake to sell whole at a cake walk or other dessert auction. It can be left at room temperature for a day or so.

To make two complete cakes, complete the recipe two separate times.

Ann Amernick became assistant pastry chef at the White House shortly after launching her career. In 1982, she became pastry chef at Jean-Louis at the Watergate. Her lengthy career also has included stints at Cashion's Eat Place, Michel Richard's Citronelle, Red Sage, and, currently, Amernick, a bakery that she co-owns, along with a restaurant, Palena,

with Frank Ruta. Ann has received three James Beard nominations for Outstanding Pastry Chef, and was twice named one of the Top Ten Pastry Chefs in America by Chocolatier/Pastry Art and Design. She is the author of Special Desserts *and co-author of* Soufflés.

Kelly Bailey's

Chocolate Bonanza Fruitcake with Mom Bailey's "Sozzled Santa" Raisin and Walnut Sauce

I began dating my husband, Brett, in culinary school. The first Christmas that I joined him at his parents' house in upstate New York, I was nervous. We were poor students (bearing no gifts), I hadn't met many people in his family (and there were *many*), and I wasn't sure what to expect. Something different, for sure, since in my own family we celebrate a Ukrainian Christmas. We have a traditional turkey dinner, but it's accompanied by smoked fish, *pelmeni* (little dumplings), and plenty of prayer. We'd even have communion before the meal with hosts that my grandmother had had blessed at our church. And we had breads, nut rolls, *kvachkes* (apricot and raspberry preserves tucked in pastry dough), a wafer cake with hazelnut butter (a torte that my grandmother doesn't have a name for), and a fruitcake—a yeasty version with apricots and candied citrus, made in a roasting pan and sliced into squares.

No matter what I had imagined eating at Brett's folks', I had never dreamed of a huge spread of wild turkey, venison, and bear (and a tour of the basement with its walk-in cooler filled with game, and a bandsaw for butchering meat). His father not only dressed deer, he saved the bones to make demi-glace . . . and tanned the hide to make deerskin gloves for our Christmas stockings. And since there were a good two dozen people for dinner, the desserts entirely covered the table (everything made from scratch): fruit pies, pumpkin pies, cakes, brownies, and then the Bailey family fruitcake, heavily soaked, a dense block packed with dried fruits. Everyone had to have a slice at the end of the meal, as well as a few cookies from a display that could rival that of a bake shop.

So the fruitcake became an annual part of my life, too. In cooking school, Brett decided to modernize the family fruitcake. He lightened it up, added a luscious whipped cream sauce with rum, and formed the cakes in little Bundt pans to make them easier to serve and eat. And then, as both of us spent years working alongside Marcel Desaulniers at The Trellis, his infectious love of great chocolate crept into the fruitcake as well, adding a really modern touch.

Now this cake has become one of my own holiday traditions, and although some of your relatives might say, "No, thank you, I don't really care for fruitcake," have them try *this* one, and see if they don't convert.

Chocolate Bonanza Fruitcake

Makes 12 mini-Bundt cakes;
an easy recipe to double

- 8 tablespoons (1 stick) unsalted butter, cut into 1-inch pieces, plus 1 tablespoon, melted
- 1½ cups plus 2 tablespoons all-purpose flour
- ½ teaspoon baking powder
- ¼ teaspoon baking soda
- ⅛ teaspoon ground cinnamon
- ⅛ teaspoon ground cloves
- ⅛ teaspoon ground mace
- ½ cup dried cherries
- ½ cup raisins
- ¼ cup candied lemon peel chopped into ¼-inch pieces
- ¼ cup candied orange peel chopped into ¼-inch pieces
- ¼ cup dried pineapple chopped into ¼-inch pieces
- ¾ cup sugar
- 3 large eggs
- 4 ounces semisweet baking chocolate, coarsely chopped and melted
- ¼ cup pure maple syrup
- ½ cup Scotch whisky
- 1 cup walnut halves, toasted and chopped (preferably by hand) into ¼-inch pieces
- 1 recipe "Sozzled Santa" Raisin and Walnut Sauce

1. Preheat the oven to 325°F. Adjust the oven racks so that one rests in the center and the second rests above it, leaving enough space for the cakes to rise slightly in the baking pans. Refrigerate two 6-cup, nonstick fluted mini-tube (Bundt) pans for 5 minutes (see Note).

2. Remove the tube pans from the refrigerator. With the melted butter, lightly grease the inside of each mini-tube pan. Be sure to coat the indentations in each pan. Return to the refrigerator until ready. (The butter needs to adhere to the nonstick surface so the baked cakes can be removed easily.)

3. In a sifter, combine the 1½ cups flour, the baking powder, baking soda, cinnamon, cloves, and mace. Sift onto a large sheet of parchment or wax paper and set aside.

4. In a medium bowl, combine the cherries, raisins, chopped lemon and orange peels, and pineapple pieces. Sprinkle with the remaining 2 tablespoons flour and toss gently.

5. In the bowl of an electric mixer fitted with the paddle attachment, combine the sugar and 8 tablespoons butter and mix on low speed for 1 minute. Increase the speed to medium and mix for 2 minutes, scraping down the inside of the bowl. Repeat the process again, allowing the butter to become very soft.

6. Add the eggs one at a time, incorporating each one thoroughly before adding the next. Scrape the inside of the bowl; the batter may appeared curdled, but will come together with the additional ingredients.

7. Add the melted chocolate and mix just to incorporate. Gradually add the maple syrup and mix just to incorporate. Scrape the inside of the bowl. Reduce the speed to low and gradually add the sifted dry ingredients; mix just until incorporated. Scrape the inside of the bowl. On the lowest speed, slowly add ¼ cup of the Scotch whisky and mix to combine. Add the walnuts and dried fruit and mix for 15 seconds to combine. Remove the bowl and mix once more by hand to ensure that all ingredients are well incorporated.

8. Fill each tube pan just less than halfway. Place the pans on the top and center racks of the oven. Bake for 15 minutes, then rotate the pans from top to center and from front to back. Bake for an additional 15 minutes, or until a toothpick inserted in the center of the cakes comes out clean.

9. Transfer the pans to wire racks and cool for 5 minutes, and then invert the pans to release the cakes. (Leaving them in the pans longer may make releasing them more difficult.) Turn the cakes right side up. Brush the top and sides of each cake with the remaining ¼ cup whisky. (For a more pronounced whisky flavor, brush the cakes with the same amount of whisky the next day.) Cool completely. The fruitcakes can be

"Sozzled Santa" Raisin and Walnut Sauce

Makes about 4 cups

⅔ cup plus 2 tablespoons Scotch
   whisky
½ cup raisins
1¼ cups heavy cream
2 tablespoons confectioners' sugar,
   sifted
½ cup walnut halves, toasted and
   chopped (preferably by hand) into
   ¼-inch pieces

1. In a small saucepan, combine ⅔ cup of the whisky and the raisins; bring to a boil over medium heat, stirring occasionally. Reduce the heat to low and simmer, stirring occasionally, until the raisins have absorbed nearly all of the Scotch. Spread the raisins on a plate to cool in the refrigerator.

2. In the bowl of an electric mixer fitted with the whisk attachment, place the heavy cream, sugar, and the remaining 2 tablespoons whisky, and whip on medium-high speed for 45 seconds, or until thickened but not stiff; there should be no peaks.

3. Gently fold in the raisins and walnuts. Cover and refrigerate until needed.

stored in an airtight container at room temperature for several days.

10. Serve the cakes at room temperature or slightly warmed (10 to 15 seconds in a microwave) on individual plates, topped with 2 to 3 tablespoons of the sauce.

❖ **Bake Sale Tips**

Place the cakes in individual vellum or wax paper bags and seal with a sticker.

The cakes are best sold without the sauce.

Note: Nonstick fluted mini-tube (Bundt) pans can be found in kitchenware, hardware, and department stores. Baker's Secret®, a widely available brand manufactured by Ecko Housewares, Inc., has a pan with six 3½- x 1¾-inch cups.

Kelly Bailey grew up in Indiana, and graduated from the Culinary Institute of America in Hyde Park in 1993. After working at the Bully Hill Winery, she and her husband, Brett Bailey, joined Marcel Desaulniers at The Trellis, where she became pastry chef and her husband served as test kitchen chef. Since moving to Williamsburg, Virginia, she has contributed to three of Marcel Desaulniers's cookbooks. She is currently pastry chef at Fat Canary.

Judy Rosenberg's
Rosie Pies

I have been told that my great-grandmother was a master baker in Czechoslovakia, although she left no recipes, because she used her God-given talent to measure ingredients: a handful of this, a pinch of that. Neither my grandmother nor my mother followed in her floury footsteps. However, my mother did inherit my great-grandmother's taste genes, which led her to the best bakeries of Manhattan: Bonté Patisserie on Third Avenue, where she purchased all of my birthday cakes (golden, buttery layers sandwiched with raspberry preserves, coated in vanilla buttercream, and adorned with frosting roses, all of which I piled on my slice); William Greenberg Bakery, famous for its rich sticky buns and linzer cookies; and Éclair, a European bakery around the corner from our house where she bought their poppy seed strudel, which I devoured. And how could I ever forget Reuben's cheesecake—the creamiest in town—and Schrafft's brownies, which, in those days, contained only the finest ingredients. My mother bought the best goodies that money could buy, and these shaped my taste buds.

Despite that "culinary sophistication," I still had mundane adolescent cravings for junky pastries that would accompany me home on the school bus each day. Devil Dogs were my favorite: tender chocolaty chocolate cakes shaped like a hot dog bun and filled with a whipped marshmallow frosting.

Now that I'm an adult, I've worked long and hard to come up with my version of this sensational confection—without the artificial ingredients. Similar in shape to a Whoopie Pie® (a tasteless, rubbery, marshmallow-filled, chocolate sandwich cookie shaped like a hamburger bun) but deeply flavorful and tender like the Devil Dog, my Rosie Pies are round, chocolate-cake cookies sandwiched with a fluffy buttercream filling and glazed with a chocolate ganache—and they're even better than my childhood memories.

Judy Rosenberg's Almond Raspberry Bars and
her biography appear on page 29.

Rosie Pies

Makes 20 sandwich cookies

For the cookies

¾ cup Dutch-process cocoa powder,
  sifted

1 cup plus 2 tablespoons all-purpose flour

1 teaspoon baking powder

½ teaspoon baking soda

12 tablespoons (1½ sticks) unsalted
  butter, softened

¼ cup vegetable oil

1 cup plus 2 tablespoons sugar

3 large eggs

1 large yolk

½ cup sour cream

For the filling

1¼ cups marshmallow cream (such as
  Marshmallow Fluff)

8 tablespoons (1 stick) unsalted butter,
  softened

1 cup confectioners' sugar

2 tablespoons heavy cream

For the glaze

¾ cup heavy cream

6 ounces bittersweet chocolate, finely
  chopped

1. Preheat the oven to 400°F. Line two or three cookie sheets with parchment paper or aluminum foil and lightly mist them with nonstick cooking spray.

2. For the cookies, in a large bowl, sift the cocoa, flour, baking powder, and baking soda.

3. In the bowl of an electric mixer fitted with the paddle attachment, combine the butter, oil, and sugar and mix on medium speed for 2 minutes, or until light and fluffy. Stop the mixer and scrape down the sides of the bowl.

4. Add the eggs and yolk to the mixture one at a time, incorporating each one thoroughly before adding the next. Scrape down the sides of the bowl. Add the sour cream and beat briefly on medium speed, then briefly on high speed (about 10 seconds total). The mixture should be very smooth.

5. Adjust the speed to low, add half of the flour mixture, and blend briefly. Stop the mixer, scrape down the sides of the bowl, and add the remaining flour mixture. Mix for 30 seconds, or until the mixture is smooth.

6. Drop rounded tablespoons of batter 2 inches apart onto the prepared cookie sheets. Bake for 8 to 10 minutes, or until the cookies spring back to the touch. Cool the cookies slightly, then transfer them to a wire rack to cool.

7. Line a sheet pan with parchment paper.

8. In the bowl of an electric mixer fitted with the paddle attachment, combine all of the filling ingredients and mix on medium-high speed for 2 minutes, or until the filling is light and fluffy; stop the mixer at least twice during the mixing to scrape down the sides of the bowl.

9. When the cookies have completely cooled, sandwich two of them with a rounded tablespoon of the filling and press lightly. Place the filled cookies on the prepared pan.

10. Finally, make the glaze. In a small saucepan over medium heat, cook the cream just to the point of simmering, then remove the pan from the heat. Add the chocolate and stir until the mixture is smooth.

11. Pour the chocolate mixture into a small deep bowl. Securely holding one sandwich cookie in your hand, dunk three-fourths of it into the glaze, then lift the cookie out of the bowl, allowing some of the glaze to drip back into the bowl.

12. Place the finished cookies back onto the pan. Rosie Pies are best the day they are prepared; however, they can be stored in an airtight container for up to 2 days.

❖ Bake Sale Tip

To make twice as many "pies," complete the recipe two separate times.

Edna Lewis and Scott Peacock's
Gingerbread Cupcakes with Caramel Glaze

I love the lineage of this recipe. It's the gingerbread from Miss Lewis's mother, which makes it close to a century old. Although Miss Daisy died when Miss Lewis was nineteen, a handwritten copy of this recipe is pressed in a notebook that Miss Lewis has to this day. The handwriting might have you think it's her mother's recipe card, but Miss Daisy didn't *have* recipes; she cooked instinctively.

When Miss Lewis and I were searching for dishes we wanted to include in our first book together, we scrounged through plantation journals, old recipe folders, family notebooks, local cookbooks—anything that would offer us an idea of great, gracious Southern cooking. We wanted the ultimate, as well as the most personally pleasing, version of all the things we grew up loving. And we settled on this recipe for gingerbread immediately; I knew instinctively that it was going to be denser and richer than the gingerbread spice cakes that were often served at cake walks and bake sales that I remember from growing up in Alabama.

So we took this recipe to my mother's house for one of our cooking, recipe-testing retreats. Some dishes, such as lemon chess pie, took us dozens of trials (I remember the endless fiddling with the sugar in that pie . . . one teaspoon more . . . okay, two more teaspoons . . .). But the first time we made this gingerbread to-gether, Miss Lewis and I both declared it to be perfect. No searching for other versions. No adding an extra measure of this or that. And another proof that it was just right: We'd serve a square of the gingerbread to folks who'd come over to visit, and they'd have a taste, and their eyes would light up. You could see it: the taste connected them to somewhere else—or some*time* else, a neighbor's house, a grandma's kitchen. They were responding nostalgically. A recipe has to have the right emotional impact along with all the other carefully balanced ingredients.

I think about this from time to time. Cooking is a dialogue that takes place be-tween a person and whatever he or she is making. Between the past and the present. Between one generation and another. So even if I make a dish that isn't exactly the way *you* remember it tasting in *your* family's version, tasting and smelling my version can reconnect you with those people and that special dish, because it turns out that what we're all looking for is not so much an ideal that's taste, but an ideal that's emotional: an echo of that time when you felt secure and loved and all things were still possible.

So this is the gingerbread of Miss Lewis's childhood and the gingerbread of my dreams: It's black, rich, spicy, and just what gingerbread ought to be—except that the day after it's made, it's even better.

Maple Walnut Tart, page 140

Quince Empanadas, page 147

Vanilla Bean Cupcakes, page 152

Apple Snacking Spice Cake, page 220

Irish Soda Bread, page 256
Lemon Marmalade, page 40

Cranberry Pistachio
Panettone, page 265

Gingerbread Cupcakes

Makes ten 3¾-inch cupcakes or one 8-inch square cake; an easy recipe to double

2 cups bleached all-purpose flour (see Note)

¼ teaspoon baking soda

2 teaspoons baking powder

½ teaspoon salt

½ teaspoon ground cloves

1 teaspoon ground cinnamon

1 tablespoon ground ginger

8 tablespoons (1 stick) unsalted butter

1 cup boiling water

2 large eggs, beaten

1½ cups molasses

1 recipe Caramel Glaze

Sweetened whipped cream, stewed rhubarb, custard sauce, or confectioners' sugar, optional, for serving.

1. Preheat the oven to 350°F. Generously butter the inside surfaces of one or more muffin tins; you'll need 10 muffin cups. (Fill any unused cups with ¼ cup water.) You can also make this recipe as a cake: butter an 8-inch square baking pan.

2. In a large bowl, sift together the flour, baking soda, and baking powder. Mix in the salt and spices.

3. Pour 1 cup boiling water into a large measuring cup, add the butter, and stir until the butter melts completely. Add this to the flour and whisk to combine. Add the eggs and molasses and whisk to combine.

4. Fill each muffin cup two-thirds full with the batter, or pour the batter into the cake pan.

5. Place the tin(s) on the middle rack of the oven and bake for 17 to 20 minutes (bake the larger cake pan for 35 to 40 minutes), or until a toothpick inserted into the center of a cake comes out clean.

Caramel Glaze

Makes enough to glaze 10 cupcakes or one 8-inch square cake

4 tablespoons (½ stick) unsalted butter

¼ cup granulated sugar

¼ cup light brown sugar (packed)

Pinch of salt

½ cup heavy cream

In a small saucepan, melt the butter over medium-low heat. Add the granulated sugar, brown sugar, and salt and stir until the sugars are moist. Cook for 2 minutes, or until the mixture thickens and turns golden brown. Pour in the heavy cream (be careful of spattering) and boil for 8 minutes, stirring constantly, until the mixture becomes a thick, creamy caramel. Spoon the hot glaze over the cooled cakes.

To make two portions of the glaze, complete the recipe two separate times.

6. Transfer the tin to a wire rack and cool for 5 minutes. Remove the individual cakes, invert them, and cool completely. Spoon the glaze over each cake and allow the glaze to set for 10 minutes. (Cut the cooled whole cake into individual portions.) At home, these are delicious served with sweetened whipped cream. They reach even greater heights with stewed rhubarb or custard sauce—or both.

❖ Bake Sale Tips

Place each cupcake in a paper baking cup. Arrange them on a platter or cake stand. If you've made the recipe in a cake pan, dust the finished gingerbread squares with confectioners' sugar.

Note: To substitute unbleached flour, re-duce the amount of flour by ⅓ cup to keep this gingerbread moist.

Among the many accolades and awards Edna Lewis has garnered over her decades in the culinary profession is the Grande Dame of Les Dames d'Escoffier International. She is the author of The Taste of the Country, In Pursuit of Flavor, The Edna Lewis Cookbook, *and the co-author, with Scott Peacock, of* The Gift of Southern Cooking. *Scott Peacock was born and raised in Alabama. He has served as chef for two governors of Georgia and at two restaurants, Horseradish Grill in Atlanta and Watershed in Decatur. He is the co-author, with Edna Lewis, of* The Gift of Southern Cooking.

Gale Gand's
Marshmallow Heart Throbs and Homemade Marshmallows

I first got to know my future husband over a marshmallow. My son and I were at a big Fourth of July party, and Jimmy, whom I knew only vaguely, was talking to a young girl about, well, how hard it was to get a really perfectly toasted marshmallow these days—and so on. I overheard his banter, and I thought to myself, well, if there's one thing my culinary skills are good for . . . So I found just the right branch and I toasted a single marshmallow, evenly tanned, warmed just to the point of being gooey, but not dripping off the branch. I presented it to him and that began our relationship; it showed me that Jimmy truly appreciated food but that he was no food snob. Perfection aside, this was still a marshmallow.

For our first New Year's Eve together, I did the entire meal in pink and white: crab legs, pink Depression glass, boiled potatoes and cauliflower, rose champagne, pink linens. I set forks on one side of the plates, knives and spoons on the other, and then a big branch next to that. Jimmy didn't get it, and I didn't say a thing until after this elaborate meal when I told him to grab his branch and join me in the living room. We made s'mores for dessert in the fireplace to celebrate what had brought us together.

So the perfect toasting stick has become a symbol for us, and marshmallows remain central in our family. We live in the woods, so there's always a bonfire somewhere. In the winter, we roast marshmallows in our living room fireplace and chuck them in hot cocoa, which is really the only drink—for kids or adults—after a few hours of playing in the snow.

Along with a simple, kid-friendly recipe for homemade marshmallows, here's a cake that I created for my son Gio's first year in public school. At the start of the school year, on the first parents' night, all the moms and dads sign up to help with various projects and field trips. I was so busy talking that when I finally made my way over to the sign-up sheets, all the holiday party baking slots were filled with other names. So I said to the room mother, "I wonder if I could still bake something." She was busy and suggested I just sign up to work on some other committee. I said, "You really do want me on one of those parties . . ." but then she got pulled away and I went home feeling as if I hadn't been chosen to play on a team.

Three days later, I got a call from Gio's room mother, apologizing. "I had no idea! Of course we want you to bake for us. I called one of the other mothers who signed up twice, and you can have either Halloween or Valentine's Day." So we both laughed, and I picked Valentine's Day and felt much, much better.

When I asked Gio what we should make, he suggested chocolate oozy cakes. I told him serving a warm cake with a liquid center wasn't exactly ideal for a classroom. So I countered, "How about a heart-shaped cake . . . and we could make homemade marshmallows for inside." Gio loved the idea: He had no idea a person could actually make marshmallows! So we made twenty-two little cakes. Gio stirred the batter. He cut out the baked hearts. He piped the marshmallow inside each one. And I mostly gave directions and added the final piped heart on top of each cake. The individual cakes have a very finished look, because you use a cutter to shape each cake into a heart. Gio was very proud to present his cakes at the class party. As far as his classmates were concerned, he was the celebrity baker.

Marshmallow Heart Throbs

Makes 10 two-layer mini-cakes

For the cakes

4 large egg whites
8 tablespoons (1 stick) unsalted butter,
    slightly chilled, cut into pieces
1 cup sugar
½ teaspoon pure vanilla extract
½ teaspoon pure almond extract
2 cups sifted cake flour

1 tablespoon baking powder
⅔ cup whole milk

For the pink marshmallow filling

¼ cup light corn syrup
¾ cup sugar
2 egg whites
1 tablespoon powdered gelatin
¼ teaspoon pure vanilla extract
Red food coloring
Red colored sugar (also known as
    "sanding" or "sparkling" sugar)

1. Preheat the oven to 350°F. Brush a 12½ x 17½-inch jelly roll pan with butter

and line it with a piece of parchment paper that extends beyond the ends of the pan (to help lift out the finished cake). Butter the parchment paper.

2. For the cakes, in the bowl of an electric mixer fitted with the whisk attachment, whip the egg whites until stiff but not dry. (You may also use a hand mixer or a whisk.) Set aside in the refrigerator.

3. Fit the paddle attachment into the electric mixer. Add the butter to a clean bowl and mix on medium speed for 1 minute, or until it is smooth. With the mixer running, slowly add the sugar and beat until the mixture is light and fluffy. Add the vanilla and almond extracts, mixing briefly to incorporate. Scrape the inside of the bowl.

4. In a large bowl, sift the flour and baking powder three times (this will lighten the cakes). Alternately add approximately one-fifth of the flour mixture and one-fourth of the milk, mixing thoroughly and scraping the inside of the bowl after each addition; start and end with the flour mixture.

5. Fold one-third of the beaten egg whites into the batter. Add the remaining egg whites and gently fold them into the batter.

6. Pour the batter into the prepared pan, place on the middle rack of the oven, and bake for 25 to 30 minutes, until the cake is firm to the touch. (You may prepare the marshmallow filling while the cake is baking.)

7. Transfer the pan to a wire rack and cool the cake in the pan.

8. Lift the cake out of the pan using the parchment paper. Cut out 20 hearts using a 2-inch heart-shaped cookie cutter. (Reserve the cake scraps to make ice cream cake balls; see Note.)

9. To prepare the filling, clip a candy thermometer to the side of a saucepan and pour in ¼ cup cold water, the corn syrup, and sugar. Bring to a boil over medium-high heat and allow the mixture to continue boiling, without stirring, until the thermometer reads 235°F (this is the "soft-ball" stage).

10. While the sugar boils, beat the egg whites in the bowl of an electric mixer fitted with the whisk attachment. Whip on medium-high speed until soft peaks form. In a small bowl, put 2 tablespoons of cold water and sprinkle on the gelatin so that it dissolves.

11. When the syrup reaches 235°F, remove it from the heat and stir in the softened gelatin. With the mixer on low speed, pour the syrup in a slow, steady stream into the whipped egg whites. Add the vanilla, increase the speed to high, and continue whipping until the mixture is stiff. Add a few drops of red food coloring to turn the marshmallow pink.

12. Scoop the marshmallow filling into a pastry bag fitted with a ¼-inch plain pastry tip. Pipe the filling on half of the cake hearts, covering the top surface entirely. Sandwich the filling by placing one of the plain cakes on top of each marshmallow-covered cake. Pipe a heart on top of each

cake: Form two teardrops that meet in a V at the narrow point. Lightly sprinkle this small marshmallow heart with red colored sugar.

❖ Bake Sale Tip

To make double the number of cakes, complete the recipe two separate times.

Note: The cake scraps can be used for another childhood favorite: ice cream cake balls. Crumble the remaining cake pieces into a large bowl. Form round scoops of ice cream, and then roll each scoop in the crumbs. Serve as is, or with a little hot fudge sauce.)

Homemade Marshmallows

Makes 3 dozen large
or 6 dozen medium marshmallows

These marshmallows are kid-friendly for floating in cocoa or roasting over fires, but adults will like dipping one side of these squares in some great melted chocolate. Let the chocolate harden, and serve these on a little plate of after-dinner treats with coffee. You can also toss them, while still a bit tacky, in colored sugars, to make a bright or pastel range of marshmallows. At Easter,

feeling ambitious, you can make your own marshmallow chicks with the marshmallow "batter," or you can pipe it into bunnies, ducks, and anything else your kids insist upon having.

¼ cup plus 2 tablespoons water
¼ cup plus 2 tablespoons light corn syrup
1 cup plus 2 tablespoons sugar
3 large egg whites
1½ tablespoons powdered gelatin
½ teaspoon pure vanilla extract
Cornstarch for dusting the pans and
    cutting the marshmallows

1. Line an 8 x 8-inch cake pan with parchment paper and lightly dust it with cornstarch.

2. Clip a candy thermometer to the inside of a saucepan and pour in ¼ cup plus 2 tablespoons water, the corn syrup, and sugar. Bring to a boil over medium-high heat and allow the mixture to continue boiling, without stirring, until the thermometer reads 240°F (this is the "soft-ball" stage).

3. While the syrup boils, whip the egg whites on medium-high speed in the bowl of an electric mixer fitted with the whisk attachment. Whip until soft peaks form. In a small bowl, put 3 tablespoons water and sprinkle on the gelatin so that it dissolves.

4. Once the syrup reaches 240°F, remove it from the heat and stir in the dissolved gelatin. With the mixer on low speed, pour the syrup in a slow, steady stream into the whipped egg whites. Add the vanilla, in-

crease the speed to high, and continue whipping until the mixture is stiff.

5. Spread the whipped marshmallow onto the prepared cake pan. The marshmallow layer should be about 1 inch thick. Let cool completely (the marshmallows may be easier to cut if left overnight at room temperature). Use the parchment to lift the marshmallow from the pan, then cut the block into 1-inch squares. Dip your knife or sharp kitchen scissors in cornstarch as necessary to ensure clean cuts. Lightly toss the individual squares in cornstarch to keep them from sticking to one another and store in an airtight container.

❖ Bake Sale Tips

Place half a dozen or a dozen marshmallow squares in plastic bags and cinch them shut with colorful ribbons.

To make twice as many marshmallows, complete the recipe two separate times.

Gale Gand, executive pastry chef/partner of Tru, caught the eye of a Life magazine photographer as a mud-pie-making six-year-old. Forty-some years later, she's still attracting attention for her desserts. The recipient of a Beard Award for Outstanding Pastry Chef, Gale appeared in Julia Child's book and PBS series Baking with Julia. Her previous culinary experience includes Charlie Trotter's, Gotham Bar & Grill, Stapleford Park Hotel, a five-star hotel near London, and Trio. Gale is the host of Food Network's Sweet Dreams and the author of four books, including Gale Gand's Just a Bite and Butter Sugar Flour Eggs.

Rémy Fünfrock's
Chouquettes
(Filled or Glazed Pastry Puffs)
and
Chocolate Carolines

When I was seven, my mother took me to a little bakery in the French countryside owned by a distant relative of ours. We were escorted into the back of the shop—where customers weren't supposed to go!—and I saw the bakers mixing the dough. I inhaled that sourdough aroma. I walked across the floury floor. I saw loaf after loaf of bread, each one rolled out by hand, put into rows inside wood cabinets to rise. I had never seen a more magical place.

Ten years later, I began my first job at the best pastry shop in Lyon, Jacques Fréry, a traditional pâtisserie with a chef who was obsessed with the quality of each ingredient as well as the perfection of each recipe. I apprenticed myself to Jacques, and then worked with Roger Vergé and Daniel Boulud, learning classic French pastries, many of which involved *pâte à choux*, an egg-based dough that's cooked on the stove and then baked into light pastries best known in America as éclairs or cream puffs.

My first experience with choux puffs was in their restaurant version, the *profiterole*, which I prepared while working at a restaurant for two years. The finished choux puffs, with a small scoop of ice cream tucked inside each one, were brought to the tables and topped with a pool of hot chocolate sauce.

But at Jacques Fréry, I learned many other forms the choux puff can take: We created *Choux Chantilly* (filled with whipped cream and dusted with confectioners' sugar); *Choux Religieuse* (filled with coffee, chocolate, or vanilla pastry cream, glazed with fondant, then stacked in pairs, and decorated with buttercream); *Choux Duchesse* (an oblong éclair filled with flavored pastry cream and glazed with fondant); the *Chouquette* (the baked choux topped with rock sugar); and *Pets de Nonne* (believe it or not, my crazy French predecessors named this fried choux rolled in sugar "nun's farts"). And we also made two more spectacular desserts with the choux puffs: *Paris-Brest*, a crown-shaped choux topped with sliced almonds and filled with praline whipped cream; and then my favorite, the dessert I would take home each Sunday tucked in a basket for my family, the *Gâteau St. Honoré*.

We only made this cake for Sundays: It's the dessert customers wanted for a fancy dinner or to take to someone else's house as a gift. And while everything

Pâte à Choux
(Cream Puff Dough)

½ cup whole milk

8 tablespoons (1 stick) unsalted butter, cut into small pieces

1 teaspoon sugar

½ teaspoon salt

1⅓ cups all-purpose flour, sifted

5 large eggs

1. In a medium saucepan, combine ½ cup water, the milk, butter, sugar, and salt and cook over high heat until the liquid comes to a boil. Immediately add the flour and stir without stopping to incorporate the flour into the liquid. Stir continuously until a smooth mass forms and the bottom of the pan is coated with a thin film, about 1 minute.

2. Transfer the dough to a large bowl. While it's still hot, add the eggs one at a time, incorporating each one thoroughly before adding the next. (Alternatively, you may do this step in an electric mixer fitted with the paddle attachment.)

❖ Bake Sale Tip

To make two portions of the choux dough, complete the recipe two separate times.

at Jacques Fréry was perfection, this cake required extra effort because the cake comes together at the last minute. Though we started very early in the morning with the puff pastry and the pâte à choux, we'd finish assembling the cake—filling the puffs with pastry cream, dipping them in caramel, assembling them in a ring on the puff pastry, and then piping in a mound of whipped cream in the center—just as the customers would be stopping in after church.

Sunday afternoons, the pastry chefs had time off, though the shop would remain open. One time, both the chef and I had gone home, but his mother, who stayed in the back of the shop, was tending the store. Now, Madame Fréry was close to eighty, so when she heard the door push open and the bell ring, a bit of time passed before she made it into the shop. She walked in and saw a boy—she said he couldn't have been more than eight years old—rushing out the door with one of the Gâteau St. Honoré from the display window. He had the cake—not even in a box—in one hand and he grabbed the handlebar of his bicycle in the other hand, and through the window she watched him quickly scramble onto the bicycle—but carefully balancing the cake at the same time—and pedal off down the street.

The next day when we all reported for work, she explained about the stolen cake. But she was too amused—or maybe flattered—by the theft to be upset.

I was tempted to offer my recipe for the Gâteau St. Honoré for this book, since it hints at the story of my life in Lyon. Then I realized that while you probably wouldn't be transporting the gâteau on the handlebars of your bicycle, this dessert still might be a little delicate for a bake sale. So here are two other recipes that use the pâte à choux—one very simple and easy to keep at room temperature; the other, filled with pastry cream, needs to be kept chilled. Both of them should appeal to eight-year-olds, eighty-year-olds, and most of us in between.

Chouquettes

Makes about 4 dozen 2-inch puffs

This miniature choux gained its popularity before the French Revolution. The cream filling (typically reserved for kings and queens) was replaced with a more economical caramelized sugar, creating a more affordable treat for the common people. Thankfully, we all deserve the royal treatment these days: pipe out a large batch and spread the wealth.

1 large egg

Pinch of salt

1 recipe Pâte à Choux (see page 177)

⅓ cup rock sugar, for glazing (available at gourmet food stores or from baking suppliers such as www.kingarthur.com)

1. Preheat the oven to 375°F and line two baking pans with parchment paper or silicone mats.

2. Prepare the egg wash by whisking the egg with the salt in a small bowl. Set aside.

3. Spoon the pâte à choux into a pastry bag fitted with a ½-inch round tip. Pipe 1-inch balls onto the prepared baking sheets, leaving 2 inches between each ball.

4. With a pastry brush, lightly dab each ball with egg wash and sprinkle with rock sugar. Place the pans on the middle rack of the oven and bake for 17 minutes, or until the puffs are golden brown and the sugar has melted and caramelized; rotate the pans halfway through the baking process.

5. Transfer the puffs to a wire rack and cool completely. Store in an airtight container.

❖ Bake Sale Tip

Package 6 to 8 pastries in a clear cellophane bag and tie with a colorful ribbon.

Chocolate Carolines

Makes 10 pastries

This time the *pâte à choux* is larger, spherical, and filled with chocolate pastry cream before it's topped with a chocolate caramel. The Caroline comes the closest to an American cream puff or éclair, but it's a bit more restrained than the overblown, hamburger-bun-size fluffs supermarkets typically offer.

1 recipe Pâte à Choux

For the egg wash

1 large egg

Pinch of salt

For the chocolate pastry cream

2 cups whole milk

½ cup sugar

1 vanilla bean, split lengthwise, seeds scraped free and reserved

4 large egg yolks

¼ cup cornstarch, sifted

7 ounces bittersweet chocolate, finely chopped

For the chocolate caramel

1 cup cane sugar
2 tablespoons light corn syrup
1½ ounces bittersweet chocolate,
  finely chopped

1. Preheat the oven to 375°F and line a baking sheet with parchment paper or silicone mats.

2. Spoon the pâte à choux into a pastry bag fitted with a ½-inch round tip. Pipe 2-inch balls in staggered rows on the prepared baking sheet. Leave a 3-inch space around each ball. Lightly beat together the egg with a pinch of salt. Using a pastry brush, gently dab only the top of each ball with egg wash. (Egg that drips down the sides will make the puffs expand unevenly.)

3. Place the pan on the middle rack of the oven and bake for 25 to 30 minutes, until the puffs are golden brown and have a hollow sound when tapped; the pastries should be firm enough so that they do not collapse after baking. Transfer the puffs to a wire rack to cool.

4. For the chocolate pastry cream, combine the milk, ¼ cup of the sugar, and the vanilla bean seeds and pod in a medium saucepan. Bring to a boil over medium heat.

5. While the milk is coming to a boil, vigorously whisk together the yolks and the remaining ¼ cup sugar in a medium bowl. Once the mixture turns pale, whisk in the cornstarch. While whisking continuously, very gradually add half of the hot milk mixture to the sugar-egg mixture, and then pour the contents of the mixing bowl into the

saucepan. Still whisking, cook this over medium heat until the pastry cream thickens and begins to boil. Once the pastry cream has boiled for 30 seconds, remove the pan from the heat. Remove the vanilla bean pod. Add the chocolate and stir until it has melted.

6. Scrape the pastry cream into a non-reactive bowl and cover the cream with plastic wrap, pressing the film directly on the surface of the cream. Refrigerate for 4 hours or until well chilled. (The pastry cream can be made up to 2 days in advance.) Fill a pastry bag fitted with a ¼-inch round tip with the chocolate pastry cream. Cut a small hole in the bottom of each choux and fill it with the chocolate cream.

7. For the chocolate caramel, combine ¼ cup water, the sugar, and corn syrup in a medium saucepan over medium heat. Stir to dissolve the sugar. Use a wet pastry brush to wash down any sugar crystals that form on the sides of the pan. Bring the syrup to a boil without stirring and cook until golden brown. Remove from the heat, add the chocolate, and stir well. Keep warm.

8. Carefully dip the tops of the filled choux in the warm caramel and place on a tray. (Keep a small bowl of ice water nearby in case any hot caramel drips onto your skin.) Once the caramel cools, the Carolines are ready to serve.

❖ Bake Sale Tip

While the Carolines are best served within 2 hours of being made, they can be kept cold in a cooler filled with ice packs. Sell the desserts individually.

Rémy Fünfrock, one of Pastry Art & Design *magazine's Top Ten Pastry Chefs in America, began his formal pastry study (after a childhood at his cousin's pâtisserie in Lyon) at Lycée Jean Rablais in Lyon and apprenticed with Pierre Hermé, among others. After several other prestigious jobs in the south of France, he served as executive pastry chef at Roger Vergé's Michelin three-star Moulin de Mougins. Since 1997, Rèmy has been executive pastry chef at three of Daniel Boulud's restaurants: Daniel, Café Boulud, and, currently, the new Café Boulud in Palm Beach.*

Dan Dye and Mark Beckloff's

Chocolate Cake

and

Carob Dog Treats

People may know us best as the founders of Three Dog Bakery, "the world's original bakery for dogs," but in our private lives, we're pretty good at baking for humans, too. For this special cookbook, we've chosen a fabulously rich chocolate sheet cake for two-legged readers (remember, absolutely no chocolate allowed for dogs, ever, since it's toxic to their systems) and, because we'd never deprive our beloved buddies of a batch of baked goods, we've added a healthful, easy-to-make cookie designed for four-legged rascals.

"Chocolate cake" couldn't have a simpler name, but that's all a recipe name was supposed to be 100 years ago. This dessert has been handed down through four generations of hardy Midwestern farm folk, originating with Mark's Great-

Grandma Kaiser, a German who came to America and settled, improbably, in Wetherford, Oklahoma, a tiny town even now, which must have been even tinier back then.

This particular cake, the delicious sum of which is far greater than its parts, has graced literally hundreds of birthdays, graduations, engagement parties, and holidays over the years. The original recipe is written on lined paper that is yellowed with age. It's faded, brittle, and held together with dried-out, discolored tape. When Mark's great-grandmother died, his grandmother, who was a home ec professor—one of the first in the state of Oklahoma—inherited the recipes, among her mother's other possessions. And when Mark's mother, more of a twentieth-century cook, moved her family to California, she got the recipe files. Today, they're here with us in Kansas City. Just looking through the recipes conjures up an image of the gardens with their fruit-laden trees and bushes that must have surrounded the farmhouse, from which she gathered the blueberries, rhubarb, strawberries, apples, pears, and other fruits that filled her cobblers and pies. Need I say Great-Grandma Kaiser had no A&P nearby?

Never in her wildest imaginings could Great-Grandma have conjured up a world of high-speed Internet access and on-demand television satellite service—this place where we all live now. But her cake—another amazing human achievement—provides a lasting link between both worlds.

Chocolate Cake

Makes one 17 x 12-inch baking pan, serving 24

For the cake

2 cups all-purpose flour

2 cups sugar

8 tablespoons (1 stick) unsalted butter

8 tablespoons (½ cup) vegetable
   shortening

¼ cup Dutch-process cocoa powder

½ cup buttermilk

1 teaspoon baking soda

2 large eggs, slightly beaten

1 teaspoon pure vanilla extract

For the frosting

8 tablespoons (1 stick) unsalted butter

4 tablespoons Dutch-process cocoa
   powder

6 tablespoons whole milk

1 teaspoon pure vanilla extract

1 pound (3½ to 4 cups) confectioners'
   sugar

⅔ cup chopped pecans

1. Preheat the oven to 350°F and lightly grease a 17 x 12-inch baking pan.

2. For the cake, in a large bowl, mix together the flour and sugar.

3. In a large saucepan, combine the butter, shortening, cocoa, and 1 cup water. Bring to a boil over medium heat, stirring occasionally. Remove the pan from the heat, add the flour and sugar mixture, and stir to incorporate.

4. In a small bowl, combine the buttermilk and baking soda. Pour the buttermilk mixture into the cake batter, add the eggs and vanilla, and mix with a whisk until the batter is smooth.

5. Pour the batter into the prepared pan and bake for 25 to 30 minutes, or until a toothpick inserted into the center of the cake comes out clean. Transfer the cake to a wire rack to cool completely.

6. For the frosting, place a small saucepan over medium heat and add the butter, cocoa, milk, and vanilla. Bring to a boil, stirring occasionally. Transfer the chocolate mixture to a medium bowl and slowly whisk in the confectioners' sugar until the frosting has a smooth consistency. (If desired, use a hand mixer.) Fold in the chopped pecans.

7. Pour the frosting over the cake and spread evenly. Allow the frosting to set for 2 hours before cutting the cake into squares.

❖ Bake Sale Tips

It's easiest to cut this cake when slightly chilled. Wrap each piece in a sheet of wax paper or clear cellophane and seal with a sticker.

To make two cakes, complete the recipe two separate times.

Carob Dog Treats

Makes 3 to 4 dozen soft cookies;
an easy recipe to double

Dogs are obviously a huge part of our lives and, as for millions of other Americans, they are family members in every sense of the word. Over the years, we've shared in some hilarious dog moments: We've hosted doggie weddings ("You may now lick the bride . . ."), where the "bow vows" were followed with three-tiered wedding cakes that we had to transport and build on site. We've joined in black-tie affairs at the Biltmore Fashion Park in Phoenix, where golden retrievers arrived in limos, wearing top hats and "tails." We've baked for countless doggie birthday parties, Dogtoberfests, and most every other holiday that's on the human calendar. (So far, no Kosher-for-Passover requests.)

But nothing holds warmer memories than our road trips, crisscrossing the country with our great Danes and Dalmatian. The girls traveled with us, whether to a grand opening, media event, or family vacation. We loved watching Sarah, Dottie, and Gracie jump into the car before our trips. They didn't care if we were headed to Timbuktu or around the block. No worries, no pre-trip jitters, just trusting the great highway of life (also known as "us") to take care of their daily needs. How simple and happy our lives could be if we all lived with that same trust, with the sense that it's always *now,* with no need for yesterday's regrets or anxieties about tomorrow.

A few days in a rented fifteen-passenger van packed with three dogs, their food, bowls, and bed, and our suitcases, tuxes, etc., gives a person plenty of time to "paws" and reflect on what's truly important—or at least as important as finding a motel that takes dogs before falling asleep at the wheel. On occasion, we need to be creative: Sneaking four hundred pounds of sleepy dogs into a motel room is not as easy as it sounds.

One morning, after a particularly long haul, we heard a knock at the motel door. "Housekeeping . . ." the woman's cheerful voice announced. It was 7 A.M. Just one of the dogs started barking in her usual baritone, and then all we heard was the click-click-clock of the housekeeper's sandals running off. We checked out very quickly that morning.

These dog treats make the ride a little more jolly, even if you're just going to the post office and back.

1 cup all-purpose flour
¼ cup whole wheat flour
½ teaspoon baking powder
¼ cup vegetable shortening
½ cup mashed banana (1 medium banana)
½ cup unsweetened applesauce
1 large egg
1 cup rolled oats
1 cup unsweetened carob chips (available at health food stores and larger markets)

Warning: Do not substitute any form of actual chocolate, which is poisonous to dogs.

1. Preheat the oven to 350°F and lightly mist two baking sheets with nonstick cooking spray.

2. In a medium bowl, combine both types of flour and the baking powder.

3. In a large bowl, beat together the vegetable shortening, banana, and applesauce. Beat in the egg. Gradually add the dry ingredients and blend until smooth. Fold in the oats and carob chips.

4. Place small spoonfuls of the dough on the prepared pans and bake for 8 to 10 minutes, until the edges of the cookies turn a light golden color; the cookies will be soft rather than like a hard biscuit. Transfer the treats to wire racks and cool completely. Store the treats in an airtight container.

❖ Bake Sale Tips

Package cookies in lots of a dozen or so in clear cellophane bags tied with a colorful ribbon and a "dog tag," clearly identifying them as dog treats. Or decorate small paper sacks with dog-themed rubber stamps, stickers, or drawings.

Dan Dye and Mark Beckloff are the founders of Three Dog Bakery. With the goal of creating dog biscuits that were both tasty and nutritious, they sought advice from veterinarians, breeders, and dog lovers, and in 1989 opened their first Three Dog Bakery store, which featured a range of healthy dog treats. Their books include Amazing Gracie, Short Tails and Treats from Three Dog Bakery, The Three Dog Bakery Cookbook, *and the forthcoming* Cooking the Three Dog Bakery Way: Drooling in the Kitchen with Dan and Mark.

Maida Heatter's
Buttermilk Key Lime Cake

n my first book, in the "Plain Loafs and Other Old-Fashioned Cakes" section, I had a recipe for a Buttermilk Lemon Cake, which I described as "light, moist, lemony, and lovely."

A day or two after the book was published, my editor received a call from an angry reader who complained that my recipe for this cake simply didn't work. I thought it was a silly call since, as you may know, I'm a demonic recipe tester and, as with all the other recipes in the book, I had made this one over and over. But I tried it again and the reader was right. It didn't work. I made it over and over and over again. I tried everything. I never did find out what was wrong, so I asked my editor if we could delete the recipe in future printings. (Actually, I asked if the first printing could be recalled. I argued, "General Motors recalls cars.") I replaced the recipe with a caraway seed cake.

When the second printing hit the bookstores, both my editor and I began getting complaints. People were calling and writing to say they had bought the book especially for that buttermilk lemon cake recipe because it was the best cake they had ever tasted and they wanted to give the book—*with that recipe*—to a friend/daughter/mother-in-law/sister. One woman wrote to say that she made a lot of money for her church by selling copies of that recipe.

In the face of all the attention, I tried the recipe several more times, but never could get it to work to my *complete* satisfaction again. And there were new books to write, and new recipes to test.

It's now almost thirty years later, and I'm glad to include this version here along with a new twist: Now that I live in Florida, I thought that instead of lemons, Key limes could contribute their uniquely fragrant tartness. (If you can't find Key limes, you can substitute fresh limes, though the flavor will be slightly different and you'll need about one-fourth as many fruits.) I hope you'll give this cake a new life, too, by sharing this book with friends, daughters, mothers-in-law, sisters.

Buttermilk
Key Lime Cake

Makes one 10-inch tube cake, serving 10

For the cake

2 to 3 tablespoons fine, dried bread
    crumbs, for coating the pan
2 tablespoons finely grated
    Key lime zest (from about
    10 Key limes)
3 tablespoons freshly squeezed
    Key lime juice (from about
    8 Key limes)
3 cups sifted all-purpose flour
½ teaspoon baking soda
½ teaspoon salt
16 tablespoons (2 sticks) unsalted
    butter, softened
3 cups sugar
5 large eggs
1 cup buttermilk

For the glaze

¼ cup plus 1 tablespoon Key lime juice
    (from about 12 Key limes)
½ cup granulated sugar
Confectioners' sugar, for dusting the
    surface of the cake

1. Preheat the oven to 325°F and place
one rack a third of the way from the bottom. Butter a 10 x 4-inch tube pan and line
the bottom with parchment or wax paper.
Butter the paper and dust all over with the
crumbs. (Alternatively, you may use a nonstick pan and line the bottom with buttered
parchment or wax paper.)

2. In a small bowl, mix the zest with the
juice.

3. In a large bowl, sift together the flour,
baking soda, and salt.

4. In the large bowl of an electric mixer
fitted with the paddle attachment, cream the
butter on medium speed for 2 minutes, or
until light and fluffy. Gradually add the
sugar and beat for 2 to 3 minutes, scraping
the inside of the bowl occasionally. Increase
the speed to medium-high and add the eggs
one at a time, incorporating each one thoroughly before adding the next; beat for an
additional 2 to 3 minutes after the last egg
has been added.

5. On the lowest speed, alternately add
one-third of the dry ingredients and half of
the buttermilk; after each addition, scrape
the inside of the bowl and beat only until
smooth; begin and end with the dry ingredients.

6. Remove the bowl from the mixer and
stir in the Key lime zest and juice.

7. Scrape the batter into the prepared
pan. Level the batter by briskly rotating the
pan, back and forth, several times. Bake the
cake for 80 to 90 minutes, or until a toothpick inserted into the cake comes out clean.

8. Make the glaze while the cake is baking. Combine the lime juice, 1 tablespoon
water, and granulated sugar in a small bowl.
Let stand, stirring occasionally.

9. Allow the cake to cool in the pan for

5 minutes, then cover with a wire rack and invert over a large piece of aluminum foil or wax paper. Remove the pan and the paper liner, leaving the cake upside down.

10. Brush the glaze all over the hot cake until it is all absorbed. Allow the cake to cool and dry. Using a small cookie sheet as a spatula, transfer the cake to a plate or cake stand. Generously sprinkle with confectioners' sugar through a fine-mesh sieve.

❖ Bake Sale Tips

Wrap the whole cake in a large piece of clear cellophane and tie with a colorful ribbon, or wrap individual slices in cellophane wrap and seal with a sticker.

To make two cakes, complete the recipe two separate times.

Maida Heatter, often described as the "First Lady of Desserts," has influenced generations of American pastry chefs and home bakers. A celebrated cooking teacher and the recipient of two James Beard Awards, Maida was named to Who's Who of Cooking in America by Cook's magazine, and inducted into Chocolatier magazine's "Hall of Fame." Maida's desserts have been served at the Four Seasons and Spago, as well as at numerous presidential luncheons, and her recipes have appeared in countless periodicals and newspapers and in a shelf of award-winning cookbooks, including Maida Heatter's Brand New Book of Great Cookies, Maida Heatter's Book of Great Desserts, *and* Maida Heatter's Greatest Dessert Book Ever. *Her legendary efforts have always been simple: rework classic recipes and achieve a timeless perfection with each cookie, pastry, or cake.*

The Best White Cake with Maple Meringue Frosting

If you know what to look for, you can see the remains of ancient sap houses dotting the Vermont landscape like rusted hulks of antique cars, doors askew, creepers headed up toward the eaves. Unlike hunting camps, which are found deep in the woods, sap houses are usually built near roads for easy access, so they are readily discovered, even by a casual observer. Many of these tumbledown shacks still come alive in late February and March when the nights are cold but the days push up over freezing, the sap running freely from the sugar maples, filling the galvanized buckets and holding tanks to overflowing.

This arrangement may sound crude but, much like cooking, there is a science to the art of sugaring. Each day begins with a measurement of barometric pressure. This will affect the temperature at which the sap boils—some days it boils at 212° F, other days at 210°F—and therefore the temperature at which the syrup is done, which is always seven degrees over boiling. A hydrometer—a glass tube that floats in a narrow metal cylinder filled with hot syrup—is also used to measure the density of the syrup, the best gauge of when it's ready for canning. Cold sap is run into the pans, the arch (a box-shaped, wood-burning stove) is fired up, and within fifteen minutes, the sap is bubbling and great clouds of steam are headed skyward through the open louvers on top of the building.

The process sounds simple enough but there are rules. First, you never start a boil unless you have enough sap. It takes a wood fire a long time to cool down and if you run out, the pans will scorch or even melt. The second rule is to burn hot and quick, reducing fifty or sixty gallons of sap to one gallon of syrup as fast as possible. This requires dry wood that has been split into small pieces. Finally, you have to pay keen attention. The sap can boil over in seconds (a dab of butter on the surface of boiling sap will instantly stop a boil-over), and stepping out, even to grab a cold beer from a snowbank, can mean disaster.

Boiling sap, for most Vermonters, is about passion, not profit. The wife of one committed sugarer figured out that her husband earned about six cents an hour. She offered him a raise to twenty-five cents if he would do some work around the house, but he knew what all sap boilers know. Sitting around a hot arch on a cold March day, sometimes boiling through the night, defies economics. The hot steam swirls, the pulsing coals blast enough heat to cause a sunburn, the sap jumps and froths in the pans, and neighbors swap stories, some of them true. We are refugees, huddled in the dark around fires, sitting in lawn chairs like lesser kings of New England, convinced that we live in a world of our own making.

In my sap house, I sit with my five-year-old son, Charlie, in front of our own small arch, watching the boil, making maple snowcones, throwing two-inch kindling onto the hot fire every few minutes. Just down the dirt road, my neighbor Tom sugars with his now grown-up son Nate, checking the taps, collecting the sap, and adjusting the float. Here we are, fathers and sons, sitting in shacks in late winter, working side by side, distilling memories into thick syrup. We follow the rules, boiling hot and fast, trying to prepare for the future. But as we stoke the fires, we sense that this easy partnership burns brightly for only a short while. Even summer tourists can see that, in time, all sap houses turn wild, roof lines sagging, stinging nettles pushing up around the foundations. That is why Vermonters know to pay attention when it matters. In these sweet short years, even a moment's inattention can have serious consequences.

Christopher Kimball's Maple Walnut Tart appears on page 140.

The Best White Cake

Makes two 9-inch round cakes

----

1 cup whole milk, at cool room
    temperature (about 70°F)

6 large egg whites, at cool room
    temperature (about 70°F)

2 teaspoons pure vanilla extract

2⅓ cups cake flour

1½ cups sugar

4 teaspoons baking powder

¾ teaspoon salt

12 tablespoons (1½ sticks) unsalted
    butter, softened but still firm

1 recipe Maple Meringue Frosting

1. Preheat the oven to 350°F and grease two 9-inch cake pans with butter. Cover the bottom of each pan with a circle of parchment.

2. In a medium bowl, stir together the milk, egg whites, and vanilla.

3. In the bowl of an electric mixer fitted with the paddle attachment, combine the flour, sugar, baking powder, and salt. Add the butter and one-quarter of the milk mixture and mix on low speed for 1 minute, or until the dry ingredients are moistened. Increase the speed to medium and mix until the batter comes together. Increase the speed to medium-high and mix for 2 minutes, stopping to scrape down the inside of the bowl once or twice. Add the remaining milk mixture in three more batches, mixing for about 20 seconds after each addition. Scrape down the inside of the bowl and beat on medium-high until the batter is homogeneous and light, about 30 seconds longer.

4. Transfer the batter to the prepared pans and place on the center rack of the oven. Bake for 25 to 28 minutes; after 12 minutes, rotate the cakes from front to back. The cake is done when it is lightly colored, slightly firm to the touch, and a toothpick inserted into the center comes out clean.

5. Transfer the pans to wire racks to rest for 5 minutes. Run a thin knife around the sides of the pans and invert the cakes onto the wire racks. Re-invert the cakes so the top is facing up. Cool completely before frosting.

Christopher Kimball is founder and publisher of Cook's Illustrated, *a national magazine for cooking hobbyists. Since 2000, America's Test Kitchen, which Christopher hosts, has been the top-rated food program on public television, reaching more than 90 million households. He is a frequent guest on* The Today Show, Weekend Today, *and the CBS Early Show, as well as a columnist for the* New York Daily News *and the Boston-based TAB newspapers. Author of* The Cook's Bible, The Yellow Farmhouse Cookbook, Dear Charlie, The Dessert Bible, *and* The Kitchen Detective, *Christopher lives in both Boston and Vermont with his wife and four children.*

Maple Meringue Frosting

Makes enough to frost and fill one 2-layer, 9-inch cake

⅔ cup Grade B maple syrup (see Note)
⅓ cup sugar
3 large egg whites, at room
  temperature
¼ teaspoon cream of tartar
¼ teaspoon salt

1. In a small saucepan, combine the maple syrup and sugar and bring to a boil over medium-high heat. (Watch carefully: This mixture tends to boil over quickly.) Lower the heat to maintain a simmer and cook for 4 minutes, stirring frequently, or until the sugar is dissolved and the syrup is slightly thickened; the foaming will subside when the pot is removed from the heat.

2. Place the egg whites in the bowl of an electric mixer fitted with the whisk attachment. (You can also use a large bowl and a handheld mixer.) Beat on medium speed for 45 seconds, or until foamy. Add the cream of tartar and salt, increase the speed to high, and beat for 1 to 2 minutes, until the egg whites are glossy and soft peaks form. Add the syrup mixture in a thin steady stream; once added, continue to beat on high for 2 more minutes.

Lower the speed to medium and beat, occasionally scraping down the inside of the bowl, until the meringue is cool, about 3 minutes. The frosting should be stiff and glossy, but not dry.

3. Place the bottom layer of cake on a serving tray, place several large spoonfuls of frosting on the layer, and smooth them over the surface. Place the second layer of cake on top of the frosted layer. Cover the top and then the sides of both cakes with the remaining frosting. The cake is best served the day it is made.

❖ Bake Sale Tips

Place the cake on a large disposable plate or tray before frosting. Wrap the cake in clear cellophane and tie with a colorful ribbon. The cake can also be sold in slices. Place each piece on a disposable plate and cover with plastic wrap. Place a sticker on top with a description.

To make two cakes, complete both the cake and the meringue recipe two separate times.

Note: Although it can be difficult to find, Grade B maple syrup will provide a fuller flavor than Grade A. Two sources are Whole Foods Markets or The Baker's Catalogue (800–827–6386; www.bakerscatalogue.com).

Fran Bigelow's
Classic Chocolate-Chocolate Icebox Cake

An icebox cake was what my mother would make for special occasions. The sight of it in the refrigerator meant we were in for a festive dinner or celebration. My mother was a master at making things always look great. Anything she served had to have visual appeal. Hot dogs in buns were served in a napkin-lined basket, mashed potatoes were always sprinkled with paprika, lettuce leaves lined trays and salad plates, even the asparagus from the can was presented on a silver tray.

I believed she had to be very skilled to make all those layers for this cake. Little did I know that it was thin store-bought cookies that would melt into the whipped cream and become this delectable chocolate dessert. Her recipe even came from the back of the cookie package. Still, this was one of the desserts everyone in America made in the 1950s, along with other favorites such as Waldorf salad, beef stroganoff, and crab casserole.

But the taste of it also reminded me of family summers spent on Camano Island, a small island off Seattle. We'd swim all day at the beach, hike, pick berries (so my mother could make blackberry pies for us), and then my sister and I would be allowed to go to the Maple Grove store and pick out our one treat for the day. Mine was usually an ice cream sandwich. I loved the combination of dark chocolate cookies with vanilla ice cream. Many of the tastes I try to recreate now come from those memories of summer and just how wonderful those treats were.

Going back to try this dessert years later, I wanted to add the taste of pure chocolate to it. I have added dark chocolate cocoa powder to the cream and a chocolate wafer that is the essence of chocolate itself.

Be sure to pay close attention when whipping the cream: It should remain just firm enough to spread, but still loose or "wet" enough to be absorbed by the crisp dry cookies. That's the magic of this cake: The cream melts the cookies and the two become a moist cake.

Classic Chocolate-Chocolate Icebox Cake

Makes one 8 x 4-inch loaf, serving 10

----

1 cup sugar

7½ tablespoons dark Dutch-process cocoa powder

3 cups heavy cream

18 Chocolate Wafer Cookies (3½-inch rounds)

Dark or milk chocolate shavings, optional, for garnish

1. Line an 8 x 4-inch loaf pan with a single piece of parchment paper (approximately 8 x 12 inches).

2. In a large bowl, stir together ⅔ cup of the sugar and 5½ tablespoons of the cocoa powder. Add 2 cups of the heavy cream and stir until the cocoa powder and sugar dissolve. (Since you will be layering the cake with whipped cream and then "frosting" it later, only a portion of the cream, sugar, and cocoa powder listed are used now.)

3. Either by hand or using a mixer, whisk the chocolate cream until it becomes quite thick. Continue to whisk until soft peaks form; do not whip excessively or the cream may become dry and will not be absorbed by the cookies and soften them into a moist "cake."

4. To assemble the cake, spread approximately ¾ cup of the whipped cream in the bottom of the parchment-lined pan.

5. The cake is formed of two rows composed of 9 wafers each, all held together with whipped cream. Spread both sides of 2 wafers with the cream, and press each one against the long side of the loaf pan; these are the first layers of the two rows. Spread the cream on one side of 14 other wafers pressing the wafer side against the cream side of the previous layer. Spread cream on both sides of the 2 remaining wafers, and slide them into place. Spread the remaining whipped cream on the top and ends of the loaf to cover the cookies completely. Cover

with plastic wrap and chill in the refrigerator for 24 hours.

6. To finish the cake, you will "frost" with a second layer of whipped cream. Either by hand or using a mixer, place the remaining ⅓ cup of the sugar and the remaining 2 tablespoons of the cocoa powder in a bowl. Add the remaining 1 cup cream and whisk until the cocoa and sugar dissolve. Continue to whisk until soft peaks form.

7. Take the cake from the refrigerator. Remove the plastic wrap and invert the loaf

Chocolate Wafer Cookies

Makes 24 cookies; an easy recipe to double

12 tablespoons (1½ sticks) unsalted butter, softened

1 cup sugar

⅔ cup dark Dutch-process cocoa powder, sifted, plus extra for rolling (see Note)

1 large egg

1½ teaspoons pure vanilla extract

1¼ cups all-purpose flour, plus extra for rolling

¾ teaspoon ground cinnamon

1. In the bowl of an electric mixer fitted with the paddle attachment, combine the butter and sugar and mix for 4 minutes on medium-high speed, or until light and fluffy.

2. Add the cocoa powder and mix on low speed until it is well combined. Scrape the inside of the mixing bowl. Add the egg and vanilla and blend thoroughly; scrape the inside of the bowl. Mix together the flour and cinnamon and add this to the batter. Mix on low speed until the dough begins to hold together.

3. Wrap the dough in plastic and chill for 4 hours or overnight. The dough should be firm.

4. Preheat the oven to 325°F. Line two baking sheets with parchment paper.

5. Working quickly on a surface dusted with equal parts flour and cocoa powder (this ensures a nicely darkened cookie), roll half the dough into a 12 x 12-inch square, approximately ⅛ inch thick. Using a 3½-inch cutter, cut out 12 circles. With a metal spatula, transfer the circles to the prepared sheets and pierce the cookies several times with the tines of a fork. Repeat with the remaining dough.

6. Place the sheets on the middle rack of the oven and bake for 8 to 10 minutes. The cookies are done when they turn dull and begin to bubble. Cool slightly, then transfer them to a wire rack to cool. Store the cookies in an airtight container for up to 3 days.

Note: "Dark" Dutch-process cocoa powder is also called black cocoa powder. Brands such as Dröste and Valrhona are available at larger supermarkets and specialty stores.

onto a serving plate. Ice the loaf with the freshly whipped cream, giving the loaf a finished look. Decorate with dark chocolate shavings or curls, if desired. As its name suggests, this cake needs to be kept refrigerated. Serve cold.

Variations

Chocolate-Malt Icebox Cake

The distinctive addition of powdered malt turns this creamy dessert into a chocolate-malt cake. Add 6 tablespoons powdered malt along with the cocoa powder during the first whipping of the cream, and add 2 tablespoons powdered malt during the second whipping of the cream.

Mocha Icebox Cake

For a coffee-flavored version, replace the cocoa powder in the first step with 1 shot of espresso or 2 tablespoons instant coffee dissolved in 2 tablespoons water. Reduce the sugar to ¼ cup plus 2 tablespoons and whisk it into the coffee. Add the cold cream and beat as in the main recipe.

In the second whipping of the cream, replace the cocoa powder with 1½ tablespoons espresso or 1 tablespoon instant coffee dissolved in 1 tablespoon water, and reduce the amount of sugar to 3 tablespoons. Follow the directions in the main recipe.

❖ Bake Sale Tips

To transport this dessert to a bake sale, place it on a platter and wrap with clear cellophane. The dessert should be transported in a cooler filled with ice packs and kept chilled during the sale. With a beautiful coat of chocolate curls—white, dark, or a combination, even—this is a beautiful cake to sell as a whole.

For doubling the recipe, whip the cream in two separate batches and prepare twice as many cookies.

Fran Bigelow is considered a pioneer in artisan chocolates in Seattle. Founder of Fran Bigelow's Chocolates in 1982, she creates a collection of award-winning, hand-dipped chocolates and caramels, which are available in her retail shops, at select stores throughout the country, or by mail order (800–422–FRAN, www.franschocolates.com). She is the author of the recently published Pure Chocolate.

Chocolate Sunburst Birthday Cake

While my mother provided us kids with chocolate—her way to relax and also indulge—when it came to birthdays, my uncle Jerry provided the cakes. He lived upstairs from us with my mom's sister, and he worked at—and eventually owned—a bakery. Uncle Pete's Bakery (some people called Uncle Jerry "Pete") produced breads and pies, but in Woonsockett, Rhode Island, you went to *his* bakery when you had something to celebrate.

I have a picture of myself on my first birthday, digging into one of Uncle Jerry's sheet cakes. It says "Happy Birthday," it has two candles, and it's decorated with the classic leaves and roses that were piped on all the cakes that celebrated the birthdays in our family. My uncle Jerry's school of baking—this was the 1950s—was not so much what went *into* the cake, but what went *on* it. These were unsophisticated, economical cakes (white cake with chocolate icing; chocolate cake with white icing) that he'd customize with whatever words a customer wanted piped among the swags and flowers of blue, green, red, and yellow icing. I can still smell the sugar of his bake shop. I can still feel the gritty sweetness, biting into a corner square of cake—every kid's first choice!—with icing on three sides as well as the middle. And the truth is, most kids from the age of one to ten love any cake as long as it's sweet and they can stick a finger into the icing.

But this Chocolate Sunburst Birthday Cake is a dessert I'd make for kids as well as kids-at-heart. It's easy to prepare, it's got all the richness we've grown to expect from chocolate these days, and the colorful sunburst on top pops out as if to say "wow." It's a round cake, which seems much more personal to me than a sheet cake. A round cake is less daunting, too: If I see a big sheet cake with my name on it I know I must have reached quite a milestone! The sunburst, too, is the right design for holding a single candle, which is helpful for those people who don't really want to see a forest of candles, like some symbolic bonfire, consuming all the years gone by.

I know some adults don't want a cake on their birthdays—they don't even want their birthdays, but I think we need all the celebrating we can get. One day, maybe I'll do an entire book of celebration cakes, include a chapter called *"You Say It's Your Birthday,"* and stock it with cakes that are, themselves, reason enough to celebrate.

So here's to you! Happy [Birthday, Anniversary—whatever fits!], from Uncle Marcel.

Chocolate Sunburst Birthday Cake

Make one 2-layer, 9-inch cake, serving 10 to 12

For the cake

16 tablespoons (2 sticks) unsalted butter, cut into tablespoons, plus 2 teaspoons, melted

1¾ cups all-purpose flour

1 teaspoon salt

½ teaspoon baking soda

8 ounces semisweet baking chocolate, coarsely chopped

1¼ cups sugar

3 large eggs

½ cup buttermilk

1 teaspoon pure vanilla extract

For the icing

1 pound (3½ to 4 cups) confectioners' sugar

32 tablespoons (4 sticks) unsalted butter, cut into 1-inch pieces

1 tablespoon finely chopped orange zest

2 tablespoons heavy cream

2 tablespoons freshly squeezed orange juice

1 teaspoon pure vanilla extract

11 drops yellow food coloring

5 drops red food coloring

1. Preheat the oven to 325°F and lightly coat the insides of two 9 x 1½-inch round cake pans with the melted butter. Line the bottoms of the pans with parchment or wax paper and lightly coat the paper with more melted butter.

2. For the cake, in a large bowl, sift together the flour, salt, and baking soda.

3. In the top half of a double boiler (or in a medium glass bowl in a microwave oven; see page 16), melt the chocolate and the 2 sticks of the butter; stir until smooth.

4. In the bowl of an electric mixer fitted with the paddle attachment, combine the sugar and eggs, beating on medium-high speed for 2 minutes, or until slightly thickened and pale in color. Add the chocolate-butter mixture and blend on low speed just to combine. With the speed on low, gradually add the sifted ingredients; mix for 1 minute, or until incorporated. Scrape the inside of the bowl. Add the buttermilk and vanilla and mix on low just to combine, then beat on medium speed for 15 seconds. Remove the bowl from the mixer and finish blending the batter with a spatula.

5. Divide the batter evenly between the prepared pans and smooth the surfaces. Place the pans on the middle rack of the oven and bake for 30 minutes, or until a toothpick inserted into the center of the cake comes out clean.

6. Remove the cakes from the oven and cool in the pans for 15 minutes. Invert the cake layers onto plates and carefully peel the paper from the bottoms of the cakes. Refrigerate the cake layers until ready to frost.

7. For the icing, sift the confectioners' sugar onto a large piece of parchment or wax paper.

8. In the bowl of an electric mixer fitted with the paddle attachment, combine the butter and orange zest and mix on low speed for 1 minute, then increase the speed to medium-high and beat for 2 minutes, or until soft. Scrape the inside of the bowl and the paddle. Beat on medium speed for 2 more minutes, or until the butter is very soft. Reduce the speed to low and add the confectioners' sugar and mix for 1 minute, just to combine.

9. Scrape the inside of the bowl and the paddle. Add the heavy cream, orange juice, vanilla, and 8 drops of the yellow food coloring; mix on low for 10 seconds, then beat on medium high for 1 minute. Remove the bowl from the mixer and use a spatula to finish blending the icing.

10. Transfer ¾ cup of the yellow icing to a small bowl. Add the red food coloring and 3 more drops of the yellow food coloring; stir vigorously with a spatula until thoroughly combined and bright orange. Transfer this orange icing to a pastry bag fitted with a small star tip.

11. To assemble the cake, remove the cake layers from the refrigerator. Spread 1 cup of the yellow icing into an even layer across the top of one inverted cake layer. Place the second cake layer, right side up, on the iced cake and press gently to level the layers. Spread the remaining yellow icing over the top cake and the sides of both layers.

12. Create a sunburst on top of the cake by piping the bright orange icing in 10 to 12 individual rays or spokes. Leave a 2-inch circle in the center of the cake with the spokes extending to the edge. Refrigerate the cake for 1 hour before serving. When you serve the cake at home, each slice should have a

"sunbeam" of bright orange icing centered on the top surface.

❖ Bake Sale Tips

This cake should be offered as a whole. Wrap it in clear cellophane, gather the edges well above the decorated surface, and tie the package with a bright orange ribbon. With its distinctive chocolate and orange colors, you might also adapt the icing pattern for an autumn or Halloween occasion.

To make two cakes, complete each part of the recipe two separate times.

Jane and Michael Stern's
Cola Cake with Broiled Peanut Butter Frosting
and
Milky Way Cake

N ext to the experts behind the tables at a bake sale, our favorite source for cake and cookie recipes is a good self-published community cookbook. Over the course of many cross-country trips, we have collected hundreds of them put out by PTAs, church groups, wives of farmers and fishermen, debutantes' mothers, and firefighters. To us, these books are a brilliant reflection of American cooking, not the upwardly mobile cuisine you find made by chefs in four-star restaurants, but the dishes good cooks prepare for their families and friends in the community. Like an oft-repeated folk song with a dozen variations, a good community cookbook stresses honesty more than originality, and its recipes will freely borrow from formulas that are tried and true. There is no shame for such a book to have twelve different versions of a cheese ball, each one just slightly different. And best of all, each recipe will be connected to a real person who lives in town, and maybe even be introduced with a story of who first made it, when it's best to serve, and who eats the most of it when it's set out on the table.

One of the first such books we ever found, way back in the 1970s while on a tenderloin-eating tour of the Midwest, was the *Oakland Iowa Centennial Cookbook*. It was filled with gooey sock-it-to-me cakes, mock Oreos, Mounds-like candies, and millionaire pies. When we came home and made the Cola Cake, we were awestruck by how perfectly simple and direct it was: moist and chocolaty but not sinfully rich like some fancy-pants mousse or flourless cake. It's the kind of chocolate cake that makes us want to have a big glass of cold milk on the side, and it is especially well suited for a bake sale because you can cut it into neat squares to be handheld and devoured while standing up. If, like us, you were a child who saw milk-and-cookie time as the highlight of your day, this is a cake that is guaranteed to put a grin on your face. In the years since "discovering" it, we have learned that many cooks, especially in the South, have similar recipes for cakes made with their favorite cola. We've never done a Coke vs. Pepsi taste-test with the recipe, but in our experience, it works fine with either one.

Cola Cake with Broiled Peanut Butter Frosting

Makes one 9 x 13-inch cake, serving 10 to 12

For the cake

2 cups all-purpose flour

2 cups sugar

16 tablespoons (2 sticks) unsalted butter, melted

2 tablespoons Dutch-process cocoa powder

1 cup cola

½ cup buttermilk

2 large eggs, beaten

1 teaspoon baking soda

1 teaspoon pure vanilla extract

1½ cups miniature marshmallows

For the frosting

6 tablespoons unsalted butter, softened

1 cup dark brown sugar (lightly packed)

⅔ cup smooth peanut butter

¼ cup whole milk

⅔ cup chopped salted peanuts

1. Preheat the oven to 350°F. Butter and flour one 9 x 13-inch cake pan.

2. For the cake, in a large bowl, combine the flour and the sugar with a wooden spoon. In a medium bowl, combine the melted butter, cocoa, and cola and pour this into the dry mix. Stir until well blended. Add the buttermilk, eggs, baking soda, and vanilla and mix until blended. Fold in the marshmallows.

3. Pour the batter into the prepared pan and bake for 35 to 40 minutes, or until a toothpick inserted into the center of the cake comes out clean. While the cake begins to cool, make the frosting, which you should apply while the cake is warm.

4. Preheat the oven to broil and place the top rack 4 to 5 inches from the heat source.

5. For the frosting, in a large bowl, combine the butter, brown sugar, and peanut butter. Stir in the milk and fold in the nuts. Spread the frosting evenly over the surface of the cake. Place the cake in the oven and broil for 20 to 30 seconds, or until the frosting starts to bubble, rotating the cake for even cooking. *Watch carefully:* You want the frosting to bubble and to caramelize slightly; do not let it scorch.

❖ Bake Sale Tip

To make two cakes, complete the recipe two separate times.

Milky Way Cake

Makes one 9-inch Bundt cake, serving 10 to 12

One of the other things we love about community cookbooks is that so many of their recipes exemplify what we call mix-'n'-match cuisine: using store-bought ingredients in novel ways. Canned soup casseroles and Jell-O molds chock-a-block with nuts and fruits are the most common variations of this creative home cookery, and one of our all-time favorites is the Southern favorite, a Milky Way cake, which we found in *Bayou Cuisine*. Is it a cake? Is it a candy bar? Like a statue of the Venus de Milo with a clock implanted in its stomach, it is two things in one and an improvement on either. It's a culinary twofer, edible kitsch incarnate.

Four 2.1-ounce Milky Way™ candy bars, chopped

16 tablespoons (2 sticks) unsalted butter, softened

2 cups sugar

4 large eggs, at room temperature

2½ cups all-purpose flour, sifted

¼ teaspoon baking soda

1 cup buttermilk, at room temperature

2 teaspoons pure vanilla extract

1 cup coarsely chopped pecans

1. Preheat the oven to 350°F. Butter and flour a 9-inch Bundt pan.

2. In a medium saucepan, combine the candy bar pieces and 1 stick of the butter; stir constantly over medium-low heat until melted. Allow the mixture to cool to room temperature.

3. In the bowl of an electric mixer fitted with the paddle attachment, cream the remaining stick of butter and the sugar: Mix for 1 minute, then scrape the inside of the bowl; mix for 1 additional minute, then scrape the inside of the bowl again. Add the eggs one at a time, incorporating each one thoroughly before adding the next.

4. Combine the flour and baking soda in a bowl. Combine the buttermilk and vanilla in a measuring cup. With the mixer on low speed, add half of the dry mix to the batter followed by half of the buttermilk. Mix for 30 seconds, or until blended. Repeat with the remaining ingredients. Scrape down the sides of the bowl and mix for an additional 30 to 40 seconds, until the batter is well blended. Add the Milky Way mixture and mix until the batter is smooth. Fold in the pecans.

5. Pour the batter into the prepared pan and bake for 1 hour, or until a toothpick inserted into the center of the cake comes out clean. Cool the cake for 15 minutes and then invert it onto a cooling rack.

❖ Bake Sale Tip

To make two cakes, complete the recipe two separate times.

Jane and Michael Stern are the authors of more than twenty books, including many about American cooking, such as Road Food *and* Square Meals. *They contribute to www.roadfood.com, a Web site they helped create, which locates the best local eateries along America's highways and back roads. Their "Roadfood" column for* Gourmet *has won three James Beard Awards, and their "Roadfood" segments appear regularly on television's Food Network. Regular contributors to NPR's "The Splendid Table," the Sterns live in West Redding, Connecticut.*

No-Mistake Red Velvet Cake with Pecan Cream Cheese Frosting

My grand-aunt raised my mother, and she had a big hand in raising me, my sister, and all my cousins. She was a baker and a cook, and a visit to her home was what I most looked forward to during a week of school. Come Friday, I'd race home, pack up my things, and walk over to her house, where I'd meet my cousins for a weekend stay. Anything you could have wanted was there. We'd be six or seven or eight kids and we'd take over the dining room, making pallets on the carpeting with my grand-aunt's old-fashioned quilts.

We were in the kitchen all the time, watching her or helping her make corn bread, sweet potato pie, fried chicken—and our favorite, crabs, because she lived next door to a crab house. We'd get to stay up until eleven o'clock Friday night so we could watch wrestling with the Mighty Igor and Bobo Brazil and the Iron Sheik while we ate boiled crab and watermelon.

Surely inspired by her, I took up baking as a hobby in junior high school. In home ec, I'd spend extra time decorating cakes. I remember my first project was a giant four-leaf-clover cake for Saint Patrick's Day. By the time I was in high school, I became the person who made the cakes for everyone in my family. And I mean my "extended family": my grandparents and all my first and second cousins, who always came to family functions. We'd have upwards of thirty people. And for each birthday, we usually did something special, like a cookout, or a low-country boil (crab, shrimp, potatoes, corn on the cob, onions—maybe crawfish), and then steamed oysters, and a dessert table with plenty of choices.

I tried to decorate each cake in a special way for each person—and I still do: the little girls like doll cakes with a Barbie tucked in the center with a big icing skirt. I remember lots of Barney cakes and Mickey Mouse cakes when those characters were so popular. And here at Elizabeth's on 37th, where we have something like twenty-two employees, I keep a calendar with everyone's birthday on it because everyone gets to request some special cake, but it's at the point where some of the people are requesting cakes for their spouses, and their new boyfriends. Birthdays are just sort of nonstop around here.

But there are two favorite desserts that everyone requests, even when it's not a birthday: One is a strawberry shortcake, and the other is this red velvet cake. The first time I tasted this cake I was at a restaurant here in Savannah, Georgia, when I was pretty little. This piece of red cake arrived at the table, redder than anything edible I'd ever eaten. It was wonderful. But when I learned to make it at home, from scratch, it was even better. Now I think of this as a festive dessert, something to save for the holidays. I've revised our family recipe a few times, after a cousin of mine told me her cake crumbled and fell apart. Now this version is perfected, and it's always a showpiece at our church bake sales and dinners. You put a red velvet cake on your table and you have a centerpiece.

Another cousin called me one day, and she said, "I want you to try something with me." She had this idea of making a red and green velvet cake for Christmas, and it turned out beautifully! Red, green, and white. Just make this recipe twice for two cakes, one with a red batter and one with a green batter (substitute a bottle of green food coloring), and then trade halves before you frost the cakes. You'll have two finished cakes—which is just right, because the minute people see this cake, their faces just light up and you won't have enough with just one!

Stephanie Hall's Strawberry Shortcake appears on page 125.

No-Mistake Red Velvet Cake

Makes one 2-layer, 9-inch cake, serving 10 to 12

----

1 cup buttermilk

1 teaspoon white vinegar

1 teaspoon baking soda

1 ounce (1 bottle) red food coloring

2 cups sugar

2 large eggs

2 cups vegetable oil

2⅓ cups all-purpose flour

1 teaspoon salt

1 teaspoon pure vanilla extract

1 tablespoon Dutch-process cocoa powder

1 recipe Pecan Cream Cheese Frosting

1. Preheat the oven to 325°F. Grease two round 9-inch cake pans and line the bottom of each pan with a circle of parchment paper. Grease the paper.

2. In the bowl of an electric mixer fitted with the whisk attachment, combine all the ingredients and whip on low speed for 1 minute, or until everything is incorporated. Scrape the sides of the bowl and increase the speed to medium and whip for 2 minutes. Divide the batter between the prepared pans and smooth the surface of the batter with a spoon.

3. Place the pans on the middle rack of the oven and bake for 25 to 30 minutes, or until a toothpick inserted into the center of each cake comes out clean. Cool the cakes in the pans for 15 minutes. Invert the cakes onto a wire rack, remove the paper,

Pecan Cream Cheese Frosting

Makes enough to frost and fill one 2-layer, 9-inch cake (about 2 cups)

5 ounces cream cheese, softened

4½ tablespoons unsalted butter, softened

3 cups confectioners' sugar

2 teaspoons pure vanilla extract

1 teaspoon heavy cream

½ cup finely chopped pecans

In the bowl of an electric mixer fitted with the paddle attachment, combine the cream cheese and butter and mix on medium speed for 2 minutes or until smooth. Scrape the inside of the bowl. Reduce the speed to low, gradually add the confectioners' sugar, and mix until incorporated. Add the vanilla and cream and mix until smooth. Fold in the nuts.

and cool completely. Flip the cakes right side up.

4. With a serrated knife, trim off the domed top of each cake to make a flat surface. Sandwich the layers with frosting and cover the sides and the top with frosting.

❖ Bake Sale Tip

To make two cakes, complete the recipe two separate times.

Stephanie Hall is executive pastry chef at Elizabeth's on 37th restaurant in Savannah, Georgia. She joined the staff in 1985 and has upheld the restaurant's commitment to fine Southern cooking. Since then, Stephanie has cooked for the James Beard House, A Salute to Southern Chefs in Charleston, and the Atlanta Ritz-Carlton. Actively involved in her church and church choir, she resides in Savannah with her husband, Jerome, and adopted daughter, Jamerice.

Rick Rodgers's

Chocolate-Cherry Fudge Torte with Kirsch Whipped Cream

In my family, good baking was a part of life, a way to celebrate family and friends. My heritage is mixed, to say the least. My mom's side of the family, the Perrys, included my grandmother from Liechtenstein, and my grandfather, who was born in Waikiki of Portuguese extraction. A native Californian, my paternal grandfather was also second-generation Portuguese, and Grandma Rodgers came from solid Irish stock with a dash of Spanish and English tossed in. I remember one of Grandpa Perry's birthdays where we had Portuguese sausage, Hawaiian poi (mashed taro root—something to give new meaning to the phrase "an acquired taste"), and pit-roasted pig, and my aunties' famous Viennese desserts. My relatives cooked food from the old country not just because they liked it or because it reminded them of the past, but because it established their individuality in our simmering Californian melting pot.

Until I was almost in college, I had a full set of living relatives, including cousins and second cousins, aunts and uncles and great-aunts and great-uncles, grandparents, a great-grandmother, two brothers, and my parents. Every one of us was entitled to a birthday party, which, of course, meant a personal choice of birthday cake. With so many parties, I got to know a huge variety of cakes, and I became quite a connoisseur at an early age. Vanilla cake filled with rum pastry cream or tangy lemon curd; chocolate with thick fudge frosting or the distinctive coconut-pecan frosting of German chocolate cake; ice cream cakes of all shades and flavors; banana cakes; spice cakes; cakes made from cake mixes; cakes made from pudding mixes—the list was as long as my family tree was tall. And there never was a bad cake in the lot.

My mother's cousin Trudy made an incredibly moist chocolate cake that made her a culinary goddess in our world. To this day, almost twenty years after her death, my relatives still cluck after tasting any chocolate cake: "Well, it's fine, but it's not as good as Trudy's!" (In the great tradition of excellent cooks, Trudy passed away with her secret.)

The combined baking talent of my great-aunts Gisela, Erna, and Trudy (a popular name with the Germanic side of the family) was formidable. The intricacies of homemade puff pastry or *Kipferln* (Viennese croissants) held no terror for these ladies. I always thought that they had brought their recipes with them from Europe. Actually, they learned to bake on this side of the ocean. They could only find work as domestics, and of course, their employers expected fabulous Viennese desserts from cooks who were born just a few hours away from the Hotel Sacher. So baking well was a question of survival. Luckily, they loved what they learned, and that love was literally baked into every birthday cake.

My mom is renowned as the family's best cake decorator. Her pièce de résistance was my sixteenth birthday cake, made in the shape of a portable record player, complete with black frosting to simulate the vinyl record. However, Mom's pies are so flaky and perfect that many family members have eschewed cake (no matter how awesomely designed) in favor of her chocolate cream or lemon meringue pies. It took me many years of practice before my piecrusts came close to Mom's. My Chocolate-Banana Cream Pie with Almond Crust is an attempt to roll everything that I love about her and her pastries into a single dessert. My Chocolate-Cherry Fudge Torte is a salute to the extravagant desserts of her aunts.

There is nothing like being exposed to quality early in life. It can be fine music, great art, a superb athletic team, or in my case, wonderful baking. But once you experience it, there's no going back. When I taste a truly delicious piece of cake that is worth every calorie and extra sit-up sessions at the gym, I still remark, "Well, it's fine, but it's not as good as Aunt Trudy's."

Rick Rodgers's Chocolate-Banana Cream Pie with
Almond Crust appears on page 106.

Chocolate-Cherry Fudge Torte

Makes one 9-inch cake, serving 10 to 12; an easy recipe to double

----

For the cake

16 tablespoons (2 sticks) unsalted butter, cut into bits, plus 2 teaspoons for the pan

¾ cup dried cherries

⅓ cup kirsch or cherry brandy

12 ounces bittersweet chocolate, finely chopped

1½ cups sugar

6 large eggs, at room temperature

⅔ cup all-purpose flour

½ teaspoon salt

For the glaze

½ cup heavy cream

5 ounces bittersweet chocolate, finely chopped

2 tablespoons kirsch or cherry brandy

¼ cup dried cherries, for garnish

1 recipe Kirsch Whipped Cream, optional, for serving

1. Preheat the oven to 350°F. Lightly butter a 9-inch round springform pan. Line the bottom of the pan with a round of wax or parchment paper. Butter the paper as well. Dust the inside of the pan with flour and tap out the excess.

2. Combine the dried cherries and kirsch in a small microwave-proof bowl and microwave at full power for 15 seconds, until the kirsch is hot. (Alternatively, you can use a small saucepan and heat on low until steaming.) Let stand until the cherries are cool and plump. Drain the cherries and reserve the kirsch.

3. Melt the 2 sticks of butter in a medium heavy-bottomed saucepan. Remove from the heat and add the chocolate. Let stand for 1 minute, then whisk until smooth. Whisk in the sugar. Add the eggs one at a time, whisking thoroughly before adding the next egg. Stir in the reserved kirsch. Add the flour and salt and mix until combined. Fold in the drained cherries. Scrape into the prepared pan and smooth the top.

4. Place the pan on the middle rack of the oven and bake for 40 to 45 minutes, until a toothpick inserted 2 inches from the edge comes out clean. (The center will not seem completely set.) Do not overbake. Transfer to a wire rack to cool for 15 minutes.

5. Run a knife around the inside of the pan and allow the torte to cool, in the pan, for at least 2 hours. (The torte's center will sink if the cake is removed from the pan before it is cooled.)

6. Remove the sides of the pan. Place a wire cake rack over the torte, invert, and remove the bottom of the pan and the paper. Place the cake, still on the wire rack, over a rimmed baking sheet, which will catch the glaze in the next step.

7. To make the glaze, bring the cream to a simmer in a medium saucepan over medium heat. Remove the pan from the heat and add the chocolate and kirsch. Let stand for 1 minute, then stir until smooth. (Don't whisk: That will create bubbles on the surface of the glazed cake). Let stand until slightly thickened but pourable, about 10 minutes.

8. Pour the glaze over the torte. Smooth the glaze over the cake, allowing the excess to drip down the sides. Smooth the sides. Allow the glaze to set for 15 minutes, and then sprinkle the dried cherries around the top edge of the cake. Refrigerate the torte until the glaze is firm, about 1 hour. Using a large spatula or small baking sheet, transfer the torte from the rack to a serving platter. At home, serve wedges of the cake with a dollop of Kirsch Whipped Cream.

❖ Bake Sale Tip

The torte can be made 1 day ahead. Cover it with a cake dome to keep the glaze pristine. Transfer the whole torte to a sturdy, disposable plate. Wrap in a large sheet of clear cellophane, forming the extra into a dome above the glazed cake. Tie with a colorful ribbon.

Popular cooking instructor Rick Rodgers has written more than twenty books, including the successful "101" series (Thanksgiving 101, Christmas 101, and Barbecues 101). *Winner of* Bon Appétit's *Outstanding Cooking Teacher of the Year Award and a frequent guest on radio and television programs, Rick lives in the New York City area.*

Kirsch Whipped Cream

Makes about 2 cups

1 cup heavy cream
2 tablespoons confectioners' sugar
½ teaspoon vanilla
2 tablespoons kirsch or cherry brandy, optional

Either by hand, in a chilled medium bowl, or in an electric mixer fitted with the whisk attachment, whip the cream, sugar, and vanilla until the cream is stiff. Stir in the kirsch, if desired. Keep refrigerated until needed.

Bundt, Pound, Angelfood, and Coffee Cakes

◆ ◆ ◆

Gina DePalma's
Apple Tube Cake
and
Pumpkin Loaf Cake
with Chocolate Chips

My mom led somewhat of a double life as a cook. She spent a period of her childhood in Italy just before World War II, but spent her years as a mother with young children in the postwar 1950s, exploring the new cooking fads that were popular with housewives of the time. I grew up with the traditional Italian cooking of her heritage right alongside recipes clipped from her favorite ladies' magazines or taken from the *McCall's* or Betty Crocker cookbooks she kept on a shelf in the kitchen: a hybrid of new and old world ways.

My mother had a select few American-style desserts in her recipe file, and this apple cake was a standout, as well as my favorite. I am unsure of the exact origin other than the tattered index card—now about thirty years old—that I copied it from. In autumn, when apples were in season and we could tolerate the heat in the kitchen generated by the lengthy baking time, I could always count on its appearance at family gatherings. Since this cake becomes moister and more flavorful after a day, it was always made on Saturday in anticipation of Sunday dinner. There it would wait, under the dome of Mom's etched glass cake stand, golden and tall, sprinkled with powdered sugar, mocking me as I watched a precious hour of TV in my pajamas before going to bed. It was torture!

Apple Tube Cake

Makes one 10-inch cake, serving 10 to 12

- 5 large Granny Smith apples
- 2 teaspoons ground cinnamon
- 2¾ cups sugar
- 4 cups unbleached all-purpose flour
- 4 teaspoons baking powder
- 1 teaspoon salt
- 1 cup freshly squeezed orange juice
    (from 5 to 6 oranges)
- 1 cup vegetable oil
- 4 large eggs
- Confectioners' sugar, optional,
    for serving

1. Preheat the oven to 350°F. Butter and flour a 10-inch tube pan with a removable bottom. (Do not use a Bundt pan.)

2. Peel, core, and quarter the apples. Cut each quarter into ¼-inch slices. In a small bowl, combine the cinnamon and ¾ cup of the sugar. Toss the apples with 3 tablespoons of this cinnamon-sugar, and set aside the rest.

3. In a large bowl, sift together the remaining 2 cups of sugar, the flour, baking powder, and salt. Make a well in the center of the dry ingredients.

4. In a medium bowl, whisk together the orange juice, vegetable oil, and eggs. Pour the egg mixture into the dry ingredients and mix well, using a large spatula or spoon, to create a smooth batter.

5. Pour half of the batter into the prepared pan, scatter half of the apples over the batter, and sprinkle with half of the cinnamon-sugar mixture. Top with the remaining batter, then the rest of the apples, and finally the remaining cinnamon-sugar.

6. Bake for 1 hour and 30 minutes, or until a toothpick inserted in the center comes out clean.

7. Transfer the cake to a wire rack and cool for at least 30 minutes before removing from the pan to finish cooling. If desired, sprinkle with confectioners' sugar before serving.

❖ Bake Sale Tips

If you'll be selling the cake as a whole, add the confectioners' sugar just before putting it on display. To sell individual slices, wrap wedges in wax or parchment paper and seal with a sticker. This is a cake that's easy to double, and it's even better the day after it's made.

To make two cakes, complete the recipe two separate times unless you have a very large mixing bowl.

Pumpkin Loaf Cake with Chocolate Chips

Makes one 9-inch loaf, serving 8 to 10;
an easy recipe to double

Halloween was a big deal in our neighborhood. People worked on their costumes for days. But when it came to giving out candy, my mother needed to be thrifty. My father died when I was six, and Mom held down a full-time job and often did other part-time jobs from home while raising us children. I couldn't understand her frugality as a little kid, though now I realize how wonderful it was. So we never had the obligatory mini candy bars that were so cute. Instead, she'd buy cheap bulk candy, and we'd spend the day before Halloween making up little paper bags, each one filled with a handful of candy corn, a couple of hard candies, some chocolate, and then tied shut with a string. So each trick-or-treater at our door received this goodie bag. We lived in a complex with garden apartments and townhouses, so hundreds of kids would come with their open Halloween sacks to each and every door.

On Beggar's Night, Mom passed out the candy, and my friends and I made a plan of action: which houses had the best loot, whose dad came to the door dressed as a ghoul, who was having a haunted house that year in their basement. It was a nightlong adventure, and then we'd come home and turn over our filled pillow cases to my mother, who would put all the candy in shoe boxes stashed in the hall closet, doling it out piece by piece so that it would last until Easter (when the next stash of candy would come along). Need I say that there was quite a lot of candy eating on the way home?

But I understood her way of thinking: You are not to waste or squander anything. Indeed, this delicious loaf cake—my first introduction to the surprising combination of pumpkin, spice, and a touch of chocolate—was the eventual reincarnation of every pumpkin we ever carved. The next morning, before the jack-o'-lantern's smile slumped into a frown, she'd snatch the pumpkin from the porch, carve it into chunks, and plunk it into her stockpot. She'd freeze some of the pureed flesh to make pies, and the rest she'd make into these chocolate-chip loaves that we'd enjoy throughout the holidays and give as gifts to our neighbors. In her honor, I do the same every year.

1½ cups unbleached all-purpose flour
1 teaspoon baking soda
½ teaspoon salt
1 teaspoon ground cinnamon
½ teaspoon freshly grated nutmeg
¼ teaspoon ground ginger
¼ teaspoon ground cloves
8 tablespoons (1 stick) unsalted butter, softened
1 cup sugar
2 large eggs
1 teaspoon pure vanilla extract
¾ cup solid pack, canned plain pumpkin or fresh pumpkin puree (see Note)
¾ cup semisweet chocolate chips
½ cup chopped walnuts

1. Preheat the oven to 350°F and lightly grease a 9-inch loaf pan.

2. In a large bowl, sift together the flour, baking soda, salt, and spices.

3. In the bowl of an electric mixer fitted with the paddle attachment, cream the butter and sugar on medium speed for 2 min-

utes, or until light and fluffy. Add the eggs one at a time, incorporating each one thoroughly before adding the next. Add the vanilla and scrape the inside of the bowl.

4. Alternately add one-third of the dry ingredients and one half of the pumpkin, mixing briefly after each addition; begin and end with the dry ingredients. Fold in the chocolate chips and walnuts.

5. Bake for 50 to 60 minutes, or until a toothpick inserted into the center of the loaf comes out clean.

6. Transfer the loaf to a wire rack and cool for 15 minutes. Invert the pan to release the loaf, then place the loaf right side up and cool completely before slicing.

❖ Bake Sale Tip

Sell this as a whole loaf or wrap individual slices in wax or parchment paper and seal with tape or a sticker.

Note: To use fresh pumpkin puree in this recipe, make certain to drain the puree through a sieve, and then squeeze it in a clean, dry tea towel. Excess water will affect the density and rising of the cake, as well as the baking time.

Born and raised in Virginia, Gina DePalma credits her close-knit Italian family for instilling a love and understanding of good food that is simply prepared from the best ingredients. After completing her apprenticeship in the pastry kitchen of Chanterelle, she decided to pursue a career in pastry. She now works with Mario Batali and Joseph Bastianich at Babbo, where her philosophy is to bring traditional Italian ingredients to the world of three-star desserts.

Joanne Chang's

Apple Snacking Spice Cake

 hen I was in fourth grade, I fell in love with my English teacher. She was kind, gentle, articulate, lovely—everything I wanted to be. If I'd been older, I would have been accused of being the teacher's pet, but at that age, we were blissfully unaware of these labels and, besides, everyone else was as infatuated with Ms. Davis as I.

At the end of the school year, I decided to make her a cake to show her how much she meant to me. I found a picture and recipe for an apple cake in one of my mom's magazines and begged her to help me make it. My mom will be the first to admit that she is an awful baker and, at nine years old, I had little, if any, kitchen acumen.

We made this cake. Four times. The first cake never rose. The second one never turned brown (we forgot the sugar). The third tasted soapy (too much baking soda?). And the fourth looked great, but never made it to the cake box: It fell on the floor when we tried to take it out of the pan.

I was in tears, Mom was frustrated, and I realized I'd never be able to show Ms. Davis how much I loved her.

Mom to the rescue! She ran to the corner store and bought a cake mix: a Duncan Hines apple spice cake. There wasn't a lot to mess up: add oil, eggs, water, and bake. This one went without a hitch and I presented the cake the next morning to Ms. Davis. She was glowing (so was I) and told me how much she would miss me. And the next day she called me at home to tell me how fabulous the cake was.

Years later I found another apple cake recipe, and, reminded of the baking fiasco of my childhood, I tried again. I've tweaked this recipe a number of times since then and now this spice cake is one of the best sellers at my bakery. I still have fond memories of Ms. Davis and how much she loved the cake-mix cake; I wish she could have tried this one.

Joanne Chang's Homemade Oreos® appear on page 36.

Apple Snacking Spice Cake

Makes one 9 x 9-inch cake, serving 10 to 12;
an easy recipe to double

----

1 cup cake flour

1 cup all-purpose flour

1½ teaspoons baking soda

½ teaspoon salt

¼ teaspoon ground cinnamon

¼ teaspoon ground ginger

⅛ teaspoon ground cloves

6 tablespoons (¾ stick) unsalted butter,
    softened

1½ cups sugar

2 large eggs

4 cups chopped Granny Smith apples
    (3 large apples)

⅓ cup raisins

1 cup chopped pecans

1. Preheat the oven to 350°F. Mist a
9 x 9-inch cake pan with nonstick cooking
spray.

2. In a large bowl, sift together the cake
flour, all-purpose flour, baking soda, salt,
cinnamon, ginger, and cloves.

3. In the bowl of an electric mixer fitted
with the paddle attachment, mix the butter
and sugar on medium speed for 1 minute, or

until light and fluffy. Add the eggs, increase
the speed to high, and mix for 1 minute.
Scrape the inside of the bowl. Reduce the
speed to low, add the flour mixture, and mix
just until the dry ingredients are incorporated; do not overmix. Fold in the apples,
raisins, and nuts by hand.

4. Spoon the batter into the prepared
pan, and place it on the middle rack of the
oven. Bake for 40 to 45 minutes, or until
firm to the touch. Cover the cake with aluminum foil after 25 to 30 minutes if the top
is browning too quickly. Allow the cake to
cool and cut into squares.

Joanne Chang, an honors graduate of
Harvard College with a degree in applied
mathematics and economics, left a career
as a management consultant to enter the
world of professional cooking. She has worked
in various baking capacities at Rialto, Biba,
Mistral, and Bentonwood Bakery in the
Boston area, as well as overseeing the cake de-
partment of Payard Patisserie and Bistro in
New York City. Flour, her bakery and cafe in
Boston's South End, opened in 2000. An avid
runner who has competed in every Boston
Marathon since 1991, Joanne also writes
pastry articles and reviews cookbooks for
Fine Cooking magazine.

Espresso Chocolate Chip Angelfood Cake

My mother's mother—after whom I'm named—didn't bake all that much. I'm actually the seventh Emily in our family: I have an old oil portrait of the first Emily, who looks as if she didn't eat many sweets—her expression isn't exactly happy—and on the back of the painting is a list of all seven Emilys, ending with me.

My grandmother's angelfood cake was just about her only dessert, but people never tired of it. I saw her make it so many times I didn't even realize it might be hard to prepare. I actually (successfully!) made it about the time most girls my age were just learning how to make brownies and chocolate chip cookies, and it wasn't until years later that I learned most ten-year-olds haven't baked an angelfood cake. It made me proud of myself and of my grandmother for teaching me. I can still picture us: my grandmother having her coffee with a forkful of her angelfood cake, and me, standing beside her, just biting into a piece I'm holding—no glass of milk, no silverware, no chair to sit in—no reason to turn this treat into a whole polite "meal."

I suppose I've always liked the idea that there was an angelfood and a devil's food: one so light and airy, and the other sinful. Maybe I think that way since I'm a twin. My mother would bake me and my twin brother our own cakes on our birthday: My brother always asked for chocolate cake with chocolate icing (devilish?), and I'd ask for something like a spice cake (angelic?). But then we'd both end up eating part of the other person's cake.

In any case, an angelfood cake is a good dessert to have in your baking reper-toire. I've added espresso and chocolate chips to my grandmother's version, maybe paying homage to her accompanying cup of coffee, as well as showing a little devilish influence. Serve it plain as an afternoon snack or gussied up with fruits or berries, caramel or chocolate sauce, or ice cream for after dinner.

Emily Luchetti's Coconut Cream Pie appears on page 104.

Espresso Chocolate Chip Angelfood Cake

Makes one 10-inch cake, serving 10 to 12

----

2 teaspoons instant espresso powder

1⅓ cups cake flour, sifted

⅛ teaspoon salt

1¾ cups (12 large) egg whites

1 teaspoon cream of tartar

1¾ cups sugar

1½ teaspoons pure vanilla extract

1¼ teaspoons freshly squeezed lemon
  juice

¾ cup chocolate chips, coarsely
  chopped

Ice cream, sorbet, fresh fruit, or whipped
  cream, optional, for serving

1. Preheat the oven to 350°F. Wash one 10-inch tube pan and dry well to ensure that the batter will climb the walls of the pan.

2. In a large bowl, sift together the espresso powder, cake flour, and salt. Set aside.

3. In the bowl of an electric mixer fitted with the whisk attachment, whip the egg whites on medium speed until frothy. Add the cream of tartar; increase the speed to high and slowly add the sugar in a steady stream. Continue whipping for 5 to 6 minutes, or until the egg whites are stiff and shiny.

4. On low speed, add the vanilla and lemon juice. Add the reserved flour mixture. When the dry ingredients are almost com-pletely incorporated, fold in the chocolate bits by hand. Mix only as much as needed to distribute the chocolate.

5. Scrape the batter into the cake pan. Cut through the batter with a knife to elimi-nate air pockets.

6. Bake for 40 to 45 minutes, or until a toothpick inserted into the center of the cake comes out clean. Invert the pan onto a wire rack and allow the cake to cool com-pletely while upside down.

7. Once the cake is cool, run a knife around the inside edge of the pan and re-

move the cake from the collar. Run a knife between the bottom of the cake and the rest of the pan. Invert onto a large plate or platter. Slice the cake with a serrated knife. At home, serve unadorned or with ice cream, sorbet, fresh fruit, or whipped cream.

❖ Bake Sale Tips

To transport the cake pieces, wrap individual slices in wax or parchment paper and seal with a sticker.

To make two cakes, complete the recipe two separate times.

Emily Luchetti graduated from the New York Restaurant School in 1980, and worked at the Silver Palate and The Manhattan Market. She moved to France, where she cooked for a year, and then settled in San Francisco to work at Stars. For three years, she cooked on the savory side at that restaurant, and then switched to desserts for the next eight years. Now pastry chef at Farallon, Emily is the author of three cookbooks—most recently, A Passion for Desserts*—and also contributed desserts to* The Farallon Cookbook *and* The All New All Purpose Joy of Cooking.

François Payard's
Apricot Cake

I grew up above a pastry shop called Au Nid des Friandises that my grandpa started in 1948. My mother met my father at the bakery, and he eventually took over and opened two bakeries in the south of France. Our family lived on top of the shop, and we ate our meals each day in the shop, so the classic breads and pastries of that region of France were part of my everyday life.

Apricots have to be among the best things southern France offers. They are tart and acidic, and nothing like the tinny apricots in syrup. Even the apricots most often available at the grocery stores here are too sweet and too soft, lacking the firm texture and acidity that is an apricot's unique beauty.

My grandfather had fruit trees surrounding the pool in the back of his house. He also owned two fig trees, five peach trees, and ten cherry trees—including a special one, the griotte cherry, which grows like an inverted umbrella and bears white and red cherries that we would steep in alcohol for an extraordinary dessert treat. But the best were his half-dozen apricot trees. We could go down to the trees before dinner, pick the ripest fruits, and bring them to the house, where my grandmother, waiting to cook dessert, would have a tart crust or charlotte mold lined with strips of bread.

This pound cake is really my dad's staple recipe, although I'm substituting my love of apricots for his love of apples. Every day he bakes fifty or a hundred of these cakes—layers of batter and apples, with apples arranged beautifully on the top—and they are so popular they're gone almost the moment they have cooled. And as wonderful as the apple pound cake can be during the winter months, in the summer months, apricots create an even more glorious cake, since the fruit—which is arranged only in a middle layer—almost melts in the oven. And the plumped raisins match even more beautifully with apricots than with apples.

We don't really have what's called a "pound cake" in France, but this comes close to an American version, though it's lighter, less sweet, and less rich. A true tribute to the apricot.

François Payard's Flourless, Butterless Chocolate Cookies appear on page 41.

Apricot Cake

Makes one 8-inch loaf, serving 8 to 10;
an easy recipe to double

⅓ cup raisins

3 tablespoons dark rum

1 scant cup all-purpose flour

¾ teaspoon baking powder

8 tablespoons (1 stick) unsalted butter,
    softened

1 cup confectioners' sugar

3 large eggs

6 to 8 small fresh apricots, halved and
    pitted

¼ cup apricot jam

1. Preheat the oven to 325°F. Butter an
8½ x 4½-inch loaf pan. Dust with flour and
tap out any excess.

2. Bring a small pan of water to a boil,
add the raisins, boil for 1 minute, then drain.
Repeat the process. In a small bowl, combine the raisins with the rum.

3. In a medium bowl, sift together the
flour and baking powder.

4. In the bowl of an electric mixer fitted
with the paddle attachment, mix the butter
and confectioners' sugar on medium speed
for 2 minutes. Add the eggs one at a time, incorporating each one thoroughly before
adding the next. Scrape the inside of the
bowl. Mix in the rum-soaked raisins. Add
the dry ingredients and mix on low speed
until blended.

5. Spoon half the batter into the prepared pan and smooth it into an even layer.

Arrange as many apricot halves on the surface, cut side down, as will fit snugly.
Smooth the rest of the batter over the fruit.

6. Place the pan on the middle rack of
the oven and bake for 60 to 65 minutes, or
until the top is golden brown and a toothpick inserted into the center of the cake
comes out clean. Cool the cake on a wire
rack for 15 minutes. Unmold the cake and
turn it right side up.

7. Thin the apricot jam in a small
saucepan with 1 to 2 tablespoons water and
warm over low heat, stirring the entire
time. Brush the warm apricot glaze over the
top of the hot cake. Allow it to cool completely before slicing into 1-inch-thick slices.

❖ Bake Sale Tip

Sell the cake as a whole or wrap individual slices in wax paper or clear cellophane and seal with a sticker.

----

*François Payard is a third-generation French
pastry chef. He cultivated his passion for the
art of pastry in his grandfather's renowned
shop, Au Nid des Friandises, on the Riviera.
In Paris, he was pastry chef at La Tour d'Argent and later at Lucas Carton; his dessert
menus helped that restaurant earn a three-star Michelin rating. In 1995, he was named
the Beard Foundation's Pastry Chef of the
Year, and in 1997, he opened his own Payard
Patisserie and Bistro (www.payard.com). His
book,* Simply Sensational Desserts, *won a
James Beard Cookbook Award.*

Roasted Orange Cakes

Orange cakes are something I first made when I was sixteen and anything but an accomplished cook. I found a version of this recipe in a magazine before I embarked on a bicycle trip from Vancouver to San Francisco, the first such excursion I'd ever tried. I started the trip with nine other sixteen-year-olds, all strangers. I was a rebellious girl who could barely ride a bike and had no friends with me. I became the person who would stop and do the shopping, who would carry the cooking equipment (all on my bike), who would figure out what we could cook over an open fire.

Not that I mean to suggest I cooked extravagant meals. We had macaroni, burgers, hot dogs, and, since we were in the Pacific Northwest, a lot of grilled salmon. Anyone who goes camping knows that desserts—other than roasting marshmallows or just slicing a watermelon—are not all that easy. But this recipe is perfect for campfires: You use the orange as a baking cup—the peel buffers the heat while it adds its own orange flavor.

You simply hollow out the oranges (a grapefruit spoon works perfectly), fill them with batter, wrap them in foil, and nestle them among the embers. You want a fire that's burned down so that the coals are warm and evenly glowing. Rotate the foil balls so all sides heat evenly. And in no time (you'll just have to pull one from the fire to see if it's done), you have these orange cupcakes with that lovely smoky scent from the fire.

At Border Grill, we even bake the filled oranges at a high heat and char the skins—we don't use foil—to add that rustic taste. And if a little batter runs over the side, that, too, adds a nice touch. This is a dessert with a little playfulness. Which leads me to wonder, how swell would other citrus fruit be, hollowed out, and baked with a little cake inside? Lemons, tangerines . . . tiny Key lime petits fours?

Try these at your next cookout, and you'll be the hit I became with my fellow cyclists. And if you're camping—or just can't be bothered one day—sure, buy a yellow-cake mix as I did on that biking trip, and use that inside the oranges.

Mary Sue Milliken's Miniature Cranberry-Pecan Loaves appear on page 238.

Roasted Orange Cakes

Makes 8 to 10 "cupcakes";
an easy recipe to double

⅓ **cup golden raisins**

⅓ **cup dark rum**

8 to 10 large navel oranges

1½ **cups cake flour**

⅛ **teaspoon baking soda**

1 **teaspoon baking powder**

½ **teaspoon salt**

8 **tablespoons (1 stick) unsalted butter,**
   softened

1 **cup sugar**

2 **large eggs**

¾ **teaspoon pure vanilla extract**

½ **teaspoon finely grated orange zest**

¾ **cup buttermilk, shaken well**

Premium vanilla ice cream, optional,
   for serving

1. Preheat the oven to 450°F.

2. In a small saucepan, combine the raisins and rum and simmer for 5 minutes, stirring occasionally, until all the rum has been absorbed. Set aside.

3. Cut a very thin slice of peel from the bottom of each orange so that it will stand without rolling (try not to cut through the pith). Cut another slice, ¾ inch thick, from the top of each orange. Scrape out any part of the orange segments that remain inside the tops.

4. With a small steak knife and a grapefruit spoon, hollow out each orange, removing the orange segments (reserving the segments for another use, if desired).

5. In a large bowl, sift together the flour, baking soda, baking powder, and salt.

6. In the bowl of an electric mixer fitted with the paddle attachment, combine the butter and sugar and beat on medium speed for 2 to 3 minutes, until light and fluffy. Add the eggs one at a time, mixing each one

thoroughly before adding the next. Add the vanilla and zest and mix to incorporate. Scrape the inside of the bowl. Alternately add one-third of the flour mixture and half of the buttermilk, stirring briefly after each addition; begin and end with the flour mixture. Fold in the raisins.

7. Fill the orange shells two-thirds full with the batter and place the "lids" on top of each orange. Wrap each orange in a piece of aluminum foil and arrange them on a baking sheet. Place the baking sheet on the middle rack of the oven and bake for 45 to 50 minutes. To check for doneness, unwrap one orange: The cake should be firm and when a toothpick is inserted into the center it should come out clean.

8. Transfer the foil-wrapped oranges to a wire rack and cool for 5 minutes, or until cool enough to unwrap. Set the unwrapped oranges on wire racks for at least 15 minutes. Serve warm or at room temperature. Spoon out bites of the cake and enjoy with vanilla ice cream, if desired.

❖ Bake Sale Tips

Place each baked orange in a white paper muffin liner and arrange them on a platter. You could also place each orange in a small cellophane bag and tie each bag with a green piece of ribbon, tucking a green leaf/label under the ribbon. Or try a black ribbon and offer these as "pumpkins" at Halloween.

Mary Sue Milliken and her business partner of twenty years, Susan Feniger, are two of American's most beloved chefs. They are the chef-owners of the critically acclaimed Border Grill restaurants in Santa Monica, Pasadena, and Las Vegas, as well as Ciudad in downtown Los Angeles. Natural teachers, the partners have created 396 episodes of Too Hot Tamales *and* Tamales World Tour *series with the Food Network, authored five cookbooks, hosted the "Hot Dish" radio feature on radio station KFWB, and launched a line of prepared foods, "Border Girls" brand at Whole Foods Market.*

Sheila Lukins's
Chocolate Tea Cake with Orange Glaze
and
Ginger Banana Bread

y Granny Block from Lithuania was my baking grandmother, and ever since I first tasted those apple and cherry pies she pulled out of the oven I have loved warm, comforting baked treats.

While living in London during the 1970s—my husband was developing a business for a large conglomerate—I came to appreciate teatime with its soothing brew, demure cakes, delicate sandwiches, and, most of all, a relaxing break. Fortnum's was lovely, the Ritz fancy and gorgeous. Some of my favorite tea spots outside London were Angelina in Paris (oh, that hot chocolate!), Emirgen Park in Istanbul, Dorset in England (strawberries, scones, and clotted cream), my friend Irina Esimova's home in St. Petersburg, Russia (crêpes and jam), and Cringletie House Hotel in Scotland. While I was never served a rich slice of a chocolate pound cake, I thought I might create one after traveling through Scotland with my colleague Laurie Griffith doing research for my *All Around the World Cookbook* and sampling a myriad of tea shops. It's excellent served with Earl Grey tea or, at the other end of the spectrum, a small scoop of orange sherbet.

The inspiration for the second tea cake came from Round Hill in Jamaica, where I met Miss Maud, whose luxurious banana bread, with its fresh-baked aroma, wafted out on the porch of her home, beckoning us to breakfast each morning. As soon as I got to my own home, I couldn't resist the addition of molasses, sugar, spice, and everything nice to come up with this teatime treat.

Chocolate Tea Cake with Orange Glaze

Makes one 9-inch loaf, serving 10;
an easy recipe to double

For the bread

8 ounces bittersweet chocolate, chopped

16 tablespoons (2 sticks) unsalted butter, softened

1 cup granulated sugar

4 large eggs

1 teaspoon pure vanilla extract

Zest of 1 orange, finely grated

½ cup sour cream

1½ cups all-purpose flour

1 teaspoon baking powder

Pinch of salt

For the glaze

½ cup confectioners' sugar

2 tablespoons freshly squeezed orange juice

1. Preheat the oven to 350°F. Lightly grease a 9-inch loaf pan. Line the bottom with a piece of parchment paper and grease the paper.

2. In a small saucepan, melt the chocolate over low heat, stirring the entire time until smooth. Let cool.

3. In the bowl of an electric mixer fitted with the paddle attachment, combine the butter and sugar and mix at medium speed for 2 minutes, or until light and fluffy. Add the eggs one at a time, incorporating each one thoroughly before adding the next. Add the vanilla, zest, and sour cream and beat well. Add the cooled chocolate and mix for 30 seconds, or until incorporated. Scrape the inside of the bowl.

4. Sift the flour, baking powder, and salt over the batter and fold into the mixture until just combined.

5. Scrape the batter into the prepared pan and place it on the middle rack of the oven. Bake for 60 to 70 minutes, or until a toothpick inserted into the center comes out clean. Cool the loaf in the pan on a wire rack for 15 minutes. Carefully invert the bread onto the rack and remove the paper. Flip the bread right side up.

6. To make the glaze, combine the confectioners' sugar and the orange juice in a small saucepan. Bring to a boil, stir occasionally for 2 minutes, then remove from the heat. While the loaf is still warm, use a

skewer to poke holes about 1 inch apart along the surface of the bread. Brush with the warm glaze, then allow the bread to cool completely before slicing.

Ginger Banana Bread

Makes one 9-inch loaf, serving 10;
an easy recipe to double

----

2 cups all-purpose flour

1 teaspoon baking powder

½ teaspoon salt

1½ teaspoons ground ginger

1 teaspoon ground cinnamon

½ teaspoon ground allspice

¼ teaspoon ground cloves

¼ teaspoon ground nutmeg

8 tablespoons (1 stick) unsalted butter, softened

½ cup dark brown sugar (packed)

½ cup unsulfered molasses

¼ cup honey

2 large eggs

½ cup sour cream

1 cup mashed ripe bananas (2 large bananas)

1. Preheat the oven to 350°F. Lightly grease a 9-inch loaf pan. Line the bottom with a piece of parchment paper and grease the paper.

2. In a large bowl, sift the flour, baking powder, salt, ginger, cinnamon, allspice, cloves, and nutmeg.

3. In the bowl of an electric mixer fitted with the paddle attachment, mix the butter and sugar on medium speed for 1 to 2 minutes, until creamy. Add the molasses and honey and mix for 1 minute until incorporated. Add the eggs one at a time, incorporating each one thoroughly before adding the next. Add the sour cream and bananas and mix on low speed until smooth. Scrape the sides of the bowl. Add the dry ingredients all at once and mix on low speed just until incorporated.

4. Scrape the batter into the prepared pan and place it on the middle rack of the oven to bake for 55 to 60 minutes, or until a toothpick inserted into the bread's center comes out clean. Cool the loaf in the pan on a wire rack for 15 minutes. Carefully invert the bread onto the rack and remove the paper. Serve completely cooled or slightly warm.

A native of Philadelphia, Sheila Lukins studied the culinary and visual arts both here and abroad. The author of U.S.A. Cookbook, *she is a chef, food writer, and cooking teacher whose contributions to the food world have been celebrated by numerous awards and citations. Her four earlier books, co-authored with Julee Russo, include* The Silver Palate Cookbook *and* The New Basics Cookbook *and have sold more than 6 million copies. In 2003, she released her sixth cookbook,* Celebrate! *Since 1986, she has been food editor at PARADE magazine.*

Warren Errol Brown's
Sassy Pound Cake with Mango Glaze

In Cleveland, where I grew up, Spice Island's herb pepper was about as adventurous as we got in the seasonings department. But when I turned ten, Tequila Junction opened up in a new mall, and although all I ever ordered there was a hamburger—without the guacamole, please (whatever that was)—one visit, I finally tasted what my dad had been ordering, and I was just stunned. Hooked. It was no more adventurous than a burrito, but that spiciness, that prickling sensation, opened a whole new world of flavor exploration for me.

As for sweets, we had three sources. One was my mother's friend Gloria Whitehead and her cakes. She's passed on now, but I will always remember her 7-Up cake, which was amazing not only because it was made from a bottle of soda, but also because I had given up soda for Lent in ninth grade and never went back to drinking it. Yet right in front of my mom, I devoured three—or was it four?—slices.

As for the other two sources, we loved Lax and Mandel's, a bakery in Cleveland where we bought rye bread, challah, chocolate rolls we called "ho-ho rolls," and a marble pound cake dunked in ganache. And we stocked the freezer with apple pies from Howard Johnson's.

My mother prepared dinner pretty much every night until I was in high school. But on weekends, I started to make my own dinners, and once in a while dinner for my folks as well. I think barbecue sauce was the first recipe I ever followed and then began changing. Improvising, tinkering—that suited me—and sauces (I think cake batter is composed like a great sauce) became a way to unwind, particularly once I began law school. And those fortuitous forays into cooking led me, albeit circuitously, through law school to my own bakery, CakeLove, here in Washington, D.C.

For many people a cake with frosting, buttercream, or icing can be too much or too sweet, but a pound cake delivers the same satisfaction in one mouthful: a rich moistness, an appealing density to bite into, and a concentrated flavor. So when I opened CakeLove, I took a basic sour-cream pound cake and dreamed up some original versions: lime, ginger, and molasses cakes; chocolate, almond, and orange cakes; citron cardamom cakes—in addition to LCD cakes, the "least common denominator" versions in vanilla and chocolate.

This Sassy Cake has a range of special components: dried orange peel (which will hold its strength though the baking process) as well as orange oil, mango puree, a combination of liqueurs (rum, Cointreau, tequila, Limoncello—which were probably left over from a party but combine into something more aromatic than the brandy in the original recipe), as well as a vanilla bean and the tartness of sour cream. In the back of my mind, I was imagining a mango margarita.

But instead of salt, I thought cayenne would provide a sweet/heat balance. While the pepper comes through immediately if you taste the batter, once it's baked, the pepper doesn't pronounce itself until you swallow, when it barely warms your throat, adding a little tingle to the lingering orange aroma.

The pepper's heat, capsicum, works in intriguing ways. In one of Harold McGee's cooking-science books, he suggests that it interacts in a chemical and physical way with the tongue. Like a gladiator's mace ball, the capsicum pierces the tongue so the heat can get into the taste buds. Sugar apparently blocks that abrasion. Whether that's folklore or real science, I can't say, but what I do know is that this sassy combination will totally engage your mouth.

Sassy Pound Cake

Makes one 10-inch tube pan,
serving 12 to 14

----

3 cups all-purpose flour

1 teaspoon cornstarch

1 teaspoon salt

¼ teaspoon baking soda

¼ teaspoon cayenne pepper

4½ teaspoons dried orange peel,
    pulverized in a coffee grinder

1 vanilla bean

12 tablespoons (1½ sticks) unsalted
    butter, softened

3 cups sugar

5 large eggs

1 cup sour cream

1 ripe mango, freshly pureed
    (½ cup for the cake, ½ cup reserve
    for the optional glaze)

1 teaspoon pure vanilla extract

1 teaspoon orange oil

1 teaspoon dark rum

2 teaspoons tequila

1 teaspoon Limoncello

2 teaspoons Cointreau (see Note)

1 recipe Mango Glaze, optional

1. Preheat the oven to 350°F. Lightly mist a 10-inch tube pan with nonstick cooking spray and lightly flour the pan. Tap out the excess flour.

2. In a large bowl sift together the flour, cornstarch, salt, and baking soda. Add the cayenne and powdered orange peel and mix well. Set aside.

3. Split open the vanilla bean and scrape free the seeds. Reserve the pod for another use.

4. In the bowl of an electric mixer fitted with the paddle attachment, combine the butter, sugar, and vanilla seeds, and mix for 2 minutes on low speed, or until the butter is light and fluffy. Scrape the inside of the bowl. Add the eggs one at a time, incorporating each one thoroughly before adding the next. Scrape the inside of the bowl.

5. In a small bowl, combine the sour cream, mango puree, vanilla, orange oil, rum, tequila, Limoncello, and Cointreau.

6. Alternately add approximately one-fifth of the sifted dry ingredients and one-fourth of the sour cream mixture to the bowl, blending after each addition; start and end with the dry ingredients. Scrape the inside of the bowl as needed.

7. Increase the speed to medium and beat for 30 to 60 seconds, or until the mixture is smooth.

8. Pour the batter into the prepared pan and smooth the top. Place the pan on the middle rack of the oven and bake for

50 to 55 minutes, or until a toothpick inserted into the center of the cake comes out clean.

9. Transfer the pan to a wire rack and cool for 15 to 20 minutes.

10. Prepare the glaze, if desired.

11. Invert the warm cake onto the wire rack and remove the pan. Place a second wire rack on the bottom of the cake and carefully turn the cake right side up. If glazing, poke a few holes in the top of the cake and brush with the warm glaze.

12. When the cake is completely cooled, transfer it to a plate and wrap in plastic and refrigerate. For the best flavor, bring to room temperature 2 to 3 hours before serving.

❖ Bake Sale Tip

To make two cakes, complete the recipe two separate times.

Note: This pound cake is moistened and flavored with 6 teaspoons of liqueurs and alcohols. Lacking the combination given here, you may use a mixture of brandy and rum. You might also try other orange-flavored liqueurs such as Grand Marnier or Triple Sec.

In November 2000, Warren Errol Brown decided to pursue his passion for baking full time. He left his position as an attorney for the federal government and in March 2002 opened his own bakery in Washington, D.C. CakeLove's specialties are made-from-scratch cakes and sweets, which are also served at his coffeehouse café across the street.

Mango Glaze

Makes 1 cup

½ cup fresh mango puree (½ mango)
¼ cup rum
¼ cup freshly squeezed orange juice
2 tablespoons sugar

Combine the ingredients in a small saucepan and cook over low heat, stirring continuously, for 5 minutes. Strain the glaze.

Black Walnut Pound Cake with a Ginger–Black Pepper Glaze

W hile you can substitute other walnuts, the aroma of black walnuts is unmistakable, especially when enhanced with this fragrant and spicy glaze made from pulverized black peppercorns and fresh ginger. You can find black walnuts at specialty food shops, nut shops, farmer's markets, natural food stores, and gourmet emporiums such as Trader Joe's and Whole Foods Markets.

Jimmy Schmidt's Blueberry Slump, the story behind this black walnut recipe, and his biography begin on page 130.

Black Walnut Pound Cake

Makes one 10-inch cake, serving 15

2½ cups black walnut pieces (1½ cups reserved for glaze)

16 tablespoons (2 sticks) unsalted butter, softened

2 cups light brown sugar (lightly packed)

1 cup granulated sugar

5 large eggs

3½ cups all-purpose flour

1 teaspoon baking powder

Pinch of salt

1 cup whole milk

1 recipe Ginger–Black Pepper Glaze

1. Preheat the oven to 325°F. Lightly mist a 10-inch springform pan with non-stick cooking spray. Line the bottom of the pan with a circle of parchment paper. Butter and flour the parchment and the sides of the pan.

2. Spread the nuts on a baking sheet and toast in the oven for 5 minutes, or until lightly golden brown. Cool completely and coarsely chop the nuts. Set aside 1½ cups for the glaze.

3. In a bowl of an electric mixer fitted with the paddle attachment, cream the butter, brown sugar, and granulated sugar for 2 minutes on medium speed, or until light and fluffy. Add the eggs one at a time, incorporating each one thoroughly before adding the next.

4. In a large bowl, sift the flour, baking powder, and salt. Reduce the speed to low and add the dry ingredients to the mixing bowl, mixing just to combine. Scrape down the inside of the bowl. Slowly add the milk and mix just to combine. Fold in 1 cup of the nuts.

5. Scrape the batter into the prepared pan and smooth the surface of the cake. Place the pan on the middle rack of the oven and bake for 50 to 60 minutes, until a toothpick inserted into the center of the cake comes out clean. Cool the cake in the springform pan on a wire rack for 1 hour before removing the cake. Cool completely, then glaze.

❖ Bake Sale Tip

To make two cakes, complete the recipe two separate times.

Ginger–Black Pepper Glaze

Makes about 3 cups, enough for 1 cake

1 tablespoon whole black
   peppercorns
1 cup light brown sugar (lightly
   packed)
½ cup finely julienned fresh ginger
   (from one 5- to 6-inch piece)
16 tablespoons (2 sticks) unsalted
   butter
1 cup confectioners' sugar
Reserved 1½ cups toasted black
   walnut pieces, chopped to
   pea-size bits

1. In a small sauté pan over medium heat, toast the peppercorns for 3 to 4 minutes, or until they just begin to smoke.

Remove from the heat. Cool and coarsely grind them. Measure and set aside 2 teaspoons; or if a more pronounced pepper taste is desired, increase the amount, to taste.

2. In a medium sauté pan, combine the sugar, ¾ cup water, and the ginger. Simmer over medium heat for 15 minutes, or until the ginger is tender. Increase the heat to medium-high, add the butter, and cook for 4 to 5 minutes, stirring often. Remove the pan from the heat and add the ground black pepper and confectioners' sugar, mixing thoroughly. Swirl in the walnuts. Let the glaze cool for 5 minutes.

3. Spoon the glaze over the cake, coating the top and drizzling some down the edges. Allow the glaze to harden for at least 2 hours before serving.

Mary Sue Milliken's
Miniature Cranberry-Pecan Loaves

◆ ◈ ◆

Every year my son Declan and I have a tradition of making holiday loaves with this easy-to-prepare batter. While it can be baked into large loaves for a family brunch, the mini loaves are just right for giving to all your kids' teachers before winter break. Wrapped in crisp cellophane and tied with string and a tag, these loaves have become a familiar seasonal treat at our house. And now, since my youngest son, Kieran, has just started kindergarten, we need to make even more loaves.

This really is a recipe to do with kids. You can leave your mixer and your food processor in the cupboard. All you need is a pair of mixing bowls and a little old-fashioned stirring—and a short list of people who are sure to be delighted by a gift of genuine artisanal baking!

Mary Sue Milliken's Roasted Orange Cakes and
her biography begin on page 227.

Miniature Cranberry-Pecan Loaves

Makes 1 loaf or 3 miniature loaves,
serving 10; an easy recipe to double

8 tablespoons (1 stick) unsalted butter, softened

¾ cup dark brown sugar (packed)

1 teaspoon pure vanilla extract

¾ teaspoon salt

1 teaspoon ground cinnamon

¼ teaspoon ground nutmeg

2 extra-large eggs

1 generous tablespoon frozen orange juice concentrate, optional

½ cup all-purpose flour

½ cup cornmeal

1½ teaspoons baking powder

1 teaspoon baking soda

One 12-ounce package fresh cranberries
(3 generous cups)
1 cup pecans, toasted and chopped

1. Preheat the oven to 350°F. Butter a 9-inch loaf pan or 3 small loaf pans.

2. In a large bowl, cream together the butter and brown sugar until smooth. Add the vanilla, salt, cinnamon, nutmeg, eggs, and orange juice concentrate, if using, and beat to combine.

3. In another bowl, stir together the flour, cornmeal, baking powder, and baking soda. Add this to the creamed butter mixture and gently beat with a spoon just until the flour disappears. Fold in the cranberries and pecans.

4. Pour the batter into the prepared pan(s) and bake for 50 to 60 minutes for the large loaf, or 30 to 35 minutes for the small loaves. The bread is done when a toothpick inserted into the center of the loaf comes out clean. Cool in the pan for 30 minutes. Turn out onto a wire rack to cool completely before wrapping.

Susan Purdy's
Chocolate Chip Streusel Bundt Cake

In my family, the jewels we pass from one generation to the next are much more valuable than those you might wear on a finger. They are more likely to be something you would stick your finger into—a bowl of chocolate cake batter, say, or a sugar cookie dough. Our family gems are recipes, passed down and precious, which evoke taste memories: the vanilla and cinnamon scent of a favorite aunt's kitchen, the yeasty perfume of challah baking in my mother's house on Friday afternoons.

In my cookbooks, I have tried to collect and preserve these recipes, and I especially enjoy sharing them with my own daughter, Cassandra, now a baker, chef, and caterer. In addition to cooking together (she learned to mix up shortbread before she could read), we both like to search for new recipes. Our quest often leads us to country auctions where we hunt for long-forgotten recipes usually tucked away in the barn or attic.

Not long ago, a summertime neighbor's homestead and farm was auctioned in northern Vermont. Gladys, the owner, had passed away and after her many children and grandchildren had gone through things, a tent-full of avid collectors gathered one hot July morning, eagerly hoping to pick up an antique chest, a china teapot, a hand-stitched quilt, even a well-used and muddy tractor.

My husband staked out a spot in the tent's shade while Cassandra and I had a quick look around. Behind the haying equipment and beneath the darting swallows lay a jumble of overflowing, unsorted boxes, stuff apparently deemed lacking in crowd appeal. In just a few minutes, we struck gold. Beside some rakes and shovels slumped a broken cardboard carton packed with 1940s *Good Housekeeping* magazines, yellowing scraps of newspaper-clipped recipes, and the real prize: a pink metal file box of handwritten recipe cards. The Family Favorites.

With feigned nonchalance, we scooped up the box and carried it to the auctioneer's tent. As always, we had second thoughts: Were we depriving family members of their heritage? We saw one of Gladys's nephews at the edge of the crowd and walked over to chat. Had the relatives really taken all they wanted? "Sure," he said, "we've been through everything ages ago, only the junk was left." Still hesitant, we waited through the stifling afternoon until nearly all the furnishings and most of the crowd had gone. As the sun was setting, our broken carton reached the podium. The auctioneer gathered it in his arms, papers spilling over. "Who'll give me five bucks?" My heart pounding, I raised my bidding paddle, and heard "Sold!" as he nodded at me. Five dollars for a lifetime in the kitchen.

Back home, Cassandra and I studied and sorted our treasure. The well-worn recipe for Best Sour Cream Coffee Cake—a faded blue ink on a pink card—was butter-smudged and curling; the word "excellent" had been penciled at the top. Our first kitchen test was the variation called "chocolate-chip-crumb," and it was a serious success. We made it once more, just to be sure it was as wonderful as we first thought. Rich, moist, ribboned throughout with chocolaty, nutty crumbs, the texture reminded me of the coffee cakes of my childhood. I couldn't wait to make it for my mother.

A couple of weeks later, Cassandra and I baked it again and brought it to her. As we sat together tasting the cake and drinking tea, my mother began to smile. "Go find my recipe box," she said, referring to the unruly shoe box that housed a roundup of vaguely filed items she rarely consulted. Without hesitation, she opened the box and pulled out a card: "Grandma's Chocolate Chip Streusel Coffee Cake." "Don't you remember this one?" she asked. And there it was, nearly identical!

We thought we were saving another family's heirloom recipe only to discover it was already our own.

Susan and Cassandra Purdy's Apricot Crumb Bars appear on page 42.

Chocolate Chip Streusel Bundt Cake

Makes one 10-inch bundt cake, serving 14 to 16

For the cake

1 to 2 teaspoons solid vegetable shortening, for greasing the pan

3 cups sifted all-purpose flour, plus extra for dusting the pan

1½ teaspoons baking powder

¾ teaspoon baking soda

1 teaspoon salt

12 tablespoons (1½ sticks) unsalted butter, softened

1½ cups sugar

4 large eggs, at room temperature

1¾ cups sour cream

3 tablespoons vegetable oil

2 teaspoons pure vanilla extract

1 cup (6 ounces) mini semisweet chocolate chips

For the filling/topping

½ cup sugar

1 teaspoon ground cinnamon

2 teaspoons Dutch-process cocoa
powder

½ cup finely chopped walnuts
or pecans

½ cup (3 ounces) mini semisweet
chocolate chips

1. Preheat the oven to 350°F. Generously coat the inside of one 10-inch Bundt pan with the shortening, taking care to coat all the pan's indentations. Dust the pan with flour, then tap out the excess.

2. For the cake, in a large bowl, whisk together the flour, baking powder, baking soda, and salt.

3. In the bowl of an electric mixer fitted with the paddle attachment, combine the butter and sugar and mix on medium speed for 2 minutes, or until the mixture looks creamy and pale. Add the eggs one at a time, incorporating each one thoroughly before adding the next. In a small bowl, combine the sour cream, oil, and vanilla, and add this to the batter. Mix on medium speed for 1 minute, or until incorporated. Scrape the inside of the bowl and mix for an additional 20 seconds. On the lowest speed, gradually add the flour mixture, beating just until incorporated and the batter looks creamy; do not overwork the batter. Fold in the chocolate chips by hand.

4. In a small bowl, mix together all of the ingredients for the filling/topping.

5. Sprinkle ½ cup of this mixture into the bottom of the prepared pan. Spoon half of the batter onto these crumbs. Then sprinkle on another ½ cup of crumbs. Cover with the remaining batter, and then top with the remaining crumb mixture.

6. Place the pan on the middle rack of the oven and bake for 50 to 55 minutes. The finished cake should be springy to the touch and a toothpick inserted into the center of the cake should come out clean.

7. Transfer the cake to a wire rack and cool for 20 to 30 minutes. Run the tip of a knife around the edge of the pan. Top the cake with a cardboard disk or flat plate and invert, lifting free the pan. Serve the cake sliced, at room temperature. Leftover portions, sealed in plastic wrap, will keep for a week or can be frozen for up to 2 months.

❖ Bake Sale Tip

To make two cakes, complete the recipe two separate times.

Susan Purdy is a Connecticut-based food journalist and cookbook author. She has written more than twenty-eight books, including Have Your Cake and Eat It, Too, *winner of the IACP/Julia Child Cookbook Award,* The Perfect Pie, *and* The Perfect Cake.

Rhubarb Sour Cream Coffee Cake

M y love of rhubarb is rooted in childhood, in Portland, in my Nana's kitchen, in the month of December, when we visited each year at Christmas. My mother's mother had a house unlike anyone else's I knew, built in the west hills overlooking Portland and the mountains. She called her backyard "the lower forty"—just as a joke, but it was a wonderful place, with a garden filled with all sorts of things, including rhubarb, which I had never seen growing or tasted anywhere else. Nana would pick her rhubarb in June, freeze it, and make us rhubarb pies for Christmas.

Nana also made gifts of her coffee cake at Christmas. It was a yeasted cake, rather like cinnamon rolls, that everyone counted on. When my brother lived in Africa for seven years, my mother even sent him cakes every Christmas he couldn't join us.

Nana was an early bird. She was up while it was still dark, doing a crossword puzzle by the light of her desk lamp in her entirely pink kitchen: the stove, the oven, the phone, her rocking chair, and even the rose-colored light from the alabaster shade. The guest room where I slept had a back stairwell to the kitchen, and I felt so excited just being there—so excited it was Christmas—that sometimes I'd be up even earlier than Nana and would wait for the light that signaled that she was up making coffee and hot cocoa. Then I'd shuffle down the stairs in my jammies with the little feet, climb in her lap, and watch her write big letters in the little boxes. We'd sip our hot drinks, and this would be our special time together.

Nana died in 1984, when I was fourteen. We cleared out and sold her house, and each of her children and grandchildren received a few things to remind us of her. I have some furniture, linens, and photographs, and on my bedside table, I have the lamp in whose pink light she worked her crossword puzzles. But now that I live Portland, of all the things she owned, what I really would have loved is one of her old rhubarb plants to grow forever in my own "lower forty."

Mandy Groom Givler's Earl Grey Truffles appear on page 78.

Rhubarb Sour Cream Coffee Cake

Makes one 9 x 13-inch cake, serving 12

For the nut filling

⅔ cup chopped pecans or walnuts

⅓ cup sugar

2 teaspoons ground cinnamon

½ teaspoon freshly grated nutmeg

For the rhubarb filling

1½ cups (6 to 8 ounces) sliced rhubarb, cut in ½-inch pieces

⅓ cup sugar

¼ cup all-purpose flour

For the cake

16 tablespoons (2 sticks) unsalted butter, softened

2 cups sugar

1 teaspoon pure vanilla extract

2 large eggs

1 cup sour cream

2 cups all-purpose flour

1 teaspoon baking powder

½ teaspoon salt

1. Preheat the oven to 325°F. Lightly grease the bottom and sides of a 9 x 13-inch baking pan.

2. In a small bowl, combine the ingredients for the nut filling.

3. In another small bowl, toss together the ingredients for the rhubarb filling.

4. For the cake, in the bowl of an electric mixer fitted with a paddle attachment, combine the butter, sugar, and vanilla and mix on medium speed for 2 minutes, or until light and fluffy. Add the eggs one at a time, incorporating each one thoroughly before

adding the next. On low speed, add the sour cream and mix for 30 seconds, or until the batter is smooth. Scrape the inside of the bowl.

5. In a large bowl, combine the flour, baking powder, and salt; add this to the batter, mixing just until incorporated.

6. Spread half of the batter in an even layer across the bottom of the prepared pan. Top with the rhubarb filling and half of the nut filling. Cover with the remaining batter, and then sprinkle with the remaining nut mixture.

7. Bake for 50 to 60 minutes, or until a toothpick inserted into the center of the cake comes out clean. Transfer the pan to a wire rack and cool completely before slicing.

❖ Bake Sale Tip

To make two coffee cakes, complete the recipe two separate times.

Mandy Groom Givler has enjoyed a thirteen-year career in the food industry as a pastry chef, teacher, and consultant. She was the executive pastry chef at Zefiro and Bluehour, two nationally acclaimed Portland restaurants. She has appeared in Food Arts, Gourmet, *and* Better Homes & Gardens, *and one of her desserts was featured on the cover of* Northwest Palate *magazine's fifteenth anniversary issue. She currently owns her own specialty dessert business called "cake" and contributes her time to the Oregon Food Bank and Share Our Strength. She lives in Portland with her husband, Michael.*

Scones, Rolls, Doughnuts, and Breads

Jerome Audureau's Pistachio and Fig Scones

Nancy Silverton's Raspberry Walnut Scones

Christine McCabe Tentori's Irish Soda Bread and
Fritelle di San Giuseppe (Saint Joseph's Day Fritelle)

Biba Caggiano's Sweet Pastry Turnovers and
Sfrappole (Fried Sweet Pastry Ribbons)

Suzanne Dunaway's Cranberry Pistachio Panettone and
Panettone Bread Pudding

Amy Scherber's Decadent Chocolate Cherry Rolls
and Soft Chocolate Twists

Carole and Norma Jean Darden's Monkey Bread and
Sweet Potato Biscuits

Michael Schlow's Great Bay's Great Cinnamon Rolls

Jerome Audureau's
Pistachio and Fig Scones

◇◆◇

My father's side of the family is from Algeria, where pistachios and almonds are among the North African delicacies. I was born when they moved back to southern France, but my mother, who is from northern France, took her passion for cooking and continued to make several African dishes at home as well. She loved her tagine, that distinctly shaped, two-part cooking vessel with a flat bowl and a lid that draws up into a tall funnel. While she simmered many kinds of meats and vegetables in the tagine, the dish I remember best is her tagine with lamb, green olives, and pistachios. Our kitchen was filled with jars of spices and nuts from Africa as well as the traditional pantry items of a Provençal home.

My mother didn't bake as much as did our nanny, Zoubida, who came with our family from Algeria to Provence, and lived with my parents for more than thirty years. Zoubida often created Arabic or Algerian desserts that featured pistachios. So growing up in France, we ate ethnic foods and local foods in the same week, from the same kitchen, with a changing houseful of siblings, guests, and neighbors who were always stopping by—that open-door, standing-invitation way of life was something else my parents brought back with them from North African culture.

The other source of this recipe was a tea shop near our house in Avignon and the two Englishwomen who made scones there. I had never had these anywhere else until I began to visit England. While I love the subtle sweetness of a scone, I've always found scones to be a bit dry. I suppose that's why clotted cream and tea are served alongside them. So when I set about making scones at

Once Upon a Tart, I wanted something more moist, something between a crumpet and a scone. The secret is simple: You must not overwork the dough. Once you have that crumble of butter and flour, you add the liquid and mix it only enough just to combine the ingredients. Lumps are fine. The dough should be sticky. It's messy. But then you plop each bit onto a baking sheet and it will rise and crisp up, and the lightness and richness will remain. In England, I'm afraid they roll out the dough and then cut out the scones, which toughens and dries them out.

Here, then, by way of Zoubida, the two British ladies at the tea shop, and my own Provençal love of ripe summer fruits, is a pistachio and fig scone that adds just enough crunch and sweetness to this teatime classic.

Jerome Audureau's Plum Crumble Tart and his biography begin on page 137.

Pistachio and Fig Scones

Makes 10 scones

⅔ cup pistachios or almonds

4 cups all-purpose flour

1 tablespoon baking powder

1 teaspoon baking soda

½ teaspoon salt

⅔ cup sugar

20 tablespoons (2½ sticks) unsalted
    butter, cold

2 large eggs

1 cup buttermilk

1 tablespoon pure vanilla extract

6 to 7 ounces dried figs, cut into ¼-inch
    pieces (about 1 cup)

1. Preheat the oven to 400°F.

2. Place the pistachios or almonds on a baking sheet and toast them for 5 to 7 minutes, until they are lightly brown and aromatic. (Watch carefully: the nuts' oils can make the nuts brown quickly.) Cool completely and chop.

3. Line two baking sheets with parchment paper.

4. In a food processor, combine the flour, baking powder, baking soda, salt, sugar, and butter. Pulse 15 to 20 times, or until no chunks of butter remain and the mixture resembles moist crumbs. Do not overmix. Empty the mixture into a large bowl.

5. In a separate bowl, combine the eggs, buttermilk, and vanilla and whisk to combine. Add the nuts and figs and mix to com-

bine. Pour this liquid mixture into the flour-butter mixture and stir with a wooden spoon just until combined; stop as soon as the flour appears to be incorporated.

6. Using a ½-cup scoop or measuring cup, drop the batter onto the prepared sheets, leaving 2 inches between each scone.

7. Place the sheets on the middle and upper-middle racks of the oven and bake for 25 to 30 minutes, switching the pans between the two racks, and rotating each from front to back, halfway through the baking process. When done, the scones should be a light golden brown on the edges and tops.

8. Transfer the scones to a wire rack to cool. They are best served the same day.

❖ Bake Sale Tip

To make twice as many scones, complete the recipe two separate times.

Nancy Silverton's
Raspberry Walnut Scones

When I thought about what I'd make for a typical American bake sale, I knew I wanted something particularly homey. Thumbprint cookies came to mind—I think every culture has a version, whether they're known as jam cookies, thimble cookies, Hussar balls, or what the French know as "pits of love." I remembered them from Girl Scouts and elementary school fundraisers. With three children, there was always some fundraiser or classroom occasion for baking, and nothing is more kid-appealing than pressing a thumb in a mound of cookie dough.

For the first four years that my husband Mark and I ran Campanile, we lived above the restaurant. I would have lived there permanently, but the kids wanted a backyard and they thought it was kooky to live above a restaurant. Although having two chefs as parents didn't often allow us to gather around the dinner table, each of our kids did acquire a somewhat unique perspective on making food, dining, and baking. For instance, one year, my son Oliver was obsessed with cooking. He would say, "I have to do my recipe." And that would typically involve completely bizarre things, which he would never end up eating. (They were truly awful.) But now we have a huge book of his "recipes," alongside cookbooks that Mark and I have written.

I'm less inclined than Oliver to throw together wild combinations looking for tastes that might be complementary or surprising. Nor do I like to come up with scientific approaches to food just to mix things up. My cooking is about what I've had before and what I've loved. It comes from the heart.

But the baker in me does love inventing textures. Whether in a savory or a sweet item, I like exploring the food's softness, crispness, moisture, sponginess, toothsome qualities. So this walnut scone recipe is the result of taking the familiar scone and giving it a slightly new feel. It has all the integrity and appeal of a breakfast or teatime scone, but it's modeled on that thumbprint cookie I wanted for this bake sale. What I especially like is how the jam is baked right onto the scone—which is rather like making a "complete scone," with no need to get out the jars of jam.

The problem to solve was how to add the raspberry jam: I didn't want it running off as soon as the scone began to rise in the oven. And I really wanted the raspberry jam to get sticky and concentrated as it baked—even a little burned at the edges to add that caramelized flavor I like.

I discovered that a flatter scone and the indentation of the "thumbprint" made an ideal pocket for the jam. Then I found that browned butter could add a unique flavor, while cornmeal could match and counter the jam's sweetness. Although you might find that folks at your bake sale will wonder what to call these thumbprinted, jam-topped scones, they certainly won't hesitate to eat one.

Raspberry Walnut Scones

Makes 14 scones

---

10 tablespoons (1¼ sticks) unsalted butter

1 vanilla bean

1 cup walnuts

2½ cups pastry flour (you may substitute 1 cup cake flour plus 1½ cups all-purpose flour)

¼ cup plus 3 tablespoons sugar, plus extra for sprinkling

¼ cup cornmeal

2 tablespoons baking powder

¾ teaspoon kosher salt

4 extra-large eggs, hard boiled, yolks only (reserve whites for another use)

¾ cup plus 3 tablespoons heavy cream, plus extra for glazing

½ cup raspberry jam

1. In a medium saucepan, melt the butter over medium-high heat. Split open the vanilla bean, scrape free the seeds, and add both to the butter. Swirl the pan to ensure even cooking. Continue cooking for 3 to 5 more minutes, until the liquid is dark brown with a nutty, toasty aroma. Transfer to a bowl, remove the vanilla pod, and chill the butter until firm, about 1 hour.

2. Preheat the oven to 325°F. Place the walnuts on a baking sheet and toast in the oven for 8 to 10 minutes, until they are light golden brown and have a nutty aroma. Cool completely.

3. Increase the oven temperature to 400°F. Line two baking sheets with parchment paper.

4. In a food processor, combine the flour, sugar, cornmeal, baking powder, and salt. Pulse to incorporate. Push the egg yolks through a fine-mesh sieve, scraping the yolks off the bottom of the sieve and into the flour mixture. Pulse a few times to combine. Cut the chilled browned butter into ½-inch cubes. Add the butter cubes and ¾ cup of the walnuts to the egg mixture and pulse several times until the mixture is the consistency of a fine meal.

5. Transfer the mixture to a bowl, make a well in the center, and pour in the cream. Using one hand, gently draw in the dry ingredients, mixing until just combined.

6. Turn out the dough onto a lightly floured surface and gently knead a few times to gather it into a ball. Roll or pat the dough to a thickness of ¾ inch. Using a 2½-inch fluted cutter, cut out 12 scones; cut the circles as close together as possible. Pinch the remaining dough scraps together, flatten the surface with your hand, and cut out 2 or 3 additional scones. Place them 1 inch apart on the prepared pan.

7. Using the back of a teaspoon or your thumb, form a depression 1¼ inch in diameter and halfway through the center of each scone. Evenly distribute the raspberry jam among the depressions. Brush the tops of the scones (not the jam) with heavy cream and sprinkle lightly with sugar. Grate

the remaining ¼ cup of toasted walnuts (use a Mouli grater or chop the nuts very finely) and sprinkle over the tops of the scones (not the jam).

8. Bake for 17 to 22 minutes, until slightly firm to the touch and lightly browned. Transfer the scones to a wire rack to cool slightly before serving.

❖ Bake Sale Tip

To make twice as many scones, complete the recipe two separate times.

Nancy Silverton is pastry chef and co-owner of Campanile restaurant and owner and baker of La Brea Bakery, both in Los Angeles. Among Nancy's books are Desserts, Nancy Silverton's Breads from the La Brea Bakery, *and three co-authored with her husband, including* Mark Peel & Nancy Silverton at Home *and* The Food of Campanile. *Her food, restaurant, bakery, and cookbooks have received a multitude of distinctions and awards over the past sixteen years.*

Christine McCabe Tentori's

Irish Soda Bread

and

Fritelle di San Giuseppe

(Saint Joseph's Day Fritelle)

I grew up in an Irish Catholic neighborhood in Chicago where Saint Patrick's Day is the most special day of the year. We would wake up, head to Saint Ita's at eight or nine, and walk downstairs to the basement where everyone in the church would have brought in their version of Irish soda bread to sell. The church would have set up fifteen or twenty tables, and they'd be crowded with nothing but soda breads—sold by the loaf, half loaf, or the slice—and maybe, maybe, a plate of chocolate chip cookies, if you were lucky. There's a long tradition of selling Irish soda bread at a bake sale. In Ireland, this bread was considered a luxury at one time: Raisins were a real treat. And butter—or any dairy—was a richness you couldn't afford every day. This bread was a celebration.

So our whole community would stand around in the basement, eating the bread, buttering slices, drinking hot tea, waiting in our Irish sweaters and tartan plaids for the parade to start.

Finally, we'd assemble for the march through our neighborhood. We'd all have brought our bicycles, strollers, and dogs. All the families with their six or ten children would march together. There was our church's dozen-member bagpipe band with drums and horns. People would dance. We would sing chorus after chorus of "When Irish Eyes Are Smiling." And though it seemed like a long parade, it only took as long as a walk around twelve blocks.

Then the church would host the evening dinner of corned beef and cabbage and beer, with an Irish band so there could be more singing and lots more dancing. (All we kids at Saint Ita's, where we also attended grammar school, took Irish dancing classes.)

As I got older and our congregation got larger, we'd have our parade, and then join the big Saint Patrick's Day parade in downtown Chicago. We'd hire a bus so that everyone, even the older members of the church, could march along with us.

Eventually, I left Chicago and wanted to start making my own Irish soda bread on Saint Patrick's Day. Though there must be a thousand recipes for this bread, most of them are pretty awful. My mother's was as bad as the rest, though I remember Mrs. Gogarty's as the best at Saint Ita's, since hers was moist and had the most raisins. But soda bread can be bland and, especially if it isn't eaten right away, a bit dry because of the baking soda.

But this version is a recipe my mother discovered more recently. Instead of having only white flour, it has some whole wheat flour to give it character, and a good amount of caraway and raisins. Now even my friends who aren't Irish have been asking for the recipe. Share this version at your next bake sale and you'll see some smiling eyes.

Irish Soda Bread

Makes 1 loaf, serving 10 to 12

----

2 cups all-purpose flour, plus extra for
    shaping the dough

1 cup whole wheat flour

½ cup sugar

2 tablespoons baking soda

1 teaspoon salt

4 tablespoons (½ stick) unsalted butter,
    cold, cut into bits

1 cup raisins

2 teaspoons caraway seeds

1½ cups buttermilk

Whole milk, for the glaze

1. Preheat the oven to 350°F. Line a baking sheet with parchment paper.

2. In the bowl of an electric mixer fitted with the paddle attachment, or in a medium bowl, whisk together the all-purpose flour, whole wheat flour, sugar, baking soda, and salt. If using an electric mixer, add the butter and mix on low for 1 minute, or until the mixture resembles coarse meal. If mixing by hand, cut in the butter with two forks or a pastry blender until the mixture resembles coarse meal.

3. Mix the raisins and caraway seeds into the flour mixture. Add the buttermilk and mix until the dry ingredients are moistened; do not overmix.

4. Turn out the dough onto a lightly floured work surface and knead for 1 minute. Shape the dough into a disk and transfer it to the center of the prepared pan. Cut a large, ¾-inch-deep X on the top of the loaf, then brush the entire loaf with milk.

5. Bake for 50 to 60 minutes. The loaf should be golden brown on the bottom, and sound hollow when tapped. Transfer the loaf to a wire rack to cool.

❖ Bake Sale Tips

Wrap the loaf in clear cellophane and tie with a colorful piece of ribbon. Label with a sticker. The loaf can also be cut and sold in wedges.

To make two loaves, complete the recipe two separate times.

Fritelle di San Giuseppe

(Saint Joseph's Day Fritelle)

Makes 24 small pastries;
an easy recipe to double

Since Saint Patrick's Day is such a big deal at my house, two days later I do something extra special for Giuseppe, my husband, who is named after Saint Joseph. Giuseppe was born outside of Milan in Lodi, where Saint Joseph's Day is as big a holiday as Saint Patrick's Day is in Chicago. So on March 19, his name day, everyone sends him cards, and phones to wish him *"buono ono mastico"* and good luck. On this day I make him Fritelle di San Giuseppe for breakfast along with the essential cappuccino for dunking or chasing these small one- or two-bite treats.

I fell in love with this recipe while working in Italy, cooking in various regions to extend my knowledge of Italian pastries. At Rampina Antica Osteria, outside of Milan, I first sampled this fritter. This recipe is specific to the Lombardia region, although variations on the crispy dough can be found throughout Italy with different shapes, sizes, and fillings.

The pastry cream filling, which is optional, makes the *fritelle* a bit more substantial: Otherwise, a dusting of powdered sugar is all you need. Think of them as little filled donut holes. Try them for breakfast or for dessert or, if you are like my husband, eat them any time, day or night. And, of course, they pack up easily for a bake sale.

4 to 6 cups vegetable oil, for frying
1½ cups all-purpose flour
2 teaspoons baking powder
¼ teaspoon ground cinnamon
Pinch of salt
2 large eggs
¼ cup sugar
½ cup ricotta
½ cup whole milk
1 cup confectioners' sugar, for dusting
1 recipe Vanilla Pastry Cream, optional

1. Clip a candy thermometer to the inside of a 3- or 4-quart pot. Add the oil and heat it until the temperature reads 355°F.

2. While the oil is heating, whisk together the flour, baking powder, cinnamon, and salt in a large bowl; set aside.

3. In a medium bowl, whisk together the eggs and sugar until the mixture is pale yellow. Add the ricotta to the egg mixture and mix thoroughly. Alternately add one-fourth of the flour mixture and one-third of the milk, incorporating each portion before adding the next; begin and end with the flour mixture.

4. Place the confectioners' sugar in a shallow plate.

5. Gently drop 5 or 6 tablespoon-size balls of batter into the hot oil (do not over-crowd the pot) and fry for 2 to 3 minutes, turning the balls halfway through the cooking process. The fritelle should be golden brown.

6. Remove the fritelle from the oil and transfer them to a wire rack with a pan placed underneath. (Alternatively, you may use a pan lined with paper towels.) When cool enough to handle, roll the fritelle in the confectioners' sugar.

7. Once the oil returns to 355°F, repeat the process with the remaining batter.

8. If you wish to fill the fritelle with cream, allow them to cool slightly and poke a little hole in each ball. Place the pastry cream in a pastry bag fitted with a ⅛-inch plain pastry tip and squeeze some cream into each fritter. Roll the filled fritelle in the confectioners' sugar.

Christine McCabe Tentori has trained in the alchemy and artistry of dessert with the most formidable names in the industry, including Joël Robuchon and Charlie Trotter. Christine reigns as the Diva of Decadence at Sugar|a dessert bar, the nation's first establishment devoted to after-dinner indulgences. Her craft has received plaudits from the New York Times, Food & Wine, *and* Bon Appétit.

Vanilla Pastry Cream

Makes 1¼ cups

¼ cup sugar
2 tablespoons cornstarch
½ cup half-and-half
½ cup heavy cream
¾ teaspoon pure vanilla extract
1 large egg yolk

1. In a medium heavy-bottomed non-reactive pot, combine all the ingredients except for the egg yolk and vanilla, and cook over medium heat for 5 minutes, whisking continuously.

2. Reduce the heat to low. In a small bowl, whisk the egg yolk. Add ½ cup of the warm cream mixture and whisk to blend. Return the egg mixture to the pot and cook for 2 minutes, stirring constantly. Remove the pot from the heat and add the vanilla.

3. Place a sieve on the rim of a medium bowl and pour the cream into the bowl. Place a piece of plastic wrap directly on the surface of the cream and refrigerate for several hours, until set. The pastry cream can be prepared 1 day in advance.

❖ Bake Sale Tips

The fritelle, like doughnuts, beignets, and other quickly fried pastries, are at their very best when eaten warm, so these could be made on location, in a cafeteria or other venue where the oil can be heated. Package each fritelle in a napkin-lined disposable cup.

Sweet Pastry Turnovers

and

Sfrappole

(Fried Sweet Pastry Ribbons)

Every time I go to Bologna, my native city, I pay a visit to Rodrigo, one of the oldest and best restaurants of the city. During one of my last visits, Giuseppe, a waiter who had been working at the restaurant for over twenty-five years, said to me, "Biba, at the end of the meal I have a surprise for you." Later, Giuseppe arrived with a platter piled high with golden, crisp *raviole*, Bologna's tender pastry turnovers, blanketed with powdered sugar. A rush of warm, happy memories engulfed me: I was a child again, watching my mother work the sweet pastry dough with her favorite long rolling pin, stretching it with secure, steady strokes until the sheet was very thin. Then she would take a wine glass to cut circles from the sheet. She would fill each circle with whatever sweet filling she had prepared according to the season and what she had on hand: chestnuts, creamy ricotta, plump raisins, pears, apples, squash, and a thickening of her homemade plum jam.

In summer, when the fruits are too wet to use in this type of filling, her raviole were filled with crushed amaretti, raisins, ricotta, and jam.

She would seal the dough and shape them into chubby raviole, and later, depending on her mood, she would bake or fry them. Even when money was very tight and she could not splurge on expensive ingredients, she would fill the raviole with just a bit of ricotta and sugar.

Nowadays we think of all that inventiveness, all that variety, as "authentic regional specialties." But these sweet turnovers were a form of improvising, made from what could be bought that day at the central food market with the little money we had. Food wasn't just about filling bellies; it was about bringing people to the table for some time together.

This turnover was a standard in the homes of most families in the Emilia-Romagna region, in the cities of Bologna, Modena, and Parma and in the countryside—and each place claimed to prepare the very best raviole. In our home, the turnovers were prepared ritually at Christmas and on other festive occasions because they would keep well for several days and could be offered to unexpected guests. They were also the treat that waited for my sister, my brother, and me after returning from school.

Needless to say, I followed in my mother's footsteps and often prepared this treat for my daughters, Carla and Paola, when they came home from school with friends in tow. And now that I am a grandmother, there are always platters of golden, crisp raviole for my children and grandchild at the holidays.

Sweet Pastry Turnovers

Makes 30 to 34 turnovers;
an easy recipe to double

¾ cup sour cherry or plum preserves
¾ cup finely minced vacuum-packed or
    canned chestnuts

½ cup whole milk ricotta
1 recipe Sweet Pastry Dough
1 large egg
Confectioners' sugar, for dusting

1. In a medium bowl, combine the preserves, chestnuts, and ricotta and blend thoroughly. Refrigerate.
2. Preheat the oven to 350°F and line two baking sheets with parchment paper.

3. Place the filling in a pastry bag fitted with a ¼-inch plain pastry tip.

4. Place 1 piece of the dough on a lightly floured work surface and flatten it with your hands. Lightly flour the dough and roll it out to a thickness of ⅛ inch. Cut out 4-inch circles from the dough. Repeat the process with the other piece of dough. (Gather the leftover pastry scraps, knead them together, and refrigerate for at least 30 minutes. Roll out this dough to make more turnovers or to form into strips as instructed in the following Sweet Pastry Ribbons recipe.)

5. Place the circles on a work surface and pipe dollops (about 2 teaspoons) of the filling into the center of each circle. Fold each circle in half, covering the filling, and press the edges together firmly to seal the pastries. Alternatively, you may seal the edges with the tines of a fork.

6. Transfer the turnovers to the prepared pan. Lightly beat the egg to create a wash and brush this on the turnovers.

7. Place the cookie sheet on the middle rack of the oven and bake for 15 to 20 minutes, until the turnovers are golden brown. Transfer them to a wire rack to cool. Dust generously with confectioners' sugar.

Variation

Amaretti Turnovers

Prepare the filling with the same amount of preserves but replace the chestnuts with 4 finely crushed Amaretti di Saronno, increase the whole milk ricotta to 1 cup, and add the grated zest of 1 lemon.

❖ Bake Sale Tip

Arrange the turnovers on a tray to sell them individually. Wrap each one in a large square of wax or parchment paper, or place two turnovers in a vellum envelope and seal with a sticker.

Sfrappole
(Fried Sweet Pastry Ribbons)

Makes 2 dozen ribbons, serving 10 to 12

1 recipe Sweet Pastry Dough
Vegetable oil, for frying
Confectioners' sugar, for dusting

1. Place 1 piece of the chilled dough on a lightly floured surface, flatten it with your hands, and roll it out to a thickness of ⅛ inch. With a scalloped pastry wheel (also called a jagger) or a sharp knife, cut the dough into 1 x 10-inch strips. Tie a loose knot in each strip, and place them on a lightly floured baking sheet or cookie sheet. Repeat the process with the remaining piece of dough.

2. Fill a medium skillet with 1 inch vegetable oil. Turn the heat to medium-high. When the oil is hot but not quite smoking, add 2 pastry knots and fry until golden brown on one side. Turn them with metal tongs and brown the other side. Total cooking time will be 1½ to 2 minutes. Do not let them turn dark. Transfer the finished ribbons to paper towels. Repeat the process with the remaining pieces of dough.

3. Pile the fritters on a serving platter, sprinkle with confectioners' sugar, and serve hot or at room temperature. The fritters will keep well, uncovered, at room temperature for a couple of days.

❖ Bake Sale Tips

Arrange the ribbons on a platter to sell by the piece. Use tongs or tissue-paper sheets for handing them out. You might also place several ribbons in individual wax paper bags and line a rectangular basket with rows of the bags.

Owner and chef of Biba Restaurant in Sacramento, California, Biba Caggiano received the Robert Mondavi Culinary Award of Excellence in 1998. Her cooking show, Biba's Italian Kitchen, is featured on the Learning Channel throughout the world, including South America, Asia, Canada, Australia, and the United States. Biba is the author of seven bestselling cookbooks, including Biba's Northern Italian Cooking, From Biba's Kitchen, *and* Italy al Dente.

Sweet Pastry Dough

Makes enough for 30 to 34 turnovers or 24 pastry ribbons

2 cups unbleached all-purpose flour, plus extra for shaping the dough

¼ teaspoon baking powder

Grated zest of 1 lemon

¼ cup sugar

8 tablespoons (1 stick) unsalted butter, cold, cut into small pieces

2 large eggs, lightly beaten

3 to 4 tablespoons sweet Marsala or white wine

1. In a food processor, combine the flour, baking powder, lemon zest, and sugar and pulse a few times to blend. Add the butter and pulse until the mixture is the size of small peas. Add the eggs and wine and pulse until the dough is loosely gathered in clumps around the blade.

2. Place the dough on a work surface and gather it quickly into a ball, but do not knead it. The dough should be pliable and moist. Divide the dough into 2 pieces, seal in plastic wrap, and refrigerate for 2 to 3 hours.

Suzanne Dunaway's
Cranberry Pistachio Panettone
and
Panettone Bread Pudding

Even with the best company in the world, Rome can be lonely during Christmas and on New Year's Eve. Families gather together, trim trees, wrap presents, eat, drink, and make merry, with the particular warmth and intensity of Italians, and it is rare for foreigners to be included in friends' family celebrations.

One holiday season, my husband, Don, and I had taken a villa to be near his children (who are Roman). When New Year's Eve was about to ring in, many of our friends had gone off to other parts of Italy. Our landlord and neighbor, Principe Ruffo, was with his family in Sicily—the scent of oranges in the air, large groups of children laughing and gathering their horns and clackers for the stroke of midnight—and I longed to be with them, eating the requisite panettone and other holiday favorites, the soft air of Sicily and family all around me.

Other friends, Marisela and Alberto, were in Spoleto with their daughters, all of them taking turns stirring polenta to be eaten with a sun-dried tomato sauce (Marisela's specialty) or sitting around their walk-in hearth, toasting their panettone (and each other) with Prosecco. My stepdaughter and her boyfriend were at parties, and Don's young son was sleeping over with cousins and friends. And here we were, destined to wander like Dante's lost souls through Rome's deserted streets until midnight, when, I had been told, people toss old china, sinks, or anything broken and used out the window to make a clean path for a new year.

Our footsteps ticked away the minutes of the old year, and finally my husband, with a mysterious smile, suggested we simply go home. The thought of our warm villa was better than gazing at shop windows full of tinsel and panettone, and home we went. We did not wish to be among the smattering of Rome's tourists, searching for New Year's Eve. We wanted to be at home in Rome, eating our own panettone and toasting the world's most beautiful and haunting city.

When we arrived at the villa, I found that my husband had laid out smoked salmon, caviar, crystal, and silver to surprise me. Suddenly we both realized that the only thing missing was the panettone! Inspired by a chilled glass of prosecco, I started my sponge, stirred up my recipe with the cranberries and pistachios that I reserve for special occasions, and as the New Year was welcomed by bell towers all over Rome, my golden loaves emerged from the oven to complete our New Year's supper.

No one had tossed any bath fixtures or pottery out the window, as far as I could tell. Instead, the sky was suddenly lit up by the brilliance of fireworks. As we watched the glorious show from our terrace, my stepdaughter and stepson called to wish us *auguri*. Then the children's mother, Gabriella, and her husband, Giuliano, rang to invite us to New Year's Day lunch with all of our loved ones and to ask if I would possibly have time to make my special panettone with pistachios and cranberries.

"I'll see what I can do," I said, and my husband and I raised a toast to family.

Cranberry Pistachio Panettone

Makes 4 small or 2 large loaves

For the starter

1 cup warm milk

2½ tablespoons active dry yeast

1¾ cups unbleached flour

1 teaspoon sugar

For the dough

1 cup raw pistachios

1 teaspoon salt, plus a few pinches

4½ cups unbleached flour, plus more for kneading and shaping the dough

1 tablespoon freshly grated lemon zest

1 tablespoon freshly grated orange zest

½ cup Candied Orange and Lemon Rind, optional

1 cup dried cranberries

2 tablespoons dark rum

1 teaspoon pure vanilla extract

16 tablespoons (2 sticks) unsalted butter, softened, plus extra for the pans

1 cup sugar

4 large eggs

2 large egg yolks (whites reserved for glaze)

1. For the starter, in a small glass bowl, combine the warm milk, yeast, flour, and sugar and stir to blend. Cover the bowl with plastic wrap and set aside for 30 minutes.

2. Preheat the oven to 350°F. For the dough, place the pistachios on a baking sheet and spray them with water, sprinkle with a pinch or two of salt, and toast for 10 minutes, watching to make sure they do not burn. Cool completely and chop coarsely.

3. In a bowl, combine the 1 teaspoon salt, the flour, lemon and orange zests, candied orange and lemon peel, if using, cranberries, pistachios, rum, and vanilla.

4. In the bowl of an electric mixer fitted with a paddle attachment, cream the butter and sugar on medium speed for 2 minutes or until fluffy. Add the eggs and yolks and beat well. Reduce the speed to low and add the flour mixture, mixing just until combined. Gradually add the starter and continue to beat on low speed until all ingredients are incorporated. The dough should not be sticky or too firm. It should look buttery and a little ragged.

5. Turn out the dough onto a floured work surface and knead for 1 to 2 minutes, pushing the dough away from you with the heels of your hands, and then folding it back over on itself. The dough will be smooth and satiny.

6. Transfer the dough to an oiled bowl, cover, and let rise in a warm place for about 2 hours, or until doubled in size. Gently turn out the dough onto a work surface and divide it into 4 equal pieces, if making smaller loaves, or into 2 pieces if making larger loaves; keep as much air in the dough as possible. Let the pieces rest, covered with a clean dish towel, for 10 minutes.

7. For the smaller loaves, butter four 1-pound coffee cans or other deep molds that are 4 to 5 inches wide. Use 2-pound cof-

fee cans to make two large panettone. Shape each piece into a smooth ball and place the dough in the mold. It should fill half the mold.

8. Beat the reserved egg whites and brush the tops of the loaves. Cover and let the loaves rise for 1 hour, or until just slightly less than doubled. (The dough may be active and rise quickly, so you may not need the full hour.)

9. Preheat the oven to 400°F.

10. Uncover the loaves, place the molds on the middle rack of the oven, and reduce the heat to 350°F. Bake for 30 to 35 minutes for the smaller molds and up to 45 minutes for the larger molds. (If, after 20 minutes of baking, the top of the bread is taking on too much color, cover loosely with a piece of aluminum foil.) The bread is done when a wooden skewer inserted into the center of the loaf comes out clean. Cool for 15 minutes, then carefully remove the loaves from the cans and place the panettone on wire racks to cool completely. Panettone will keep fresh for up to a week in a plastic bag; freeze them for up to 6 months.

❖ **Bake Sale Tips**

While you can serve the panettone toasted on Christmas day or during the holidays with a glass of Vin Santo, these small loaves are also perfect for bake sales. Place the panettone on decorative doilies; collar them with a layer of parchment paper and then seasonal wrapping paper; wrap them in two layers of clear cellophane with tissue paper squares or tinsel between the layers; tie the tops with decorative ribbon and holiday greens.

To make twice as many loaves, complete the recipe two separate times. You can, however, make the starters together.

Panettone Bread Pudding

Serves 6; you can double this recipe easily, making twice the amount in a larger baking dish (allow for a slightly longer baking time), or in smaller, individual dishes (allow for a slightly shorter baking time)

----

6 tablespoons (¾ stick) unsalted butter, softened

Six ½-inch slices panettone

3 large eggs

3 large egg yolks

1½ cups whole milk

1½ cups heavy cream

¾ cup sugar

2 tablespoons Cognac or rum

½ teaspoon pure vanilla extract

1. Turn the oven on to broil. Using 1 teaspoon of the butter, liberally grease a 9-inch baking dish.

2. Butter both sides of the panettone slices with the remaining butter and toast each side under the broiler until golden. Arrange the slices in the prepared dish.

3. Preheat the oven to 350°F. In a medium bowl, whisk together the eggs and egg yolks.

4. In a large heavy saucepan, heat the milk and cream over medium heat until bubbles form around the edge. Remove the pan from the heat and quickly whisk the warm milk into the egg mixture. Return the mixture to the pan and whisk constantly over very low heat until thickened. Add the sugar, Cognac or rum, and vanilla and stir to combine.

5. Cool the custard slightly, then pour it through a sieve over the panettone slices, pressing down on the slices to help them absorb the custard.

6. Set the dish in a large roasting pan and place it on the middle rack of the oven. Fill the roasting pan with hot water to come halfway up the sides of the baking dish. Bake for 30 to 35 minutes, just until set and nicely browned on top. Remove from the water bath and let sit for at least 15 minutes before serving. Refrigerate the remaining servings.

❖ Bake Sale Tip

Package portions of the bread pudding in clear disposable bowls wrapped in clear cellophane and tied with a colorful ribbon. Keep the pudding chilled.

Suzanne Dunaway is the author of No Need to Knead: Handmade Italian Breads in 90 Minutes, *which was nominated for a James Beard Award, and the founder of Los Angeles'* *renowned Buona Forchetta Handmade* *Breads, which began in her home kitchen and* *now bakes up to 15,000 loaves a day. Her most* *recent book,* Rome, at Home, *was published* *April 2004. Her illustrations have appeared in* The New Yorker, Bon Appétit, Gourmet, *and the* Los Angeles Times. *She lives in Los* *Angeles but is frequently in Rome.*

Candied Orange and Lemon Rinds

Makes 1 cup; an easy recipe to double

1 cup chopped or finely slivered
orange and lemon zests (all bitter
pith removed from peels)
1 cup sugar

1. Place the zests in a small heavy pot and pour in boiling water just to cover. Simmer on medium heat for 15 minutes, or until the zests are slightly translucent and tender. Drain well and rinse.

2. Return the zests to the pot and add the sugar and ¼ cup cold water. Bring to a boil and cook for 3 to 4 minutes, until the liquid is a thick syrup. Pour the mixture out onto a smooth, oiled surface. Separate the candied rinds so that they form a single layer in which they can cool and crystallize.

3. Once the rinds are somewhat dry (they'll still be tacky), separate the bits and store them in a small plastic tub in the refrigerator or freezer. As candied rinds will last indefinitely, this is a good recipe to double.

Amy Scherber's
Decadent Chocolate Cherry Rolls
and
Soft Chocolate Twists

My father worked for Pillsbury at their headquarters in Minneapolis for thirty-five years. He did sales and marketing for all the grocery products. At home, our family of six was always testing Bake-Off recipes or trying out new items like toaster pastries or crescent rolls that would pop out of a tube; this had to have sparked my interest in baking. I remember we baked "magic pockets" with marshmallows inside that would disappear during baking. We sampled different sweet rolls with various icings. This was in the 1960s and 1970s when refrigerated dough products were becoming popular. (He also brought us Poppin' Fresh dolls, a Poppin' Fresh bank and beach towels, and all the other collectibles—many of which I still have.)

My mother was a full-time mom who was constantly cooking (when she wasn't doing the laundry or ironing): She read food magazines, planned her menus, and baked all kinds of bars, pies, and cookies. She was queen of the kitchen, but she did allow us to help once in a while. For instance, on Sunday mornings, I began to make coffee cakes; I was probably fifteen, and my mother would say, "Oh, it's the weekend, and I don't feel like bothering," and that would be my cue to browse through her cookbooks. My two main sources were the Pillsbury's three-ring binder cookbook with the tabbed sections or my mom's recipe box with her favorite dishes written out in her own neat handwriting.

Chocolate featured in many of those recipes. My dad would eat anything that even mentioned chocolate, the gooier the better. Mom was famous for her tunnel of chocolate fudge Bundt cake. We always had s'mores, dripping with chocolate, at the campfire circle we made in the little woods at the back of our yard. Hot fudge sundaes were frequently dinnertime desserts. And then when we piled in the big station wagon for our family vacations, we'd always seek out the local bakeries in Utah or Wyoming—or wherever we were—hoping to find fresh doughnuts; and my dad and I would vie for the chocolate-glazed ones.

When I first created these chocolate rolls about ten years ago, everyone was surprised by them because they were as satisfying as a brownie, but, being bread, they weren't half as fattening or as rich. Just out of the oven, the bread is soft with bits of slightly melted chocolate.

The chocolate twists are another yeasty invention with dough and chocolate. Maybe being an unofficial test kitchen for Pillsbury inspired me always to try something new.

Decadent Chocolate Cherry Rolls

Makes 12 rolls

----

2 teaspoons active dry yeast (slightly less than one ¼-ounce package)
½ cup very warm water (105° to 115°F)
1 cup brewed coffee, at room temperature
1 large egg, separated
1 tablespoon unsalted butter, softened
3 cups unbleached all-purpose flour, plus extra for kneading and forming the rolls

⅓ cup Dutch-process cocoa powder
⅓ cup sugar
1½ tablespoons kosher salt
1½ cups (8 ounces) coarsely chopped bittersweet chocolate
1 cup dried sour cherries

1. In a large bowl, combine the yeast with the warm water. Stir with a fork to dissolve the yeast and allow to stand for 3 minutes.

2. In a small bowl, combine the coffee, egg yolk, and butter. Add to the yeast mixture and blend.

3. In a medium bowl, whisk together

the flour, cocoa powder, sugar, and salt. Gradually add the flour mixture to the yeast mixture, stirring until a shaggy mass forms and all the flour is moist and sticky. If the dough feels stiff, add up to 2 tablespoons water.

4. Transfer the dough to a lightly floured work surface and knead for 7 to 8 minutes, until smooth and elastic. Shape into a loose ball, cover with plastic wrap, and let stand for about 10 minutes to relax the flour's gluten strands.

5. Unwrap the dough, flatten it, then stretch it gently with your fingers to form a rectangle about 1 inch thick. Sprinkle the chocolate and cherries evenly over the dough. Fold the rectangle into thirds as you would a business letter and knead for 2 to 3 minutes, until the chocolate and cherries are well distributed. If some of the pieces pop out of the dough, they can be incorporated after the first rise.

6. Shape the dough into a loose ball and place it in a lightly oiled bowl. Cover the bowl tightly with plastic wrap and let rise at room temperature for 1 to 2 hours, until the dough has doubled in volume.

7. Line two 12 x 17-inch baking sheets with parchment paper or silicone mats.

8. Gently place the dough on a lightly floured work surface, pressing any loose chocolate or cherries into the dough. Divide the dough into 12 equal pieces. Shape the pieces into rolls: Cup your hand over the dough and roll the ball against the table to tighten. Place 6 rolls on each baking sheet, leaving several inches between each roll. Cover loosely with oiled plastic wrap and let rise at room temperature for about 1 hour, until doubled in volume.

9. About 15 minutes before baking, preheat the oven to 400°F and place one rack in the top third and a second rack in the bottom third of the oven.

10. Once the rolls have doubled in size, mix the egg white with 1 teaspoon water. Brush all but the bottoms of each roll with the egg wash. Place one pan on each oven rack. Using a mister, spray the top and sides of the oven six to eight times and quickly close the oven door.

11. Bake for 10 minutes, then reduce the oven temperature to 350°F and rotate the pans from top to bottom and front to back. Bake for an additional 10 to 15 minutes, until the rolls feel firm but not hard when lightly pressed. The bottoms should have browned slightly and the crust should be thin and soft, rather than crunchy. Transfer the rolls to a wire rack to cool.

❖ Bake Sale Tips

Once the rolls are completely cool, package half a dozen in a clear cellophane bag, tie with a colorful piece of ribbon, and add a descriptive label. You could also sell the rolls individually by placing each one in a large white paper baking cup and then inside a small cellophane bag.

To make twice as many rolls, complete the recipe two separate times.

Ice Cream Sandwiches

For an even more unusual treat, make an ice cream sandwich from slices of the Decadent Chocolate Cherry Rolls. Slice the rolls into ¾-inch-thick disks and lightly toast them. Let them cool completely, then sandwich your favorite ice cream between two disks.

Soft Chocolate Twists

Makes nine 10-inch twists (but worth doubling, since the recipe requires repeated rising)

----

1 teaspoon active dry yeast (less than one ¼-ounce package)

¼ cup warm water (105° to 115°F)

¼ cup vegetable oil

3 tablespoons sugar

1 large egg, plus 1 egg for the egg wash

1 large yolk

3½ cups unbleached all-purpose flour, plus extra for forming the dough

1 tablespoon kosher salt

2 ounces fine-quality bittersweet chocolate, chopped into small bits

1. In a small measuring cup, mix the yeast with the warm water and stir to dissolve. Let the mixture stand for 3 minutes (small bubbles will form). Pour the yeast mixture into a large bowl along with ¾ cup plus 1 tablespoon cool water (75°F), the oil, sugar, egg, and egg yolk and whisk to blend.

2. Combine the flour and salt in a bowl and add to the yeast mixture. Using your fingers, mix the dough into a sticky mass. Once the flour is incorporated, transfer the dough to a lightly floured work surface and knead for 5 minutes. The dough will remain sticky; it will not be smooth. If the dough feels stiff or dry, knead in additional cool water, 1 tablespoon at a time. Transfer the dough to a lightly oiled bowl, cover with plastic wrap, and let rest for 20 minutes.

3. Return the dough to a very lightly floured work surface and knead for 7 to 8 minutes. The dough should become supple but not too firm. Clean the oiled bowl, then lightly oil it again. Place the dough inside, cover with plastic wrap, and allow the dough to rise at room temperature (about 75°) for about 2 hours, until it doubles in volume. (The dough should not spring back when poked; the dent should remain.)

4. Scoop the dough gently onto a very lightly floured work surface. Gently deflate the dough and pat it into an 8 x 12-inch rectangle; the long dimension should extend forward, away from you. Sprinkle the chopped chocolate to coat the dough's surface completely and then press it into the dough. Fold the dough like a business letter: bring down the top third of the dough, then fold up the bottom third. Pat it down and flatten the dough with your fingers.

5. Place this new rectangle on a work surface or baking pan, cover with plastic

wrap, and allow to rise for about 50 minutes, until soft and slightly puffy.

6. Trim a tiny bit of dough from both ends of the rectangle to make straight edges.

7. Line a baking sheet with parchment paper. Stretch the long dimension of the rectangle until it reaches a length of 10 inches. Gently score the dough crosswise into nine 1-inch-wide strips, then cut through each strip completely. As you lift each strip from the work surface, give it a single, gentle twist (do not stretch the dough to lengthen it) and place it on the prepared pan, forming a row of 9 twists that touch one another.

8. Whisk the remaining egg with 1 teaspoon water and brush the dough; reserve the remaining wash. Cover the twists with plastic wrap and let rise at room temperature for about 30 minutes, or until nearly doubled in volume.

9. While the twists are rising, preheat the oven to 350°F.

10. Gently brush the twists a second time with the remaining egg wash and place the pan on the middle rack of the oven. Bake for 10 minutes, then rotate the twists and bake for another 6 or 7 minutes, watching carefully. The twists should be golden brown but still slightly soft. Slide the row of twists off the baking pan and onto a wire rack to cool.

❖ Bake Sale Tips

While these taste great when they are slightly warm and the chocolate is still soft and melted, they can also be placed, when cooled, on a disposable platter, wrapped with clear cellophane, and tied with a colorful ribbon.

To make twice as many twists, complete the recipe two separate times.

Amy Scherber, founder and baker of Amy's Bread, launched the bakery in June 1992 in a small storefront in Hell's Kitchen, New York City, with five employees and big dreams. Now the bakery has more than 100 employees, three cafés, and two production kitchens that make breads, old-fashioned layer cakes, sweets, and sandwiches. Amy has been recognized nationally for her commitment to making handmade traditional breads and has received numerous, awards, including TimeOut New York's award for Best Bread in New York City, and Women Chefs and Restaurateurs Golden Bowl Award Recognizing Excellence in the Baking and Pastry Arts.

Carole and Norma Jean Darden's
Monkey Bread
and
Sweet Potato Biscuits

Monkey bread came into our lives with Bill Cosby. We had just published our first cookbook, *Spoonbread and Strawberry Wine*, when he called us at the catering business we had just begun and asked that we prepare a dinner for a few friends at his home in Manhattan. He maintained a residence in New York City during those years that *The Cosby Show* was being filmed out in Queens.

Mr. Cosby wanted something specific: He wanted a dinner to evoke his own childhood favorites, and he had a particular menu in mind. As we remember it, we prepared cold lemon soup, salad with edible flowers, broiled red snapper, grilled vegetables, a plain pound cake, and then two things we'd never made before: a lemon sweet potato pie, and monkey bread. In fact, we'd never heard of monkey bread. Mr. Cosby had no recipes for any of this; he just remembered that he loved these foods and wanted them for this dinner.

When we hung up the phone, we were excited and also a little nervous. But a young lady in the kitchen where we were working knew about monkey bread and explained that it was a simple, buttery bread made in small balls but baked as a whole so that guests pull apart individual "rolls." Before she had even brought in a recipe, we had received a letter from Daisy Young, who was the mother of the mayor of Atlanta, Andrew Young. She had received our book as a gift and wanted to share one of her own family recipes with us, since our book is all about the tradition of sharing recipes. Coincidentally, her recipe was for monkey bread.

Ms. Young's recipe called for raisins and sugar in the dough, so you'd roll each of the dough balls in butter and sugar before tucking them into the pan, but Mr. Cosby didn't want that. He remembered just a simple bread. So our recipe, evolved from two versions, is a loaf of buttery rolls baked into a ring-shaped bread that makes for a very friendly presentation.

Our meal met with Mr. Cosby's approval, and it was a delight cooking for his family. They all enjoyed the selections from his childhood memories, and the lemony sweet potato pie, which we had to invent, has nearly become a legend here at Spoonbread. And he even invited us to cook for him again.

Monkey Bread

Makes one 10-inch round loaf, serving 10

3¾ to 4 cups all-purpose flour, plus extra
    for kneading

3 tablespoons sugar

1 teaspoon salt

½ ounce (2 packages) active dry yeast

1 cup whole milk

16 tablespoons (2 sticks) unsalted butter,
    plus 2 teaspoons, melted, for the bowl
    and dough

3 large eggs

1. In a bowl of an electric mixer fitted with the dough hook, combine 1½ cups of the flour, the sugar, salt, and yeast.

2. In a saucepan, heat ¼ cup water, the milk, and 1 stick of the butter just until the butter is melted. (This liquid should not boil; allow it to cool, if necessary, so the heat will not kill the yeast.) Pour the liquid over the flour and mix on low speed. Add the eggs all at once. Increase the speed to medium and mix for 3 minutes. Add the remaining flour and mix just until the dough comes together.

3. Transfer the dough to a floured work surface and knead by hand for 5 to 6 minutes, until it is elastic and smooth. Place the dough in a large bowl greased with 1 teaspoon of melted butter; pat the top of the dough with the additional 1 teaspoon of melted butter. Allow the dough to rise for 60 to 90 minutes, or until it has doubled in size.

4. Punch down the dough, then knead it briefly on a lightly floured work surface. Melt the remaining stick of butter and pour it into a bowl. Brush the inside surface of a 10-inch tube pan with some of the melted butter. Break off 2-inch pieces of dough and roll each piece between your palms to form a ball. Dip each piece into the melted butter and place it in the prepared pan, tucking the pieces beside and on top of one another. Cover the pan with a clean cotton dish towel and allow the dough to rise for 45 to 60 minutes, or until almost doubled in size again.

5. Twenty minutes before the bread has finished rising, preheat the oven to 375°F and adjust an oven rack so that it sits in the lower third of the oven. Place the pan on a rimmed baking sheet (to catch any dripping butter) and bake the loaf for 45 to 50 minutes, or until the top is golden brown.

6. Remove the monkey bread from the oven and turn it upside down to cool for 15 minutes. Remove the piping hot bread from the mold and serve it right side up, suggesting that guests pull individual "rolls" from the ring.

❖ Bake Sale Tips

Transport the Monkey Bread on a large disposable plate or platter, wrapped with clear cellophane and tied with a colorful ribbon.

To make two loaves, complete the recipe two separate times.

Sweet Potato Biscuits

Makes 10 to 12 biscuits;
an easy recipe to double

As children we ate sweet potatoes in every possible form. Not a week went by that we didn't have a basic baked sweet potato. (And it was *rare* that we had regular white potatoes.) Fried sweet potatoes for breakfast. French fried sweet potatoes, cooked up in a frying pan. Sweet potato balls, mashed and rolled in nuts. As often as we could, we'd have sweet potato pie. And there was sweet potato pudding, which, on special occasions, we'd have crusted with gooey baked marshmallows. Tacky as fifties recipes may be, that one happens to be one of the few that really holds up. And with a little splash of rum in it, those creamy potatoes are even more divine. Or, sinful, really!

Certainly we'd heard of sweet potato biscuits, but we never had them. We had other biscuits, and nearly every day. If there was one thing to choose from all the foods we've cherished, it would have to be the biscuit. It's a miracle food. Nothing is more evocative of childhood, of love and family and eating times together and carrying on a family tradition, than the smell of biscuits filling the house. Our mother was the biscuit maker, and biscuits were so much a part of life in the kitchen. Sunday mornings especially. We were brought up to be great believers in breakfast, particularly on Sunday, when the morning included biscuits plus eggs, bacon, and maybe scrambled brains, or fried fish or fried salt fish, or fried pork chops, or maybe a little of all those things. Coming down to breakfast on Sunday mornings was truly an adventure.

So sweet potato biscuits were inevitable. Now this is a simple recipe, but one that took a lot of experimenting in order to make the result as satisfying as a biscuit just needs to be. If you can find the smaller sweet potatoes, they tend to be sweeter and more tender.

> 2 cups sifted all-purpose flour, plus extra
>   for rolling
> 3 teaspoons baking powder
> ½ teaspoon baking soda
> ¾ teaspoon salt
> 3 tablespoons brown sugar
> ½ teaspoon ground cinnamon
> 8 tablespoons (1 stick) unsalted butter,
>   cold, cut into 1-tablespoon pieces
> 1 cup baked, peeled, mashed sweet
>   potato (1 large or 2 small potatoes)
> ⅔ cup buttermilk

1. Preheat the oven to 425°F.
2. In a large bowl, sift together the flour, baking powder, baking soda, salt, brown sugar, and cinnamon and, using two forks or a pastry blender, cut in the cold butter. The mixture should resemble cornmeal.

3. In a small bowl, combine the mashed sweet potato with the buttermilk and stir into the flour mixture until the dough is moist.
4. Form the dough into a ball and turn out onto a lightly floured work surface. Lightly pat the top with flour as well, since the dough is sticky. With a floured rolling pin, roll out the dough to a thickness of ¾ inch. Cut with a floured cutter and set the biscuits on an ungreased baking sheet. Pinch together the dough scraps, flatten with the palm of your hand, and cut out a few more biscuits.
5. Place the baking sheet on the middle rack of the oven and bake for 10 to 15 minutes, until lightly browned. Serve warm.

Norma Jean Darden and Carole Darden are the authors of Spoonbread and Strawberry Wine, *a treasury of recipes and family history first published in 1978 and reissued in 1994, and again in a new edition in 2004. Norma Jean runs Spoonbread, Inc., a successful catering company. Carole worked as a child therapist for many years, and now runs a small family real estate business. Both are graduates of Sarah Lawrence College and live in New York City.*

Michael Schlow's
Great Bay's Great Cinnamon Rolls

astry, for everyone, is a guilty pleasure. A "giving in" to what you just can't resist. So whatever you've decided to indulge in should reward you with utter deliciousness.

When I see a warm cinnamon roll passed in a basket of breakfast breads or set out on a brunch table, it's difficult *not* to take one. There's such a hominess to the yeasty, cinnamon smell—there's an element of aromatherapy about it. Something gets triggered in your heart, and I don't know anyone who can resist one (and I don't know anything more disappointing than a lousy cinnamon roll that dashes all that anticipation to pieces).

Although I come from German ancestors on one side and Russian-Polish ancestors on the other—many of whom came to America before the Second World War and turned to baking bread and making candy to support their families—I don't always have patience for the exacting science of pastry. But I surround myself with people who do take the time to create these pleasures, which I'm not about to deny myself or my guests. Nor should you. These cinnamon rolls should work wonders at breakfast, but malls everywhere suggest that they're perfect for snacks any time.

Michael Schlow's Pineapple Strudel and his
biography begin on page 129.

Great Bay's Great Cinnamon Rolls

Makes 14 rolls

For the dough

1 ounce fresh yeast or one ¼-ounce
  package active dry yeast
2 cups warm whole milk (105°F)
½ cup plus 1 tablespoon sugar
1½ teaspoons salt
1 tablespoon ground cardamom
2 large eggs
5½ to 6 cups all-purpose flour, plus extra
  for forming the rolls
7 tablespoons unsalted butter, melted
  and cooled

For the filling

7 tablespoons unsalted butter, melted
1 cup dark brown sugar (packed)
1 tablespoon ground cinnamon

For the glaze

4 ounces plain cream cheese, softened
½ cup confectioners' sugar
2 to 3 tablespoons whole milk
½ teaspoon pure vanilla extract

1. For the dough, in the bowl of an electric mixer fitted with the paddle attachment, combine the yeast and milk and mix on low for 1 minute to dissolve the yeast. Add the sugar, salt, cardamom, and eggs and blend all the ingredients together. Replace the paddle with the mixer's dough hook. Add the flour and mix on medium speed for 3 to 4 minutes. Add the butter and continue to knead the dough for 15 minutes, or until smooth and elastic.

2. Cover the bowl with a cotton towel and let the dough rest while preparing the filling.

3. Combine all of the filling ingredients and mix to form a "wet sand" texture.

4. Lightly butter a baking pan or mist with nonstick cooking spray.

5. To assemble the rolls, dump the dough onto a lightly floured work surface and roll it into an 8 x 14-inch rectangle. The long side of the dough should be parallel to the table where you're working. Spread the filling into an even layer over the entire surface of the rectangle. Roll up from the long edge of the dough to form a 14-inch log. Pinch the seam to seal the roll. Slice into 1-inch-thick disks. Place each spiral on the prepared pan, leaving ½ inch between each roll. Cover the rolls with plastic wrap that has been misted with nonstick cooking spray. Let the rolls rise in a warm place for about 45 minutes, or until they touch each other.

6. Place the pan on the middle rack of the oven and bake for 25 to 30 minutes, or until the rolls are golden brown.

7. Make the glaze while the rolls bake. In the bowl of an electric mixer fitted with the paddle attachment, mix the cream cheese and sugar on medium speed for 2 minutes, or until smooth. Scrape the inside

of the bowl. Add the milk and vanilla and mix again until the glaze is smooth.

8. Transfer the pan of rolls to a wire rack to cool. Using the tines of a fork, drizzle a generous amount of glaze over the rolls. Alternatively, you may spoon the glaze on top of each roll, spreading it with the back of the spoon.

❖ Bake Sale Tips

Sell the rolls, attached to one another, in cellophane-wrapped packs of 4 or 6, or seal each roll individually in a vellum envelope and label it with a sticker.

To make twice as many rolls, complete the recipe two separate times.

Afterword with Grandma Hat's Butter Cookies

Crescent Dragonwagon

For twenty-two years, my late, much-loved husband, Ned Shank, rhapsodized about Grandma Hat's Butter Cookies and swore he'd make them someday.

Grandma Hat's Butter Cookies were a Shank family legend. Ned described them with a strange mixture of enthusiasm (for the cookie itself) and wistfulness (for the impossibility of recreating such perfection). "They were so good!" he'd exclaim. "They were buttery and crisp, almost paper thin. Oh!" He'd shake his head, sigh. "I think they were the best cookies I ever ate. But no one could make them like Grandma Hat."

With that same odd emotional conjunction, he told me about Grandma Hat's visits to the family home, then in Piedmont, California. Grandma Hat—Hattie—was his father's grandmother, so she was really Ned's great-grandmother. He remembered her glamour, sophistication, the smell of perfume as she leaned down to kiss him, the fur collar of her coat brushing his cheek. He remembered her bustling in at the holidays,

gift-laden, and how, among the boxes, there would always be a dress box from one of the department stores she frequented, and that in that box, layered carefully between sheets of wax paper, would be an enormous batch of the butter cookies. Now, despite the fact that the Shanks had Grandma Hat's recipe—at least, sort of—no one had attempted it in years.

This is a story not only about butter cookies, but about fear, courage, life, death, love, and the curious way we human beings often put off doing the things, small and large, we say we most want to do. Some of us spend our whole lives thus. But some, the brave ones, postpone for a while, then get down to business. My husband was one of the brave ones.

Brave may seem an odd word to apply to baking cookies. But where human postponement is concerned, little is simple. Putting off, I've come to believe, nearly always has to do with fear. Moreover, these were no ordinary cookies, and Ned's—

indeed his whole family's—feelings about them were not ordinary. There was a mythic quality of doomed longing: Eden-has-vanished-and-we-can-never-return-and-nothing-can-be-that-good-again-so-why-even-try?

Here's where fear, the dark inadmissible soil in which procrastination is rooted, comes in. Much easier, if less honest, to say "someday" or "if only I had the time," than "What if I try and I fail?" "What if I'm disappointed?" "What if I do succeed, and everyone's mad or jealous?"

Or even, "What if I can't make the cookies as well as Grandma Hat did?" Or "What if they're just not as good as I remember?"

Making the butter cookies was part of an astonishing period in the life of Ned Shank. Between November 1999 and November 2000, "someday" ceased to exist for Ned. He jumped in, with both feet and both hands, brain and heart, thinking and feeling—and began doing virtually all he'd postponed, dream by dream.

He had always wanted to write; his first book was published. He had always wanted to create commentaries for NPR; he did one. He had always wanted to act; he played Malvolio in a community theater production of *Twelfth Night*.

Most of all, he had always wanted to draw and paint. Wanted it so badly that indeed, he didn't admit it fully to himself for a long, long time. Said, instead, if pressed, he wanted to be a cartoonist. Maybe. *Someday.* He'd always been able to whip out little free-hand sketches without hesitation, so good, funny, and lively, that others (especially his wife) would say, "Ned! You have so much natural gift! Why don't you develop it?" He'd look away and say, "Naaaah."

In January 2000, he invited himself to a weekly life-drawing session some local professional artists were holding. He told me later that during breaks, several said to him, "Ned, I didn't know you'd gone to art school!" "I didn't," he told them. They, too, expressed amazement to him (and later me) at the freedom of his natural gift. But they were not as amazed as Ned himself. When he came home after that first session he said to me, "Now I finally know what I have been put here to do."

Over the next year he created more than five hundred drawings, paintings, and sketches, the pen, pencil, charcoal, or paintbrush in his hand seemingly driven. The work was gorgeous, bold, filled with energy. A single confident line told the story not just of a model's back, but how she felt about herself. A cityscape, the buildings blue, green, yellow, radiated joy and magic. "Why did I put it off so long?" he asked himself, then answered himself: fear of failure, certainty of parental disapproval. ("Being an artist," his mother told him once, "means being a bum.")

And, he said, "Really, I couldn't have begun any sooner than I did. I had to deal with all that stuff inside. I had to grow up."

Is it crazy to think that making the butter cookies was part of how he dealt with "all that stuff"—that is, fear and postponement?

No. Consider: Ned made the cookies he'd talked about for decades for a Hanukah party in December 1999—a month before he started painting. Not only was he finally making the cookies, he was cooking, period, for a public potluck, instead of me—I, a cookbook author, long the designated family cook.

"I just don't know if they'll come out," he worried.

"Well, don't you have the recipe?" I asked. "You just follow it, right?"

"Oh, I have the recipe," Ned said. "Remember? It's in that family collection my mother gave us. But something's wrong, I think. No one could ever get those cookies to come out like Grandma Hat's. My mother tried, a number of times."

I thought it over. "Maybe," I said, "it's what Charlotte calls a 'mother-in-law recipe.'" Charlotte is Charlotte Zolotow, my mother. Mother-in-law recipes, according to her, were what a grown-up son's mother gave her daughter-in-law, the son's wife. They were always for some dish the son had loved. The wife would try dutifully to reproduce it in her own kitchen. "But," my mother said, "the mother-in-law always leaves something out. An ingredient, some little fine point or technique. That way, it's never as good as the way mama made it."

"Could be," said Ned thoughtfully. "Why don't you look at it and see if you spot something glaringly wrong?"

The fateful recipe was in a cookbook put together by Ned's mother, Georgene, circa 1989, for Ned and his siblings. The recipes

were typed, in a three-hole red notebook, arranged by categories, with Georgene's notes alongside. At the front of the book were photocopies of recipes given to Georgene by friends or relatives. Thus, the recipe for Grandma Hat's Butter Cookies appeared twice. The handwritten version, obviously from Grandma herself, was noted "For Georgene"; the elegantly curled "C" on the word "Cookies" was the script of an era when handwriting was "penmanship." Later, next to the typed version, Georgene had noted, "Impossible to recreate them as delicious and as THIN as hers."

I cast a professional eye at the recipe. "Ned!" I said. "Hey, this is easy! She didn't put down that you cream the butter and sugar first! She just has it that you kind of dump everything together—no wonder no one else could get them right!"

I rewrote the directions in keeping with standard cookie-baking procedure. With deep, serious attention, Ned followed it. Bingo! Success!

The cookies were superb: delicious, fragile, paper thin, as good as Ned remembered. At the Hanukah party, everyone marveled over them and praised Ned extravagantly. They vanished as quickly as the cookies Grandma Hat had brought annually to Piedmont. Ned was ecstatic: with the cookies, with actually making them at last, with the way they'd turned out. "You know," he announced, "I think I'm going do these once a year, at the holidays, like she did."

That, as I've said, was in December 1999. The next month, he started painting. There

Grandma Hat's Butter Cookies

Makes 12 dozen cookies

24 tablespoons (3 sticks) unsalted
    butter, softened
1½ cups sugar
2 large eggs
1 teaspoon pure vanilla extract
3 cups unbleached all-purpose flour
1 teaspoon baking powder
¼ teaspoon salt
Whole pecans, chopped nuts, or
    cinnamon-sugar, optional

1. In the bowl of an electric mixer fitted with the paddle attachment, combine the butter and sugar and beat on medium speed for 2 minutes, or until the mixture is light and fluffy. Add the eggs one at a time, incorporating each one thoroughly before adding the next. Add the vanilla and mix to combine. Scrape the inside of the bowl.

2. In a large bowl, sift 2 cups of the flour, the baking powder, and salt. Reduce the mixer's speed to low and add the flour mixture, beating for 30 to 40 seconds, just until the mixture is smooth. Add as much of the remaining 1 cup of flour as needed to create a firm dough. Scrape the inside of the bowl and fold in any remaining flour by hand. Divide the dough in half. Place each piece on a separate sheet of wax paper and form each piece into a cylinder that is 14 to 15 inches long and about 1 inch in diameter. Enclose each log in the wax paper, and then seal each one tightly in plastic wrap. Refrigerate the dough for several hours until firm. The dough may be kept in the refrigerator for 4 days, or frozen for 1 month.

3. Preheat the oven to 350°F.

4. Slice the logs into ⅛-inch (or thinner) coins and place them on an ungreased cookie sheet, leaving ½ inch between the cookies. If desired, press a whole pecan in the center of each, or sprinkle with chopped nuts or cinnamon-sugar.

5. Place the cookie sheet on the middle rack of the oven and bake for 8 minutes, or until the edge of each cookie is golden and crisp. Allow the cookies to cool for 1 minute and then gently transfer them to a wire rack. (The cookies will be harder to remove if they cool completely on the cookie sheet.) Store in an airtight container.

followed eleven months of Ned joyfully knocking down one long-postponed wish after another. He was a happy man, and I— I was never happier or prouder to be his wife than I was that year.

On November 30, 2000, Ned went out for a bicycle ride, the same ride he habitually took three times a week most weeks. It turned out not to be to the Conoco station by the lake, the one where they rent canoes, which he had nicknamed "Canoe-Co." It was into eternity.

Without warning, Ned was gone from this earth, as vanished as our shared life, forever. My heart will probably pulse with grief at this for as long as I live, even as I am happy in the new life I am constructing without him. And yet, it will also pulse with gratitude and joy: For twenty-three years I loved and was loved by, knew and was known by, Ned. And though he didn't get to make Grandma Hat's Butter Cookies every year, he did make them that once, perfectly.

Mostly, I find more happiness than sorrow in that.

I hope you'll make these cookies—as well as any other delicious thing you want to make in, and of, your life—not someday, but right, right now.

Crescent Dragonwagon is the author of forty books, including cookbooks such as Passionate Vegetarian *and* Dairy Hollow House Soup and Bread *(a Julia Child Award and James Beard Award nominee), children's books such as* Half a Moon and One Whole Star *(a Coretta Scott King Award winner), and novels such as* The Year It Rained *(a New York Times Notable Book). With her late husband, the writer and historic preservationist Ned Shank, she co-founded Dairy Hollow House, a country inn and restaurant in the Ozark Mountains, which is now the nonprofit Writers' Colony at Dairy Hollow.*

Index

Pastry cream, 126
    in Basque custard cookie cake,
        117–18
    chocolate, for Carolines, 179–80
    in fritelle di San Giuseppe,
        257–58
    in strawberry shortcake, 125–26
    vanilla, 258
Pastry flour, 14
Pâte à choux (cream puff dough),
    177
Patent, Greg, 30–34
Payard, François, 41–42, 223–25
Peaches
    bourbon peach sauce, brown
        sugar cheesecake with, 111–12
    lattice-top sour cream peach pie,
        88–90
    super peach dumpling, 95–96
Peacock, Scott, 167–70
Peanut butter
    choco-peanut butter oatmeal
        chipsters, 39
    frosting, broiled, cola cake with,
        202
Peanuts, in Mexican bread pudding,
    143–44
Pecan(s)
    in apple snacking spice cake, 220
    apricot-cherry coconut bars,
        32–33
    in Aunt Sylvia's rugelach, 6–7
    in bananas Foster cake, 135–36
    bianco fudge with cranberries,
        orange, and, 84
    frosting, 183
    -graham cracker crust, for brown
        sugar cheesecake, 111–12
    Mexican wedding cookies
        (polvorones con canela), 24
    in Milky Way cake, 202–3
    miniature cranberry-pecan loaves,
        238–39
    pecan cream cheese frosting, no-
        mistake red velvet cake with,
        206–7
    pecan pralines, 72
    pecan prune cake, 4
    in rhubarb sour cream coffee
        cake, 244–45

Pepper
    Aztec fudge, 83–84
    ginger-black pepper glaze, black
        walnut pound cake with,
        236–37
    sassy pound cake, 234–35
Peppermint patties, 74–76
Peppermint patty brownies, 74
Pie(s), 86–108
    apple, smooshed, 2–3
    buttermilk chess pie, 101
    chocolate-banana cream pie with
        almond crust, 106–8
    chocolate chess pie, 101
    chocolate raspberry chess pie, 101
    coconut cream, 104–5
    crusts: almond, 107; cream pie
        shell, 98; flaky crust dough, 92;
        pre-baked pie shell, 105
    rhubarb-strawberry-rose, 98–99
    sour cherry, fresh, 90–92
    sour cream peach, lattice-top,
        88–90
    super peach dumpling with
        butterscotch sauce, 95–96
    sweet potato, old-fashioned,
        102
Pineapple
    in Mexican bread pudding,
        143–44
    strudel, 129–30
Pistachios
    cranberry pistachio panettone,
        265–66
    pistachio and fig scones, 250–51
Pizza dolce di ricotta (sweet ricotta
    cheesecake), 120–21
Plum(s)
    plum crumble tart, 137–39
    preserves, in sweet pastry
        turnovers, 260–61
    wild plum ice cream, gingersnap
        ice cream sandwiches with,
        62–64
Polvorones con canela (Mexican
    wedding cookies), 24
Popcorn
    caramel corn, 69–70
Poppy seed(s)
    cookies (mohn kickle), 50

crisp poppy seed thins (korjas), 46
filling, homemade, 48
hamantaschen, 47–48
Pound cake(s)
    apricot cake, 225
    black walnut, with ginger-black
        pepper glaze, 236–37
    chocolate tea cake with orange
        glaze, 230–31
    sassy pound cake with mango
        glaze, 234–35
Pralined almonds, 75
    in peppermint patty brownies, 74
Pralines, pecan, 72
Prunes
    pecan prune cake, 4
Pudding. See Bread pudding
Pumpkin loaf cake with chocolate
    chips, 216–18
Purdy, Cassandra, 42–43
Purdy, Susan, 42–43, 239–42

Q
Quinces
    quince empanadas, 147–48
    roasted, 146

R
Raisins
    in apple snacking spice cake, 220
    in apricot cake, 225
    in chocolate bonanza fruitcake,
        162–64
    in choco-peanut butter oatmeal
        chipsters, 39
    in Irish soda bread, 256
    in Mexican bread pudding,
        143–44
    in mohn, 48
    in roasted orange cakes, 227–28
    sozzled Santa raisin and walnut
        sauce, 163
Raspberries, raspberry preserves
    almond raspberry bars, 29
    Aunt Sylvia's rugelach, 6–7
    blackberry-raspberry slump, 133
    raspberry puree, 89
    raspberry walnut scones, 253–54
    that Baltimore cake, 157–58
Ravago, Miguel, 23–24, 142–45

About Share Our Strength

Though America is the wealthiest nation on earth, thirty-three million of our citizens cannot maintain a healthy, productive life because they are chronically or intermittently hungry. Many experience sustained bouts of profound hunger, while others endure monthly or weekly periods of poor nutrition. Some have no access to sources of healthy foods. Roughly half of these individuals work. Nearly 40 percent of those suffering are children.

Celebrating its twentieth anniversary, Share Our Strength is the nation's leading anti-hunger organization that taps into the strength of individuals and corporations to find new, creative, fun ways to raise money to fight hunger. It mobilizes thousands of individuals from every walk of life—chefs, restaurateurs, coaches, civic leaders, writers, soccer moms, kindergarten classes, and corporate leaders—and organizes their talents and resources into a powerful anti-hunger

force. Share Our Strength then grants the money raised by this volunteer force to the most effective nonprofits in America and abroad.

Share Our Strength oversees several unique fundraising programs. Taste of the Nation®, presented by American Express and Jenn-Air, is the largest culinary benefit to fight hunger in the United States. Completely volunteer-run and organized, each Taste of the Nation event is different, taking on the unique personality, culture, and cuisine of its host city. Thanks to sponsors and volunteers, 100 percent of the event's ticket proceeds go to fight hunger. Taste of the Nation has raised over $60 million, supporting 450 groups working to end hunger and poverty.

The Great American Bake Sale® teams Share Our Strength with *PARADE* magazine in a national, groundbreaking program that encourages Americans of all ages to help end child hunger in America by holding a bake sale and donating the funds to Share Our Strength. In 2003, the inaugural year of this innovative program, the Great American Bake Sale™ raised more than $1 million thanks to the hard work, creativity, and support of over 375,000 people who baked, bought, or sold at Great American Bake Sales throughout the country.

For the last decade, Share Our Strength has also provided direct service in the area of nutrition education. Operation Frontline®, nationally sponsored by Tyson Foods, mobilizes volunteer chefs, nutritionists, and financial planners to teach six-week courses in healthy cooking and food budgeting to individuals at risk of hunger. Today, classes run in more than ninety communities across thirteen states and the District of Columbia.

To find out how you, too, can share your strength, please visit www.strength.org, or write to Share Our Strength, 1730 M Street NW, Suite 700, Washington, D.C. 20036.

"All of us have diverse strengths we can share. The challenge lies in creating vehicles that enable each distinctly talented person to do so, especially that vast majority who may not think of themselves as community activists, civic leaders, or social entrepreneurs. It's not just about volunteering or trying to be a better person. It's about making your community a better place."

—Bill Shore, executive director